***Faḍl al-`alimi `ala-l-`abidi ka fadli `ala adnakum***

*The superiority (faḍl) of the learned over the [mere] worshipper*
*[i.e., one who merely prays, fasts, etc.]*
*is like my superiority over the least of you.*

*Saying of the Prophet*
*(Quoted in In Mājah, Sunan, Muqaddimah, 17, and Tirmidhi, al-`Ilm, 19)*

***Qiblah Books,***
*an imprint of Threshold Books,*
*is committed to publishing works*
*of spiritual significance and high literary quality*
*on Islamic subjects.*
*Threshold Books have sewn bindings*
*and are printed on acid-free paper.*


1 2 3 4 5 6 7 8 9 10
ISBN: 0-939669-70-9
Library of Congress Cataloging Card: 98-39399

224 p. 8.5"
1. Islamic Law—.Popular works
2. Islam—Handbooks, manuals, etc.
I. Abdul-Rauf, Feisal.
III. Title.
PK6481.M8E52 1998
340.5'9—dc21

To Lisa Nakashima,
May God fill your heart with His
Grace & Wisdom.
Y. A. Rauf
8/4/2011

# ISLAM

Lisa,

## A SACRED LAW

Thanks for your Superb Service
8/4/2011
NYC

### What Every Muslim Should Know About The *Sharī'ah*

May God always bless you

Feisal Abdul Rauf

QIBLAH BOOKS
*An Imprint of Threshold Books*

## Invocation

*Bismillah irrahman irrahim*

WE BEGIN BY INVOKING THE NAME OF ALLĀH, the All-Merciful, the All-Compassionate, and thereby invite all to enter collectively into a state of worship, a state that not only brings us closer to the Divine, but via this intimacy to acquire a receptivity to Divine inspiration. This is in fact our fundamental task: to bring our shahāda, that *lā ilāha illallāh* [our testimony that there is no god but The One God] out of our subliminal consciousness, and to translate it into all of our activities. For when our actions become imbued with this awareness, they dovetail with Divine intent. We therefore submit our intellects, minds, hearts and, most important, our souls to the awareness of Allāh's intimacy and closeness to us, for closer is He to us than our jugular vein. With this awareness and submission to His power we too become empowered. For the solutions to the dilemmas posed in our lives today require not only an intellect, but a *submitted* intellect, together with a heart and soul, surrendered to a loving relationship with their Creator.

## General Notes

It is practically impossible to be consistent when one tries to render, translate and transliterate Arabic terms into English. However, I have tried to adhere to the following general rules:

1. Transliteration: I generally follow the Arabic pronunciation over the Arabic form. Therefore we shall write ash-Shāfi`i rather than al-Shāfi`i, and *bismillah-irrahman-irrahim* over *bismillah-arrahman-arrahim.* This rule may occasionally be broken when one writes "`Alī b. Abu Talib" over the more correct "`Alī b. Abī Talib."
2. Plural forms. Although one wants to be consistent, English-speaking Muslims are so wont to render the plurals of madhhab and fatwā as madhhabs and fatwas over madhāhib and fatawa. Such commonly used Anglicized plural forms may creep in.
3. Qur'ānic translations are generally my own.
4. Upon reading or hearing the name of the Prophet Muḥammad, the devout Muslim always exclaims: "Peace and blessings be upon him (*ṣalla Allahu `alayhi wa sallam*)." For the sake of convenience of writing we shall not insert this respectful greeting, on the understanding that the Muslim reader will respond in such a manner.
5. Dates mentioned in the form 751/1350, for example, denote AH and AD respectively.

## Acknowledgments

To Dr. Faroque Khan, whose invitation to the 1995 convention of the Islamic Medical Association of North America, held in Kuala Lumpur, Malaysia, resulted in the conception of this book. To my father, Dr. Muḥammad Abdul-Rauf, whose initial reading and encouragement urged me to publish this work. To Yūsuf Nureddin, whose many comments and hours of discussion helped in the structural formatting and editing of the work. To Khadijah Jennings, who added helpful comments. To Alī Abdul Azeem, whose professional copyediting made this book abide by the rules of his profession. To Dr. Ahmad Kostas, for his helpful comments and important reminder regarding an aspect of Maliki law. To my wife, for her cheerful patience and many useful comments. To Kabir Helminski, for making this book a reality. To my murids and my Jum'ah audience who called this knowledge forth.

Finally, my gratitude to Shaykh Muzaffer Ozak al-Khalwati al-Jarrahi and Shaykh Hamzah ibn `Abbas al-Qadiri for their blessings and *barakah.*

# CONTENTS

## **Preamble:**

# WHY SHOULD YOU READ THIS BOOK?

American Muslims are challenged in dealing with real-life issues in America. You may have been a home buyer wondering if mortgage interest is permitted (*ḥalāl*); you may be a physician concerned about how to deal with life-and-death medical ethical issues like abortion or where to draw the line on treating an aging sick person. Or you may be a Muslim man wondering if growing a beard makes you a better Muslim, or a Muslim woman trying to figure out appropriate Muslim dress codes and modes of behavior while living in a modern Wesern society. The underlying dynamics of these issues, if not the specific issues themselves, as posed here, have been discussed and addressed by Islamic thinkers and jurists from early on in Islamic history. This book is not intended to give you pat legal opinions or judgments (*fatwas*) on these issues, but to help you *think* about the underlying dynamics of problems like these, so that you can follow and examine any arguments presented to you on such questions for their worthiness. It is to help you recognize what is essential and central to your faith, and to differentiate this from what is nonessential and peripheral. If you master the contents of this book, you will fathom the *basic philosophy of the Islamic law*—generally known as *uṣūl al-fiqh,* which is presented here in as simple and clear a language as possible—and you will have the tools that have been used by jurists to think about these issues and proceed towards decisions that are juridically correct.

Most Muslims do not have time to read volumes of scholarly Islamic literature. What you need are the insights into the *Sharī'ah* that really matter—those that will help you make better personal decisions that fit the practice of your faith into the present day.

And you want those insights to be presented in a concise, organized and intimately readable manner. This short book attempts to meet both of these objectives. Among the realizations that will come to you is that Islamic law is not some rigid, inflexible list of do's and don'ts that put you into a strait jacket; it is more like a well-engineered car, rigid where it needs to be and flexible where it needs to be, so that it can meet its objective of taking you towards an increasingly deeper and more intimate relationship with your Creator.

We think you can benefit from this book regardless of your current knowledge of Islām. If you are a beginner, this book will introduce you to the principles of Islamic law that to a large degree reflect a highly developed common sense. These principles, however, are powerful tools. When making decisions, they will help you develop your thoughts logically and view the central issues more clearly.

And if you are a student of Islām, we believe you will also find this book informative. However much you may have studied the Qur'ān and the Ḥadīth (see Appendix I C), you may not fully appreciate how all the "pieces of the *Sharī'ah*" fit together. But this book is written not so much for scholars as for the average Western-educated Muslims who want to practice their faith as fully and with as much understanding as they can.

Some contemporary Muslim writers, in their attempt to be modern, believe that we must ignore the lessons developed by our forebears in the development of Islamic jurisprudence and go back solely to the Qur'ān and the Ḥadīth, and some even go so far as to assert that we should only consider the Qur'ān alone and ignore the Ḥadīth. Although their argument is based on a justified reaction to fossilizing tendencies, such a radical position cannot be defended by anyone who is familiar with the wisdom contained within the corpus of writings on Islamic jurisprudence (*fiqh*). This wisdom reveals an integral, well-thought-out system and *philosophy* of law built upon the eternal lessons of the Qur'ān and the Ḥadīth. And notwithstanding the historical differences of opinion among the founders and jurists of the Islamic schools of jurisprudence, there has in fact been a growing body of consensus of jurisprudence by the great Muslim thinkers down the ages, many of whom were also in key court positions. Such individuals had to deal with the real day-to-day problems of life; they thought and wrote decisively and incisively, yet with enormous care and sensitivity on these subjects.

This book intends to bring out of camouflage this consensual outline of jurisprudence in such a manner that we can indeed detect its integral unity and faithfulness to the Divine impulse embodied in the Qur'ān and Ḥadīth, and its remarkable ability to cope with the new problems offered by life. This consensual outline is in fact the cream of the collective genius of Islamic juridical thought; it is *the way of thinking*—thus *the philosophy*—of the *Sharī'ah*, known in Arabic as *uṣūl al-fiqh.* In the process of examining this philosophy you will get an overview of the Islamic worldview—through the lens of the *Sharī'ah* of Islām—that is well within your reach.

# CHAPTER I

## WHY IS THE SACRED LAW (SHARĪ`AH) IMPORTANT TO MUSLIMS?

The *Sharī'ah* is important to Muslims because it is the operative formula by which the Muslim determines what is good or ethical. The Muslim's pursuit of happiness is ultimately linked to the simultaneous and reciprocal notions of pleasing God and being pleased with Him.[1] This comes about by accepting the Creator, God, as our Lord and aspiring to gain His acceptance of us (the word for acceptance in Arabic is *riḍa*), and may be further explained by looking at the word islām, which means surrender. Muslims who define their Islamicity by their degree of surrender to God gauge their capacity to achieve the good by their capacity to achieve a maximal surrender to the ideals, prescriptions and prohibitions of the Qur'ān and Ḥadīth. By doing so, they conform their behavior to God's preferences, since a good individual or a good society is defined as an individual or society that maximally conforms to Divine intent. To the Muslim, this surrender or conformity with Divine intent describes a process that begins with the *shahāda*, the formal and contractual ritual of bearing witness that there is no god but God, and that Muḥammad is the Messenger of God. Good and right action begins with good and right thinking, and the *Sharī'ah* embraces the creed, the set of beliefs, that a Muslim upholds as constituting good and right thinking. Although a person who utters the *shahāda* is legally accepted as a Muslim by merely uttering these words, its very phrasing strongly suggests

---

[1] See Qur'ān, verses 89:27–30, which read: "O confident soul! Return to your Lord, pleased and pleasing (by and to God respectively: *rāḍiyatan marḍiyyah*).

that the Muslim's testimony of faith should reflect his personal experience of the Divine. The unfolding personal experience of the *shahāda* continues to demand from the Muslim not only obedience to what God explicitly directs, but it also nudges him towards attempting to acquire a way of thinking, an attitude and state of mind, that is consonant with God's preference and explicit decrees. And to those among the Muslim community who have been so inclined, it has urged them to develop a jurisprudential theory which expresses and brings out the logical pattern, or mindset, of these Divine decrees.

A complementary reason for the *Sharī'ah*'s importance is because it *defines* religion as such. An authentic religion *is* a Divine ordinance, and thus a sacred law. Without a sacred law, religion cannot exist in realized form within the heart and mind of its practitioner, and becomes like a soul without a body; it is out of this world without taking you there. So if you want to be in the world and proceed safely out of it, a *Sharī'ah* is the vehicle to transport you. Since religion is realized only in its practice, a believer utilizes the *Sharī'ah* to approach his Lord. God tells us:

> *And We have set you on a road of [Our] Commandment*[2] *(a Sharī'ah, or a Sacred Law of [Our] Command, Sharī'atin min al-amr); so follow it, and follow not the whims of those who know not. (45:18)*

God designed us so that our primary function is to worship Him. *Sharī'ah* means a road, and remember that since the Arab context is that of a desert, this "road" will take us to water. The

---

2 Other meanings are "a law that embodies Our command." This verse follows a few verses in which Allāh speaks of what He granted the Children of Israel of spiritual bounty, specifically of scripture, wisdom, prophethood, and "clarifications of the Commandment" (*bayyinātin min al-amr*), which we can take to include the Ten Commandments, the most important of which is the first commandment to worship Allāh alone with no partner, and to make no image of Him. Thus *Sharī'atin min al-amr* refers to the law given to Prophet Muḥammad which carries, embodies, fulfils and manifests, and continues, or "carries on the work" ordained by the Divine Commandment (previously given to Moses in the trenchant form of the Ten Commandments, which in all respects is a branching out of the primary commandment to worship only one God).

implied imagery of the term *Sharī'ah* is that our life is like one in a desert, with God analogous to the oasis we need. Thus the primary focus of the *Sharī'ah* is on humankind's *journey* towards intimacy with our Creator, and that the *Sharī'ah*'s purpose is to establish religion (*dīn*), which means to establish the links between God and Man. Though not as evident in our desert metaphor, a road has lanes, and rules for the flow of traffic; otherwise accidents will occur. The rules of traffic flow are not meant to limit our freedom; they are designed for safety of travel so that we can travel quicky. The rules of the *Sharī'ah* are the same; they are meant to allow us to travel spiritually very quickly without accident.

*Sharī'ah* is therefore the body of Divine guidance, its structure, format and construct. A human soul with its accompaniments of mind and emotion needs to be carried and contained in the envelope of a body, well defined and well constructed, in order to be alive and functional. Without a *Sharī'ah*, a religion can be termed, if not "dead," certainly much less alive,[3] for the religion then lacks the medium by which it brings its power to bear effectively upon those who need it. And since a sacred law cannot be divorced from the task of judging, including in its embrace the roles of those who understand, uphold, apply and enforce the religious law, these roles are of vital importance.

This brings us to a third reason that makes the *Sharī'ah* important to Muslims: it protected the integrity of the faith of Islām throughout the vicissitudes of history. Even today, it is the law of Islām that is arguably the most important element in the struggle waged between traditionalism and modernism with its secular notions. Man is notorious for changing God's rules and dictates, for seeking to reduce the eternal to suit the temporal, and by so doing, reducing its power to transform him towards what is better. Man wants God to come down to him and his level, to reduce the eter-

[3] When we speak of enlivening religion, we must bear in mind that religion does not exist in the abstract sense as a disembodied entity separate from man. Although we speak of religion as an independent entity, religion becomes religion only when practiced in human behavior and embraced in human hearts. Thus the *Sharī'ah*'s purpose is to enliven and to maintain in a maximal state of aliveness the soul of man.

nal into the temporal. What God wants is that Man rise up to the Divine level, to draw our temporal into the eternal. This polarity is contained in the ensemble of the Islamic *Sharī'ah* and its inner transformative content of Divine remembrance (*dhikr*).[4] The *Sharī'ah*, as a developed form and formula of behavior, is the body of Islamic religious expression and provides us with what is unchangeable of Divine revelation for the salvation and well-being of both the eternal and temporal in humankind. It is a rope thrown down to us, intersecting the timely with the timeless, meshing them in the best possible manner, and whose intent is to transform, or raise up and subsume the temporal in man into the eternal, to bring the timely in him in line with the timeless. In other words, the *Sharī'ah* processes you so that you will get to where it's more enjoyable to be, with God, the angels, the Prophets and the close ones who are God's very good friends (or saints, known in Arabic as *awliyā'ull āh*).

Comparing Islām to Judaism and Christianity—its predecessors among the Abrahamic religions—is instructive in this regard. Judaism eviscerated the spiritual dimension from the Sacred Law, thus leading to the need for Jesus Christ to present himself upon the scene to correct this imbalance. However, in succeeding generations Christianity, in its attempt to focus on the spiritual and make itself palatable to previously unbelieving societies, eviscerated the Sacred Law from the spiritual dimension, with the result that the spiritual dimension could not maintain its integrity against the onslaught of different human cultures and succeeding epochs. A sacred law is important in protecting the spiritual dimension of the faith, and this fragmentation resulted in the need for the Prophet Muḥammad's coming on the scene to present the perfected marriage of Sacred Law with spiritual content. The *Sharī'ah* is on one level the crystallization of Islamic *spiritual* values, and at another level it is the protector of these spiritual values.

---

[4] For a more involved discussion on Divine remembrance, see my forthcoming book *Dhikrullah: Tasting the Presence of God.*

To the extent that there exists a *polarity* between some elements of the *modern* Western mindset and the Muslim mindset, it can be rendered as the battle between a philosophy that seeks freedom *from* religion and religious expression and one that seeks freedom *of* religion and religious expression. Muslims have no theological basis to dispute those who seek freedom of religious expression.[5]

## A. The Objectives (*maqāṣid*) of the *Sharī'ah*

There were many jurists from the various schools who wrote books on the aims of the *Sharī'ah* and on the interests and causes upon which it was established. Among them were the Shāfi`i jurist Al-`Izz (`Izz ad-Din) ibn `Abd as-Salām, the Hanbali jurist Ibn al-Qayyim al-Jawziyyah (d. 751/1350), the Maliki jurist Abu Ishāq ash-Shātibī and others. Centuries before the European notion of separation of Church and State and all the talk about religious versus secular, these very intelligent and wise men recognized such a conceptual separation and divided the body of *Sharī'ah* rules into two categories: **religious observances** and **worldly matters.** The first, dealing with questions of worship, they observed to be beyond the scope of modification. The second relating to the worldly interests of mankind, covers the following three categories:

1. **Criminal Law:** This includes crimes such as murder, larceny, fornication, drinking alcohol, libel.

[5] This does not fully explain the primary difference between the Western ideal and the traditional Muslim mindset. The Western ideal is a government that allows freedom of religion and religious expression, without endorsing any one religious group or practice. Historically, governments with majority Muslim populations endorsed the Islamic faith over others, even while allowing other religious groups freedom to practice their faith.

2. **Family Law:** This category, also known as the Laws of Personal Status, covers marriage, divorce, alimony, child custody, inheritance.

3. **Transactions:** This covers property rights, contracts, rules of sale, hire, gift, loans and debts, deposits, partnerships, and damage to property.

Al-`Izz ibn `Abd as-Salām stated that the purposes of the *Sharī'ah* are as follows:

> *All obligations refer to the interests of God's creatures in this world and the next. God is not in need of people's worship, nor is He benefited by the obedience of those who obey, nor is He harmed by the disobedience of those who disobey.*[6]

In other words, we worship God not for His benefit, but for our benefit. The purposes of the rules governing worldly transactions can be discerned by reason. They are based upon bringing benefits to the people and protecting them against evil, and upon the principle that, fundamentally, benefits are permitted while evils are forbidden. Most jurists subscribe to this view. There were a few exceptions, however, like Dāwūd aẕ-Ẕahirī who did not distinguish between religious observances and worldly transactions but considered both of them as religious observances that may not be discerned by reason.[7]

---

[6] Qawā'id al-Aḥkām fī maṣālih al-Anam (Cairo, 1934), vol. II, 70.

[7] This does not mean that they *could* not distinguish between the two categories, but that they *would* not make such a distinction the basis for adhering or not adhering to the rule; for if a law relating to a worldly matter was to be based on a reason that we came up with, then when the reason is no longer there, the law could be freely violated or ignored. As an example to illustrate this, the dietary laws of the Qur'ān prohibit the eating of pork products (pork, ham, bacon), but do not state the reason for this prohibition. If we deduce that the reason for this prohibition is the danger of contracting trichinosis, then we may conclude that, if we destroy the danger of trichinosis, eating pork products would be permitted. The Zahiri position that "worldly matters are to be considered as religious and that the reason cannot be discerned" means, first, that unless God states His reason, we really do not know the reason why God prohibited it, and second, that even if we succeed in eliminating the danger of contracting trichinosis (which we, not God, assert as being the reason behind the prohibition), the prohibition of eating pork products still stands. This is what is meant by categorizing the prohibition against eating pork as a "religious" prohibition and observation, and not as a

One of the most sensible definitions of the purposes of the *Sharī'ah* was given by Ibn al-Qayyim al-Jawziyyah who said,

> *The foundation of the Sharī'ah is wisdom and the safeguarding of people's interests in this world and the next. In its entirety it is justice, mercy and wisdom. Every rule which transcends justice to tyranny, mercy to its opposite, the good to the evil, and wisdom to triviality does not belong to the Sharī'ah although it might have been introduced therein by implication. The Sharī'ah is God's justice and mercy amongst His people. Life, nutrition, medicine, light, recuperation and virtue are made possible by it. Every good that exists is derived from it, and every deficiency in being results from its loss and dissipation.... For the Sharī'ah, which God entrusted His prophet to transmit, is the pillar of the world and the key to success and happiness in this world and the next.*[8]

Jesus proclaims in the Bible that man was not made for the Sabbath, but that the Sabbath was made for man. Muslim jurists make the same point: Man was not made for the *Sharī'ah*, the *Sharī'ah* was made for man. Therefore they recognized that the *Sharī'ah*, being placed for the benefit of humankind, had certain aims and human rights that it sought to protect, and these they called the "Objectives of the *Sharī'ah*" (*maqāṣid ash-Sharī'ah*); so much so that certain laws may under certain circumstances be overruled if any of these five objectives is in jeopardy. **These five are: protection of life, religion, property (or wealth), offspring (or lineage and progeny) and mind (i.e., sanity, reason/intellect).**[9]

---

"worldly" one. Muslims as a rule do not apply this type of logic to this example, but more usually to the area of financial transactions.

8 Ibn al-Qayyim al-Jawziyyah, *I'lām al-Muwaqqi'īn 'an Rabb al-'Ālamīm* (Cairo, n.d.), vol. III, 1.

9 Thus, for example, although the consumption of meat of an animal that was not slaughtered (but died of natural causes or an accident) is generally prohibited, in a time of famine it may be consumed for survival. The objective of protection of life makes it allowable under these circumstances. Another example is that medication that contains alcohol may be consumed at a time of illness to effect a cure, although the consumption of alcohol is prohibited.

Adhering to the *Sharī'ah* should enhance these five aims, which the jurists have implicitly equated with what we Americans typically call "the pursuit of happiness." Never should the *Sharī'ah* jeopardize your life, deprive you of your religion, rob you of your wealth, endanger your family or your children, nor drive you crazy.

Yet we ought to bear in mind that the concept of "good" is ultimately relative, and is relative to the point of view, time of view and component of view. There is what is good for our soul, our body, our mind and our feelings. What is good for one component is not always good or bad for another; for example it is not always true that what is good for my body is good for my mind. There is also the good of the individual versus that of society, or the good of one individual versus that of another. And what may be good for one individual or society at one point in time may no longer be good for the same individual or society at another point in time. (For example, I love well-marbled steaks, but they are bad for my health. Exercise is good for my body and for my mind, but something about me hates to do exercise. An example of a good varying with time would be like the problem of an old school friend: if he drank Coca Cola when he was sick it would make him better, but if he drank it when he was well it made him sick.) Thus we observe the need for a formula to nest our valuations of good in some typical order: the eternal over the temporal, for example, and to balance the various determinations of good. This is in fact what we do as individuals, and is also what any society seeks to do in the enacting of its laws. And this is what the *Sharī'ah* aims to do. Its objectives (*maqāṣid*), as delineated above, are concerned not only with the interests and rights of one individual over the others, but in extending these rights towards society at large. The *Sharī'ah* embodies an ideal code of human behavior, not only in ritual practices of the faith, but also regarding law and morality, and is the Muslim's guide to right conduct.

God is Absolute Being, His attributes are absolute, and His goodness is absolute. Therefore what God decrees is absolutely good. And since our soul is closer to God, because that is where God deposited His Breath within the human envelope, what is good for our soul is a higher (or "more absolute") good, and thus entails a higher priority over what is good for other components of our being (mind, body, and emotions). If you have a choice between eating prime rib every night and having a heart attack due to high cholesterol, or eating swordfish and doing physical exercises every day, what would you do? Most of us give up the prime rib, because a few moments of eating pleasure isn't worth dying for. As important as your taste buds are, they are not more important than your life, so we go for the fish and the exercise. Your soul is eternal, thus what is good for your soul is eternally good for you. The *Sharī'ah* places God, and by extension the soul of man, at the center of the determination of what is good, with the simultaneous objective of providing what is good for the rest of man's components in accordance with their relative levels of importance. It is therefore concerned with what is nutritious for the soul, that which provides for its growth and development, and is equally concerned with our avoiding what is poisonous for our souls, that which results in its regression. The *Sharī'ah* thereby provides a formula which assists man in determining the relative degrees of good within an overall, integrated framework that *balances* the temporal and the eternal, and optimizes the relationship between the body, mind and soul.

Going back to the proposition posed at the beginning of the chapter, that the good can only be measured by the degree of accord with God's dictates, then we are forced to conclude that a good individual, and a good society, can only be defined as one that abides by Divine dictates and criteria, and that the *best* individual or society is defined as that which is *maximally* in accord with these criteria. Muslims therefore believe that the best society was that of Madina at the time of the Prophet, and that the best Muslims were the Prophet's companions. The challenge this posed to Muslims after the time of the Prophet was to define the nature of the Prophet's society and companions in terms of the perennial good. We cannot just take all aspects of sixth-century Arabia that were part of the Prophet's norms and impose them on later times. *Uṣūl al-fiqh* represents the attempt to craft an operative formula, extracted from the Qur'ān and the norms of the Prophet's practice (known as *sunnah*), that would provide Muslims of succeeding generations with the means to attain the good that was expressed by the Prophet and his ideal society.[10]

God places a high premium on judging in accord with His dictates, and for developing a nation where laws apply to all equally, and where those who are in charge of upholding the law do not set themselves or any other group above the law—for then corruption sets in.[11] The corruption of the individual or a society that abandons Sacred Law is amplified in one of the key Qur'ānic passages regarding the relevance, evolution and meaning of Divine Law, (5:41–50) where Allāh speaks frequently of the act of "judging." In this passage, God criticizes previous generations who "raced towards disbelief, among those who say with their mouths 'We believe' while their hearts don't believe;" who "altered God's Words from their placements;" indicating somehow that they altered their divinely ordained *Sharī'ah,* placing their own values above that which God had established. The Qur'ān continues to describe them as "listeners of lies, devourers of ill-gotten property," an accusation that a Muslim tries carefully to avoid incurring.

---

[10] This ideal of Madinan society at the Prophet's time and for the next few generations found expression later in the Maliki school of thought, that based part of its criteria on deciding a matter by subjecting it to the norms of Madinan society.

[11] It is interesting in this regard that Qur'ānic prescriptions prescribe increased punishments for those who are on a higher level in society, the converse of what most societies practice. For example, verse 33:30 reads: "O wives of the Prophet, whoever of you commits manifest evil, the chastisement will be doubled for her;" whereas the punishment for slaves is one half that of the free. Once the Caliph `Umar caught a drunkard and had him lashed 80 lashes; after he sobered up the next morning he came to `Umar and exclaimed that he had been wronged, for he was a slave and should have been given only half the punishment, whereupon `Umar was deeply troubled that he had not examined the case in greater detail.

## B. The Participants' Responsibility before God in an Islamic Court

A key difference between American, or any secular, law and Islamic law lies in the definition of "natural law." In a secular society, the notions of equity and justice are considered to stem from natural law, without explicitly and *necessarily* rooting these terms in a value system originating with God. In Islamic law, Nature—being a creation of God and expressing values placed therein by the Creator—is not considered as something that stands in opposition to God. Natural law, no matter how one defines the term *natural*, is therefore *necessarily* an explicit manifestation of Divine law. To a Muslim jurist, natural law is a *de facto* expression and subset of Divine law, and to speak of natural law as something that just enters into human minds without speaking of God is merely to tacitly admit the values of Divine law without mentioning the name of God. And since God has spoken via His Scripture and Prophets, His revealed law not only encompasses the notions of natural law, but grounds it and extends it.

An ideal in the United States was to develop a concept of law that extracts the "common denominator of goodness" from all prior historical expressions of law, and to fashion it into a system that permits people from all religious and cultural backgrounds to coexist as full and complete equals in a state that protects all of its citizens against the imposition of beliefs and values of any one religious and cultural background upon them against their will. This was the greatest contribution of the American Constitution to the advancement of human rights in this world, so much so that most people in the world aspire to live in a nation that embodies the protections of human and individual rights that Americans enjoy. In Islamic parlance, one may even posit that the American Constitution and Bill of Rights sought to express the eternal nonparochial and super-cultural values of Divine—and thereby Islamic—law.

However, God's role in the explicit philosophical construct of the law makes a big difference between the *modus operandi* of a righteous Muslim judge in a Muslim court and a righteous Western judge in a Western court. The judge who sits in judgment in an Islamic court sits in lieu of God as His worldly representative (*khalīfah*), and is held responsible by God to His values.[12] The Muslim judge *explicitly* "reports to God." The judge who sits in a Western court is only *explicitly* responsible to the Constitution, the interpretations of a civil law and its rules. All the participants in a Muslim court, including lawyers, are held responsible before God for upholding equity and justice, whereas secular lawyers are not so explicitly obliged before God. The common conception of an excellent lawyer as one who is able to defend his clients even when they have knowingly committed the most heinous of crimes, professional code of ethics notwithstanding, serves to undermine the execution of justice. A legal defense team containing such clever lawyers may force a righteous judge to render a judgment that he knows to be wrong or not sensible. Islamically, such a person would not be a good lawyer.

---

[12]The worldly court is a "worldly representative" of the Divine Court, which will mete out absolute justice on the Day of Judgment. Although God rewards and punishes, the worldly court is only responsible for punishment, not out of a love of punishment, but as a necessary evil to keep society orderly, cohesive and immune from the socially fragmenting repercussions of crime and lawlessness.

# CHAPTER II

## HOW THIS BOOK CAME ABOUT

In the summer of 1995, I was invited to deliver a paper at the annual convention of the Islamic Medical Association (IMA) of North America, held that year in Kuala Lumpur, Malaysia.

Doctors have to deal with some really thorny problems, and that year, the convention selected a few real-life problems for discussion. Their overarching aim was to answer the question: Can we develop a problem-solving format that would assist Muslim physicians in addressing the rise of medical ethical dilemmas? In addition to the dramatic and controversial type of issues like cloning, abortion, surrogate motherhood, or when to terminate life support on someone lingering as a human vegetable, physicians daily face life-and-death issues that don't make the news. The following case of 92-year-old Grandma Fatima[13] is an example of the more common day-to-day medical dilemma.

Grandma Fatima had lost a lot of weight, was frail, and after the last bitter winter, developed colds easily. Her memory loss was significant; she did not remember the names of her own children, let alone her grandchildren. Most of the time she stays in her bedroom, and her family took turns nursing her. Having developed flu-like symptoms and fever, she had difficulty breathing. The family took her to the hospital, where she was diagnosed with pneumonia, and as suffering from an inadequate supply of oxygen. Her breathing was difficult and painful, and her heart was beating at a rate of over 100 beats per minute. During the course of her hospitalization and intensive care, she developed multi-organ failure, including kidney failure. The kidney doctors (nephrologists)

---

[13] All names are fictitious to protect the identity of the individuals.

recommended dialysis; the internists questioned the validity of such high-tech intervention. The family loved Grandma Fatima, and they wanted to do all they could to express their love towards her, but they didn't know what to do. They sought the guidance of the Imam and the senior Muslim members of their community. The question the doctors raised was: should the advanced age and the mental status of Grandma Fatima play any role in deciding the type of long-term care? Is expending great sums of money to keep her alive worth the effort?

Another example was 19-year-old Salim. The poor fellow has had repeated bouts of bronchitis and pneumonia, requiring hospitalization. He suffers from the genetically acquired disease cystic fibrosis (an inherited disease, present from birth, characterized by a tendency to chronic lung infections and an inability to absorb fats and other nutrients from food).[14] A new genetically engineered medication, Recombinant Human Dnase, is known to relieve severe respiratory problems. The monthly cost of this medicine is $1,200. This medicine, while improving quality of life, has not been shown to affect long-term survival. Salim's Yemeni immigrant parents, being poor, coulsdn't afford the medication and requested the help and support of the community in obtaining the medicines. The community elders pondered over the dilemma of allocation of limited resources. They have an annual budget of $10,000 from which to allocate funds. The choices they face are between helping Salim vs. helping a larger number of children with their crying need for food, clothing and basic medical needs. What should they do?

---

[14] When cystic fibrosis (CF) was first identified in the 1930s, before effective antibiotics were available, almost all sufferers died in early childhood. More recently, however, and particularly since 1975, the outlook has changed dramatically. With more advanced methods of diagnosis and treatment, including the use of a wide range of antibiotics, over two thirds of CF sufferers now survive into adult life, although few of them are in perfect health. CF remains a serious and potentially fatal disorder.

The question my host Dr. Faroque Khan presented as we sat in his kitchen over tea was, what is "the Islamic viewpoint"[15] on these types of problems? Is there in fact such a viewpoint? And if not, can one be formulated to help guide Muslim medical practitioners in dealing with this genre of problems? Since the convention was going to be held in Malaysia, I thought "Good! The Prime Minister of Malaysia, Dr. Mahathir Muḥammad, is himself a medical doctor. He is also known to be very interested in encouraging the development of Islamic Law to deal with modern problems. His take on questions like these would be most enlightening. Why not ask him?" Better yet, invite him to attend and open the convention, and probe him on these questions.

Anyway, Dr. Khan wouldn't let me off the hook; my reputation with him as the Imam of a New York City mosque was at stake. Couldn't I shed some light on these matters? He showed me some of his published articles in the IMA journal, and I was impressed to learn that his paper on brain death as the determinant of death had been adopted as the legally accepted standard by the medical establishment in some Middle Eastern nations. So I was forced to ponder these questions and rush to my references, as every Imam in America worth his salt is forced to do from time to time. And as I did, I was reminded that we Muslims in America are faced daily in our professions and in our personal lives with a number of matters that—as lay people—we have not been taught *how to think about*, much less how to deal with. And if we can't think about them correctly, we will not deal with them correctly. The result is a muddled controversy within at least a segment of

---

15 Or, as the question is often phrased, "What does *Islām* say about these matters?" It may be noteworthy to point out that Arabic and other non-English speakers do not commonly phrase the question this way. They tend to ask: "What does the Qur'ān say," "What does the Ḥadīth say," or more usually "What does the *Sharī'ah* say," or "What is the *hukm* in this matter?" In this very language construct lies the implicit recognition that the Sacred Law, or *Sharī'ah,* is the governing and deciding source. It is not the theology of Islām that embraces its Sacred Law, but its Sacred Law that embraces its theology. When we use the expression a "proper Islamic solution, or viewpoint," we do so with the understanding that what we are really after is a solution that is in accord with the Sacred Law of Islām.

the Muslim community, usually caused by any one of the following:

1. Uncertainty and lack of clarity in many Muslims' minds about the definitions of the underlying concepts. For example, the `Id's falling on a Sunday or a Monday in one part of the Islamic world compared with another is a result of the Islamic lunar calendar's "shifting date-line."[16]
2. Lack of awareness on the part of the Muslim public on matters that have already been settled by Muslim jurists and are not deemed controversial in their eyes. Here the controversy is more socio-political than juridical. For example, matters of dress codes and whether one should in general follow United States laws.
3. Classically controversial items, on which juridical opinion is divided. An example is whether any rate of interest, no matter how small, is in fact *ribā*, and therefore *ḥarām* (prohibited).[17]
4. New matters we tend to deal with on an ad-hoc basis as they arise. Examples are advances in medical technology which force us to reconsider and refine important concepts like the moment of death.

---

[16] See Mohammad Ilyas, *New Moon's Visibility and International Islamic Calendar for the American Region, 1407H–1421H, 1995*, published by International Islamic Calendar Programme, Penang, Malaysia, for a more detailed description. Whereas the International Date Line which zigzags across the Pacific Ocean is fixed, resulting in the date always starting in the Pacific slightly east of Japan, if one follows the Islamic lunar notion of the day beginning where the new crescent is first sighted, then the new date can begin anywhere. Therefore sometimes the new month may begin in Eastern Asia, sometimes in Africa, and sometimes in America, with the result that the `Id may be celebrated in the USA and Western regions one day prior to its being celebrated in the Eastern part of the world like Indonesia and Japan.

[17] Although most scholars are inclined to assert that any form of a return on funds constitutes *ribā*, and that the current banking system based on paper and now paperless money reeks of *ribā*, Shaykh Muḥammad Tantawi, the current Shaykh al-Azhar and previous Grand Mufti of Egypt, issued a *fatwā* allowing the Government to borrow from its subjects and reward them as they see fit, since this was in the public interest. The Government considered this as an endorsement of interest paid on its bonds.

Although we can talk about issues like these theoretically, it becomes very difficult to deal with the human reality in a gratifying way when it presents itself. Here is a question a dear brother posed to me in our masjid recently which underlines this *experiential* difficulty:

Masjid ul-Iḥsān in New York City is a community of African Americans located in a low-income neighborhood, and operates a school, Madrassat ul-Iman, with an enrollment of 120 students. Their rent is $3,000 per month, which amounts to $36,000 per year (as there is a summer school program, the Institute is open year round). This rent is a lot of money for a financially struggling community. The landlord gave this Muslim community the option to purchase the building. To exercise this option the community would have to take out a mortgage. Purchasing the building would give the Community some real estate assets and leverage for economic growth. Many in the community want to purchase the property; they are not satisfied with sinking so much of their hard-earned money into a rental arrangement. They feel it is *senseless* to pay all of this money and yet not have ownership. However, the Imam of the community states emphatically that mortgages are *ḥarām*—strictly prohibited under Islamic law. What is "the proper Islamic solution?" If they do not purchase the building the community has little chance for economic growth and development. Their rent will keep going up indefinitely instead of being capped by a mortgage payment that could amortize the purchase price, and perhaps one day even will jeopardize the ability of the school to continue to operate at all. Does it make sense to jeopardize the teaching of Islām to all these kids because mortgage interest is *ḥarām*?

Interest on loans is the basic issue here, whether they are mortgage loans, car loans or student loans. Muḥammad Ayman, who graduated from college as a pre-med and was accepted into medical school, was faced with this dilemma too. The tuition alone is about $25,000 per year, not to mention his food and board for another four years. His middle-class, immigrant Egyptian parents have just given $40,000 of their hard-earned savings to see him through his Bachelor's degree after sending four other children through college. They cannot possibly afford to spend another $150,000 for medical school. Student loans are readily available for him, which grant him the opportunity to pay the money back comfortably after he graduates and starts earning a doctor's six-figure income, which averaged $184,000 in 1995. Should we deny him the opportunity to be a successful and highly paid professional doctor because interest on a student loan is *ḥarām*? Does this make *sense* in today's world? Does this serve the better interests of the Muslim community and help us advance in the world?

Contemporary options like these, and some others created by modern technology, are forcing us to think of the morality of issues that were not posed to us before. Issues like surrogate motherhood, for instance, emanate from the ability of modern technology to provide us with options not available in the past—options that must be addressed if we are to move on as a society in this rapidly evolving world. As you think through issues like these, you will realize that many Muslims feel it is legitimate to inquire about "the Islamic viewpoint" or "proper Islamic solution"[18] regarding these options. Furthermore, if "Islamic viewpoints" have not yet been established, many Muslims believe that they certainly ought to be.

Must there be an "Islamic perspective" to every question, and is such a perspective necessarily unique? May there not be more than one solution equally "Islamic"? And on what assumptions does such a perspective rest?

## Why Study uṣūl al-fiqh?

*Uṣūl al-fiqh* is the intellectual or scientific structure of the *Sharī'ah.* Any attempt to develop an "Islamic viewpoint" on the issues of the day requires applying a mind grounded in its appreciation and understanding. In this day and age when Muslims are

---

[18] For example, that if interest is *ḥarām*, that there should therefore be an "Islamic" solution that addresses the real need of the borrower.

gathered together from all parts of the world, it helps Muslims enhance their awareness and recognition of what is essential and central to their faith, and learn to differentiate the peripheral from the essential. *Uṣūl al-fiqh* can be somewhat likened to the laws of natural science; they can be considered to be "eternally modern," although they may have been "discovered" in time and within a historical context.

An analogy will explain this point. When you study biology, you not only study the observable biological world, but by observation you notice that there are certain patterns the biological world obeys, even though each life form differs from another. And although *we* did not create the biological world—Allāh the Creator did—the science of biology is a *human perception and understanding* of that reality out there. Our knowledge may be incomplete, and in some instances incorrect, but over time as more and more biologists deepen their research and discuss among themselves the results of their studies, we weed out our incorrect understandings, and our base of correct or firm knowledge grows and expands. Over years, biologists may argue over many issues, and disputes and controversies occur over issues like whether evolution really exists and how it ought to be defined, but in time a growing consensus prevails within what is generally accepted as the science of biology. And its usefulness lies in helping us understand God's creation. For example, by applying our understanding of the laws or science of biology, we can work with God, so to speak, to breed new hybrid forms of plant and animal life that may be more useful to us. When we do this, we are not really overcoming or denying biology, we are enhancing the quality of our life with our knowledge and understanding of biology.

*Uṣūl al-fiqh* is analogous. The *Sharī'ah* is God-given, and it comprises prescriptions and prohibitions embodied in the Qur'ān and the Ḥadīth, for these two sources are respectively God-given and God-modified when the occasion warranted.[19] We therefore *know* that the Qur'ān and Ḥadīth are endorsed by God. And like the biologists in the above example, some interested and very smart people began to study the *Sharī'ah* and discovered that there were in fact some principles or laws underlying the *Sharī'ah*. This study became a *science*, and became known as *uṣūl al-fiqh*. It includes the philosophy, theory, understanding, rationale and impulse of the *Sharī'ah*. And just like biologists or any other class of scientists, the scholars of *fiqh*, known as *fuqahā'* (singular *faqīh*) had differences of opinion on matters some of which are of greater, and some of lesser, consequence to the average Muslim. However, in time, a growing consensus developed, as in the above mentioned example of biology, and the growing science of *uṣūl al-fiqh* became increasingly accepted by Muslim scholars (*'ulamā'* singular *'ālim*) as a valuable science. Understanding *uṣūl al-fiqh* not only gives you an understanding of the reasoning behind the *Sharī'ah*, but its value becomes particularly evident when it enables you, in new circumstances and when faced with modern dilemmas, to apply your reasoning to arrive at a *comfortably correct* decision.[20]

---

[19] One example of this is Surah 73, verses 1 through 4, where the Qur'ān commands the Prophet to "stay up half the night, more or less, and recite the Qur'ān." Although the command is to the Prophet, his companions who sought to emulate him and loved doing so, also put this Divine command into practice. This was in the beginning of the Prophet's mission, when the sum total of verses revealed could comfortably be recited in an hour or so. As the Qur'ān continued to be revealed, and as the Prophet's responsibilites increased with the growth of the Muslim community, it became increasingly difficult to recite the whole Qur'ān in half of an evening, and the last verse of this Surah rescinded this requirement, saying the following: "Your Lord knows that you stay up close to two-thirds of the night, or half or a third of it, as do a number of those with you (referring to the companions of the Prophet)...He knows that you are not able to do it, so He has relented towards you, so recite what is comfortable to recite of the Qur'ān (that is, what is reasonable to recite in an evening)... (verse 20).

[20] The scientific analogy may need some explication. Scientific laws are not absolute in the sense that they are given to us by God; they consist of the human attempt to discover and express natural laws in human language and formulas. The sum of these laws, as a body of science, has to be logically consistent, and as time goes on, earlier beliefs about these laws stand to be corrected as scientific knowledge, tested by experiments in real situations, advances. Also the body of scientific knowledge grows as discussions and sometimes passionate disputes and arguments occur. With time, however, consensus develops among the scientists on the controversial issues of the day as

The outcome may not always be unique; a particular answer may be valid in one location and not so in another, or at some point in time and not forever, and may be particular to you and not to someone else. This not necessarily unique outcome was one of the factors that led to the rise of different schools of law in the first place and explains why they held different opinions on certain issues. But in most cases and over time, each school considered the other as equally legitimate. There is latitude of opinion within Muslim orthodoxy on what is right and acceptable to God. Just as whether you pray with your hands crossed on your chest or down by your sides are both acceptable to God, most differences between the schools of law are of this okay-to-be-different category. So even if we come up with new opinions regarding new issues, it is necessary to be courteous to each other and regard the other opinion as equally orthodox, especially if the reasoning is within the bounds of *uṣūl al-fiqh*.[21]

---

differences of opinion get ironed out. Applying the principles we learn from this science, we develop a technology that is useful in advancing the quality of our lives.

Analogously, the injunctions of the *Sharī'ah* are God-given and further expanded by the Prophet. Jurists in later centuries began to examine this body of injunctions and prohibitions and sought to "discover" underlying principles and laws of the *Sharī'ah* to develop a logically consistent science of the *Sharī'ah*. This science is *uṣūl al-fiqh*. Differences of opinion occurred, but in time, after centuries of interaction, a growing consensus took place. By understanding this science we can apply it to situations—some of which may be new—to find answers to questions that, although not originally addressed directly in the Qur'ān and Ḥadīth, are consistent with the deepest laws and principles of the *Sharī'ah*.

[21] *Uṣūl al-fiqh*, was developed over the years by the founders of the major schools of law, both Sunni and Shi`i, and their prize students, although Imam ash-Shāfi`i (150/767–204/820) is generally considered to be its founder in the sense of being the first one who attempted to codify the bases of the *Sharī'ah*. In time the collective understanding of *uṣūl al-fiqh* merged towards a consensus. Although *uṣūl al-fiqh* had its roots in the Qur'ān and the Ḥadīth, the contribution of Imam ash-Shāfi`i significantly crystallized, added to and propelled the science of *fiqh* along certain directions, although not all of his opinions became accepted into the mainstream of collective thought on the subject.

We shall try to describe *uṣūl al-fiqh* in such a way that the average Muslim can understand it and see how it may apply to their very own problems. But bear in mind that in following a line of thought that results in one particular opinion or another, we are not necessarily formulating a *fatwā* (a definitive and binding legal judgment upon you). A pediatrician would never dream of performing heart surgery on you, but may not be averse to writing a medical book for the lay person so that you would be able to figure out if that pain in your chest is coming from your heart or from that very special birthday dinner you had. (Heartburn is not a heart problem but a stomach problem, the terminology notwithstanding.) By informing yourself before you proceed to get a medical opinion, you can better use the information and ask intelligent questions that will help you work better with your doctor to cure yourself, because now you can understand what he is trying to do. After all, your life is involved. This is how I prefer that you understand the aim of this book. Because the Islamic community in the USA is a cross-section of the world Muslim population, spanning all of the schools of law, and is a religious minority placed in a rapidly evolving American society spanning the spectrum of circumstances, the *fatwā* business in the USA can be tricky. And since opinions are very much a function of circumstances, and can change with them, it is important that these varying circumstances be taken into account.

For example, in Masjid al-Farah in New York City, the mosque in which I preach, we deal with many converts and young Muslims born into Muslim families. Being new to the practice of Islām, even when born into Muslim families, they may find the sudden imposition of practicing *all* of the Islamic rituals onerous, and may eventually walk out after a few months or years. Being more concerned that the individual acquire and taste the transformative and disciplinary powers of prayer, fasting and the other joys of worship, and anchor it on a very strong foundation of belief and love of God, we encourage our congregation to taste the Divine Presence which urges the human soul to then desire worship and taste its sweetness. Then they do as best as they can, and do not overdo. Too much of a burden can make the individual walk out completely. For instance, we encourage those who cannot pray five times a day to pray three times a day and combine their prayers rather than not pray at all. And to help working people find a way of praying while at work, we advise them to combine the noon and afternoon prayer, and if ablution is difficult, give them an appropriate solution (an easier method of ablution, or *tayammum*). Such an approach is based on the historical fact that the ensemble of Islamic rituals was revealed over a twenty-two-year period, and on the Prophet's advice to "assume unto yourselves such work as you are able to perform,"[22] and to "refrain from doing that which I have prohibited, and carry out that which I have ordered you to do within the limits of your capabilities."[23] Should we expect a new Muslim to assume in one day what took the Prophet's companions years to assimilate? The transformative process is not an overnight one, and acts of worship take root most deeply when the worshipper does it from the inside out, out of love for God, for such love of God feeds the desire to worship. Our focus is therefore on how to increase our congregation's love for God, for love feeds the urge towards discipline far more effectively than discipline feeds the urge to love.

---

22 `Ayni, *Umdat,* XI, 85.

23 Muslim, *Ṣaḥīḥ*, VII, 91. A variant reading is in Bukhāri, *Ṣaḥīḥ*.

## CHAPTER III

# HOW CAN WE RESPOND TO MODERN DILEMMAS?

First we have to figure out what we're doing, and see if we can come up with some kind of a recipe that enables us to analyze, think and see what the issues at hand are all about. Then the next thing we need to do is to develop our qualifications for this task.

If you live in Washington and decide to go to Miami, you will open your road map and look for roads going south. You wouldn't consider going north unless you wanted to go to New York or Boston. Similarly, there are some general remarks we can make about how to respond to the dilemmas we face. We have to narrow our consideration to single issues that we can talk about. There are three ways to respond to dilemmas like these:

1. **The ostrich approach**: hide my head in the sand and pretend that the problem doesn't exist. If you were to ask me "What do we do about Dr. Khan's medical dilemmas?" and I was in the ostrich mood, I would answer along the lines of "What dilemma? Dr. Khan has no such problem! He is a good Muslim, has a good family, is a devout man, etc., and Muslims don't live with moral dilemmas. The Prophet taught us to stay away from gray areas. You must be talking about some medical issue, and I'm no doctor. Go away, and don't bother me." Burying my head in the Qur'ān and *Ḥadīth*, I would quote verses that say how the Muslims are the best nation brought out from humankind, and as such we don't go looking for problems; that's the devil's work. This approach works for many Muslims because it is simple and doesn't require much hard work, but you probably wouldn't feel that this answer quite satisfied your question.

2. **Build a Muslim society**: establish a set of solid, religious, cultural, ethical, business and economic standards around us and live adhering to our Divinely ordained values. If it was good enough for the Pennsylvania Dutch and the Orthodox Jews to live in enclaves, why can't it be good for us? If the Italians can have Little Italy, we can have Little Muslim City. This is the next best thing to emigrating and living in a traditional Muslim country. We'll have shops selling *ḥalāl* meat, give interest-free loans to each other, and live around our mosque. This approach does not prevent all the thorny issues that face us in the modern world from approaching, but it successfully deals with a number of real problems while it attenuates the rest.

3. **Develop a methodology to integrate ourselves with the society at large without losing our religious integrity and identity.** This is the precedent of our forebears in the field of Islamic jurisprudence like Imam Abu Hanifah and ash-Shāfi`i, who lived in Iraq and Egypt, nations that had ancient and cosmopolitan histories. Their efforts sought to integrate the new faith of Islām with the ancient cultures. This option is the most difficult option, because it takes very hard work. But if you believe that God is almighty, and the faith of Islām is overwhelmingly compelling in its Divine content and power, then you know that God is behind you, and with God behind you, how can you fail? Integrating the Islamic impulse with modern culture cannot be more difficult for us than the task Imam Abu Hanifah and ash-Shāfi`i faced with the ancient Egyptian and Mesopotamian cultures. Besides, we have the benefit of learning from, and reflecting on, their contributions and those of many other Muslim scholars down through the ages.

This option is exercised in either of two directions:

a) One is to work with the society at large to grant us Islamic options. Because of this effort and Muslims' growing marketing and political clout, airlines now serve "Muslim" meals, caterers serve *ḥalāl* meat and alcohol-free wine and beer, some banks are beginning to provide "*ribā*-free Islamic" banking options, and alternate-side-of-the-street parking is suspended in New York on Islamic holidays. The exciting thing about this posture is that it also helps educate non-Muslims on our values, and how many of these values are good for any society, Muslim or non-Muslim.

b) The second approach is to examine the logic of each case and determine where and how we can fit it into the general situation. For example, kosher meat is clearly *ḥalāl* because it is slaughtered in the Islamic fashion and the Deity in whose name the animal is slaughtered is the same God we worship. But a former director of the Islamic Center in New York, in the early 1970's, issued a *fatwā* declaring that supermarket meat was *ḥalāl*. Among his reasons given was because the animal was slaughtered by Christians, and they believe in the same God we do (thus the animal was not consecrated in the name of a god that Muslims deny).[24] Another example is given in the dress codes. We do not have to dress in Middle Eastern clothing to be perfect Muslims, as long as the *decency* of our clothing is in line with Islamic values. And how about men having to keep beards? We'll see how to deal with this one when we discuss the category of custom as a source of law. (See the discussion following page 82 on Customs).

In practice, we tend to blend all options, sometimes sweeping problems under the rug, sometimes acting like we are building a Muslim society, and in the remaining situations examining those aspects of modern society that do not conflict with Islamic law.[25] Here is where the road map needs a little explanation on how to navigate. But because we have a wealth of information bequeathed to us by these great Imams and their followers, what we are doing

---

[24] Many Muslims have difficulty with this interpretation because they do not consider the meat sold in supermarkets as slaughtered by people who are "Christian" in the sense of being *believers*; also they question the methods of slaughter used for supermarket meat. For more on this see Appendix V, "The Transvaal Fatwa."

[25] An excellent example of this blend is the attempt in the USA to develop Islamic courts that are recognized by the Uniited States legal system. Just as the legal system recognizes Islamic marriages conducted by Imams who are licensed by the state to perform marriages, the intent here is to develop Islamic courts to address the needs of the Islamic community, especially in the area of personal law, whose decisions would be recognized and enforced by the state. For more on this, see the work of Azizah al-Hibry.

is not entirely new. We are indeed standing on the shoulders of intellectual giants.

First we must bear in mind what a solution to our dilemma requires. Our attitude cannot be an arrogant "I know what God's opinion is!" but a humble "I suspect that this is most likely what God means by such and such verses." The great scholars uttered the caveat *wallahu a`lam*, (and God knows best) to acknowledge that there is always a possibility that they might be wrong, and this is good behavior and proper courtesy before God.

In thinking about our dilemmas, it is important to identify the nature and category of the question or dilemma. The reason is that the types of problems mentioned at the beginning of the book raise issues that are not always clearly within the jurisprudiential domain. Let us explain what we mean by "nature" and "category" of the dilemma by examining some examples.

In Grandma Fatima's case, the family and doctors collared the poor Imam to help decide whether the nephrologist or the internist was right. Most Imams I know have to look in a dictionary to figure out what a nephrologist is, let alone have the faintest notion what a dialysis machine looks like. The Imam is not qualified to make a medical decision as to whether to follow the nephrologist's or the internist's advice; this is the doctor's job. When I decided to review the medical dilemmas to see how many were purely legal issues—questions of *fiqh*—I realized that other issues were critically involved. For instance, in Salim's case, the question as to whether the $10,000 the community had budgeted should be spent on him or on the many poor but healthy kids sounded very much like the problem of an old scholarly family friend whose wife ribs him over how much money he spends on books, which *she* claims he could read in the library anyway, while she needs a new washing machine for doing the laundry, which *he* says could be done in the corner laundromat. If he could spare $500 he could afford a really great washing machine, have an extra couple of hundred dollars to buy a few nice books, and he wouldn't have this problem. This sounded to me just like Dr. Khan's problem!

All I had to do now was to figure out a polite way to tell Dr. Khan that he was short $10,000, a difficult thing to tell *one* American physician, let alone a whole conference-full of them. If the community were rich and resourceful enough, would this dilemma exist? This is an example of a dilemma resulting from financial insufficiency emanating in turn from advanced medical discoveries that cost a lot of money. Looking at Salim's case this way, the *ethical* aspect of the dilemma emanates from the new medical discovery of the recently genetically engineered medication Recombinant Human Dnase, which *makes available* the option—previously not available—of treating him. Had it *not* been invented, no amount of money would have helped him, so availability of sufficient funds would not have been an issue. The point we are making here is that the ethical dilemma which stems from insufficiency of funds is often a new and humanly created, or secondary, dilemma. Before the invention of the printing press and electricity, when neither book printing nor washing machines were available, the very concept of the "financial insufficiency" presented by the example of our scholarly friend and his wife did not yet exist. Technological advances "create" a growing need for more funds, so in a sense technology creates an ever expanding potential for ethical dilemmas. How do we deal with these, and where do we stop?

Another way of saying this is that a person like Imam ash-Shāfi`i, suddenly transported into our times from the ninth century, would find a lot of our ethical dilemmas to be new and awe-inspiring; they did not exist at his time. Understanding our creative capacity to continually generate such ethical dilemmas is necessary if we are to articulate a dilemma-solving methodology that is gratifying and not morally burdensome. This is particularly important if we are to develop gratifying answers to new situations arising from technical advances in the field of finance and economics. (If we adopt approach number two described above on page 24, where we live like the Pennsylvania Dutch and dispense with modern technology, a lot of these dilemmas disappear!)

As we examine the dilemmas listed for the physicians to discuss, we discover that we can break the problems down into the following categories:

- Philosophical/conceptual
- Ethical/moral
- Technical, or professional (i.e., dealing with a given profession like medicine, economics, etc.)
- Jurisprudential/legal
- Financial /allocation of resources

To bring home the importance of separating the issues, we'll examine another case presented at the convention: that of a 24 year-old woman who was 23 weeks pregnant, and who developed "brain death" (this is the medical term) after prolonged epileptic seizures without any recovery of consciousness. The physicians continued life-support systems for three weeks and delivered a 26-week live baby after bedside Caesarian section. The legitimate and fascinating question raised was: if brain death is equivalent to "real death," then how could a "dead person" give birth to a live child?

As compelling as this question was, for it probes into the definition of death, it is not a "*Sharī'ah*" question as much as it is a philosophical or conceptual question. Marveling at a medical or biological reality is not a *fiqh* question. That's like asking an Imam how come a baby can be conceived in a test tube. An Imam has got to be careful that in their desire to respect him for his knowledge, doctors don't ask him a biological question, for that is not his realm of expertise. If there is an ethical or *fiqh* question here, it is whether keeping the woman physically alive until her fetus is viable, and then discontinuing life support, violates any ethical or religious norms. That's the *faqīh*'s domain, and anything beyond that is definitely outside his area of qualification.

So we see how important it is to phrase the question accurately so that we know in whose domain it lies, and if it is a question of *fiqh,* to phrase the question in such a fashion that it deals with the legal aspect of things, and not with the scientific or medical dimension. Overlapping often and almost always occurs between these categories, that is, the dilemma often blends two or more of the above categories (conceptual and biological), or one dilemma may be caused by another (usually money problems causing other problems). Or perhaps the wrong question is asked of the Imam. *This is not always obvious to many, even to the family and physicians involved.* Usually one issue predominates, and by identifying both the category and the order of the predominating issue, we find it much easier to address the dilemma. Bearing this in mind, we find that by implementing this approach, the dilemma sometimes disappears because we gain clarity on the issues that need to be addressed and the priorities involved. In other cases, the dilemma persists, and it does so because the competing values have the same order of priority; yet we still gain clarity on the issues we need to grapple with and resolve. The objective of trying to achieve the greater, or greatest, good becomes more clearly recognized and thus more easily worked towards.

Next, we have to have a sufficient grasp of relevant subject matter to be able to deal with the issues, both from a technical standpoint and from a religious and philosophical standpoint. For example, if I am a medical practitioner and have questions that relate to life and death, I have to understand not only the field of medicine, but also the meaning of life and death and related concepts from the Qur'ānic and Prophetic standpoint. If I have to judge between a nephrologist and an internist on behalf of a 92-year-old woman, I'd better know what they do, and where my domain of qualification lies. Or if I'm concerned about economic dilemmas, then I need to understand not only economics, but also the economic value system of the Qur'ān, how this Qur'ānic value system was further amplified by the Prophet and how it relates to the latest in economic theory. And if the matter is one about resources, we've got to think about: a) the relationship and extent that our dilemmas were created by our technical advances and discoveries, b) how we can increase our resources, which consist not only of funds but any creative means that can go into solving the problem, and c) the rights and claims that different individuals have upon available resources. Here is where the interdisciplinary cooperation comes in: we have to combine the expertise of the Imam with that of the doctor, the economist, or the political scientist to come up with gratifying solutions. It is at this juncture, where we are to combine these disciplines into a workable system that solves current dilemmas, that our need is most acute.[26]

What is often not noticed is that our predicament frequently lies in the difference between thinking and acting. As difficult as thinking might be, it can often be more difficult to *act* in the situation in accordance with what we know to be the correct course. Invariably the situation is fraught with a complex psychological framework within which we have to act. We may have to decide whether to spend the money on a new car or on new furniture, or perhaps on our child's college education instead of our own legitimate needs. We may conclude that the right answer is to just let Grandma Fatima pass away, sending her on her way into the next life in a supporting atmosphere of love, but psychologically we cannot avoid "doing everything possible" to express our love for her and avoid any feeling of emotional guilt, especially if we can personally afford to put her on dialysis and stretch her days further. The ultimate deciding factors sometimes have to do with feelings and issues that are beyond rational analysis. We frequently spend out of a desire to express love even when we know the outcome is bleak, because it is emotionally satisfying. We spend to satisfy something within us, even when it is ostensibly done for the sake of others.

When you are removed from a situation, you find it less difficult to pronounce judgment than if you are personally involved; for then you really empathize with the person in question. You may still maintain your opinion, but will be more compassionate. For example, you may strongly believe that surrogate motherhood is immoral and wrong. But let us consider the following case.

---

[26] This is why in today's world the Islamic scholars are in agreement that the *mujtahid* of today can rarely be one person, but a committee of qualified individuals who bring together the requisite skills.

I happen to know a very successful 42-year-old woman in Singapore who has repeatedly tried to have a child. Every time she gets pregnant, she miscarries after a few months. Her problem is not in getting pregnant, but in being able to carry the pregnancy to full term. She and her husband want a child so much that they are willing to consider grafting her fertilized egg into the womb of a woman who is willing to carry the baby to term for her, and pay her a fee. For $10,000, a very affordable sum for her, she can get a choice of young healthy 20-year-old Indonesian girls who would be delighted to carry the baby for her because that amount of money is enough for this village girl to live a very good life. They argued their position on the following grounds: A Muslim mother is permitted under Islamic law to give her baby to another woman to breastfeed her, and there are certain conditions that have to be recognized.[27] Can an analogy to this wet-nurse custom be made for grafting her unborn baby into the young woman's womb, and analogous conditions extended? They asked, *what Islamic juridical basis denies them this option*? And although the general consensus is that surrogate motherhood in this sense is prohibited, they sought, and needed, to understand the rationale behind this prohibition.[28]

Although a thorough analysis of any new issue needs to be made, and clear guidelines established before a decision can be made on its legality, we have shown that analogies can be made to legally acceptable courses of action. The rule of necessity and need has dictated many a juridical decision less on the application of a specific law than on the need for equity and compassion. And although surrogate motherhood may be construed in some quarters

---

[27] Among the conditions are that marriage is prohibited between the child who has been suckled from a wet nurse and the child of the wet nurse. Also the wet nurse has no rights of inheritance from the suckled child.

[28] For a more detailed analysis of why this issue is considered unacceptable, see Hassan Hathout, *Islamic Perspectives in Obstetrics and Gynaecology*, 1986, Faculty of Medicine, University of Kuwait, pp. 131-135. One cannot help but be reminded of the Prophet's ḥadīth when asked by Jibril what were the signs of the last day, and one of the signs the Prophet gave was that a slave woman would give birth to her master. This ḥadīth suggests the technology now available, where a couple implants their embryo into a rented womb.

as being valid on the basis of some analogy, it may yet be prohibited on the basis that it will lead to greater evil than benefit, such as problems with custody, confusion of the child as to who its parents are, etc.[29]

We've already seen in the couple of examples given above, that one need not be an expert in such fields as philosophy, economics and medicine to recognize and identify the different areas of issues and questions involved. Having differentiated between the doctor's job, the treasurer's job, and the Imam's job, and having understood the concept of the "separation of the domains" pertaining to each problem, we are sensitized to the reality that the ethical or jurisprudential challenge is often hidden. This is the quandary that we all enter into when we have to make up our minds about something. Although we would prefer to be able to hedge our bets and leave all doors open, life doesn't always give us these options. We sometimes have to choose one over another, facing the tough question, "How do I act, and what do I do, in this situation?" The nature of the dilemma, and the proper solution in almost every case, is clarified by asking the question "Does this course of action make *sense*?" Does it make *sense* to keep a brain-dead woman alive on life-support systems till we perform a C-section and deliver her baby? Does it make *sense* to spend our budget of $10,000 on the sick 19-year-old? Does it make *sense* to put 92-year Grandma Fatima on dialysis? Does it make *sense* for Masjid ul-Iḥsān to keep on paying rent when for the same amount of monthly payments they can own the building? Does it make *sense* for Muḥammad Ayman not to take the student loan and become a successful doctor? We could almost title this book on *fiqh*—and *fiqh* itself—as "The Islamic Search for Juridical Sense and Sensibility as the Determinant of Human Action."

If you examine the decisions of the first four Caliphs, who were also eminent Companions of the Prophet, their actions were

---

[29] Such a decision may be obtained by applying the Maliki principle of *sadd adh-dharā'i'*; i.e., preventing the legal and permitted means to an objective deemed illegal or prohibited. This is discussed later in the section on the Sources of Islamic law.

always sensible. Even when they acted in a way that appeared to differ from a Qur'ānic or Ḥadīth ruling, it was based on what can clearly be seen to be the deeper values of the Qur'ān and Ḥadīth. When, for example, the second Caliph `Umar ibn al-Khaṭṭāb terminated the tradition of paying new converts from the zakāt revenues, it was not on harsh grounds. During the earlier days, becoming a Muslim was hazardous to one's life and to one's wealth: it usually meant one had to emigrate from Mecca to Madinah, in the process often leaving behind one's assets which were confiscated by the unbelievers. Paying the new convert (known as *mu'allafati qulūbuhum*) was therefore an obligation of the community to offset losses incurred because they opted to act in accordance with their spiritual imperative. If becoming a Muslim meant losing your wealth, the nascent Muslim community felt obliged to help you get back on your feet, thus the Qur'ānic injunction to support the *mu'allafati qulūbuhum* from the treasury. But after the Prophet's death, when Islām became the religion of the majority and its empire expanded west into Egypt, east into Persia and north into Syria, many found it opportune to seek money for becoming a Muslim. Under such circumstances it made sense to discontinue this Qur'ānic instruction, which the Caliph `Umar promptly did. His ruling does not really violate the deeper sense of the Qur'ānic teaching, nor does it revoke the Qur'ānic advice to aid new Muslims who suffer for their entering the faith.

*Uṣūl al-fiqh* is the attempt to codify the sense and sensibilities of the Qur'ān, the Ḥadīth, and the principles and precedents expounded by the first four Caliphs. From this emanates a set of sensible imperatives that together draw a picture of "sensible action" extending from these textual sources. This constitutes the Muslim's moral, ethical and equitable framework.

# CHAPTER IV

## WHAT IS *IJTIHĀD* AND WHO IS THE *MUJTAHID*?

The activity of trying to think about and then solve legal problems and dilemmas is called *ijtihād* (often translated as interpretation or interpretive effort), and the person doing it is a *mujtahid*. Do not confuse this word with *jihād*, usually translated as holy war.[30] The technical definition of *ijtihād* is the *effort* expended in formulating *fiqh* (religious understanding, particularly of the law). It is used in two senses, each requiring that the *mujtahid* leave no stone unturned, and expends his or her very best effort, and deploys the best of one's intellectual, physical and financial faculties:

1. The first sense of the term *ijtihād* is to infer with a high degree of probability[31] the rules of the *Sharī'ah* from the textual sources (i.e., the Qur'ān and Ḥadīth). Here the effort is to discover God the Lawgiver's intention from His speech and actions, and is sometimes concerned with the discovery of that which is not self-evident or has been left unexpressed. (This is like the work of a research scientist who tries to discover the laws of science which are God's laws of creation.) You may call this sense of ijtihād the effort to develop the science of *uṣūl al-fiqh*.

---

[30] *Jihād an-nafs*, war against one's lower self, is a psychological war one wages in order for the higher self to have control over the lower self, as described in a Prophetic ḥadīth.

[31] The caveat "with a high degree of probability" is not so much intended to introduce an element of speculation into *ijtihād* as it is an admission of our imperfection. Zero probability of error is only granted to the Qur'ān and the inspired utterances of the Prophet. Thus, it is an acknowledgement that the result of our effort, though probably correct, is not without the possibility of error. Also, and no less important, it is an admission that more than one correct answer is possible.

2. The second sense of the term *ijtihād* is the implementation of the science of *uṣūl al-fiqh* and applying it to particular situations and issues, that is, the formulation of a legal opinion or judgment (*hukm shar`i*).[32] This is comparable to the work of an applied scientist or engineer who applies scientific rules to real-life situations: building bridges, power plants, cars, etc. In this sense, *ijtihād* is the opposite of imitation (*taqlid*), which means to follow the opinions of others without understanding or scrutiny, or to use the polite definition of al-Āmidi, "to accept the rulings of others when such rulings are not coupled with a conclusive argument."[33]

Although *ijtihād* is primarily an intellectual effort, it may involve all supportive logistical activities, such as the financial expenses and physical effort required to travel to a library, school or teacher.

The difference between *fiqh* and *ijtihād* is that *fiqh* refers to the *understanding* of religious law, and a *faqīh* is one who has this understanding; whereas *ijtihād* refers to the *effort* expended in developing the science of *fiqh*, that is, of deducing the rules and rulings, or arriving at a judgment (*hukm*, or *fatwā*) for a given case.

One analogy that may help you understand the Muslim's urges and predicament in meshing his understanding of the *Sharī'ah* with his life, is to consider what we do with our cars. We all know you wouldn't service your new Mercedes unless you were qualified, although you certainly would stick your head under the hood and ask all kinds of seemingly intelligent questions, because you just can't figure out how you spent all this money on such a fine car only to have car problems. And while the mechanic gives you the answers, talking about variable assist steering, hydraulic devices and pneumatically operated systems, you are nodding your head while all the stuff goes right over your head. So it makes per-

---

[32] *Shar`i* is the adjectival or adverbial form of *Sharī'ah*, meaning of the *Sharī'ah*.

[33] Ā midi, *Al-Ihkām fī Uṣūl al-Aḥkām*, (Cairo, 1347 AH), III, 166.

fect sense that, convinced as you are that you have the best religion on Earth, Islām being the "latest model" of God's religion revealed to us, etc., you should stick your head between the pages of your translations of the Qur'ān and Ḥadīth, and ask all kinds of intelligent and relevant questions. And if you're an Arab you generally find it impossible to resist the temptation that you are even more qualified, for after all you speak and read Arabic, the language of the Qur'ān and the Prophet. But just as reading and understanding English isn't enough to make you understand your car manual and qualify you to be a car mechanic, reading and understanding Arabic is in no way sufficient qualification for you to be a *mujtahid*. As tempting as it is to be your own *mujtahid*, you should learn what *ijtihād* involves before allowing yourself or anyone else to perform *ijtihād* on your faith without suitable qualifications. Just as you don't want a tire to blow out at highway speeds, you don't want your religion to blow out on the highway of life, for what is dangerous to your soul has longer-lasting repercussions than what is dangerous to your body. How will you know what it takes to be a *mujtahid*? Those wise jurists from the past gave us a checklist; just tick the following to see how qualified you or your *mujtahid* is:

1. You must be a *faqīh* (jurist who understands religion). If the problem has to do with a specific profession like medicine or economics, then the *faqīh* must be sufficiently knowledgeable in the profession or in the facts relating to the question at hand. (Now you can relate to the poor Imam's position in having to decide if the nephrologist's decision to do dialysis on Grandma Fatima is preferable over the internist's recommendation to call it quits. Without a threshold level of understanding of medicine, his comprehension of the case cannot be complete.)
2. If you know the rules of the *Sharī'ah* in detail but are unable to exercise your judgment in the inference of the rulings (*aḥkām*) direct from their sources, you are not a *mujtahid*. The emphasis here is on the ability to *apply* the rules, in addition to knowing the theory. (This is like someone who is a scientist but not a

car mechanic; he may understand the laws of dynamics and the principles of how cars operate, but does not know how to apply these laws to fix your Mercedes. Don't ask him to fix it, for your car would still be likely to stall on you.)

3. Your endeavor as a jurist must involve a complete and total expenditure of effort. No stone must be left unturned.
4. You must be an upright Muslim with a good character: trustworthy, mature, wise, just and competent. (Just as you wouldn't trust your car to a repair station with a bad reputation, you have to be careful as to whom you ask to render an opinion for you.)
5. You should be well-versed in the sources of the *Sharī'ah*, the technique of accessing those sources, and such helpful tools as proficiency in the Arabic language, exegesis (*tafsīr*), the causes, contexts and circumstances of Qur'ānic revelation (known as *asbāb an-nuzūl*), knowledge of the *Ḥadīth* and their relative authenticity, and the principles of repeal of rules. (Would you hire a mechanic who does not have all the required tools to service your car well?)
6. You should understand the aims and objectives (*maqāṣid)* of the *Sharī'ah,* which include the considerations of public interest (*masalih*). **We have mentioned the five primary objectives: protection of life, religion, property, offspring, lineage and reason/intellect**. You should also know the general maxims of *fiqh* such as the maxim of removal of hardship (*raf' al-ḥaraj*), the maxim of certainty prevailing over doubt, and that of necessity and need, etc. Decisions made have to be sensitive to, and respect, these aims and objectives. (Your mechanic should understand that your objectives in having a car are not just to have a shiny beautiful car adorning your driveway that your neighbors can ogle at and admire: you want a car to drive in; it should be reliable and safe when driving at highway speeds; it should start promptly in cold weather and hot; it should not stall on you on hot summer days, and it should be comfortable, well-heated in the winter, air-conditioned in the summer, etc.)

Basically, the *mujtahid* has to be a good thinker and sufficiently well informed religiously.

Do we really need to learn all of this? Do you have to be a design engineer just to fix a flat tire or the distributor cap in your car engine? Of course not. The qualifications above are indispensable only for a full-fledged *mujtahid* whose *ijtihād* aims to cover *all* questions of jurisprudence. These prerequisites are not demanded of other *mujtahids* for it is sufficient that a *mujtahid* for any one particular question be competent in its sources and in the matters consequent to it. You can be just a tire shop that fixes flat tires or a car audio expert who knows all about car audio, but know nothing about fuel injection and how it works. That's why the *mujtahids* are classified into several categories.

## A. Categories of Mujtahids

1. *Mujtahid muṭlaq*: interpreters of the *Sharī'ah*. These were those who established the independent schools of law, like Abu Ḥanīfah (d. 150/767),[34] Mālik (d. 179/795), Ash-Shāfi`i (d. 204/820) and Ibn Ḥanbal (d. 241/855), who founded the four Sunni schools that have continued till this day, and al-Awza`i (d. 157/774), Dāwūd aẕ-Ẕahirī (270/883) and aṭ-Tabarī (310/922), founders of the now extinct schools (*mujtahid jarīr*). The Imam Ja`far aṣ-Ṣādiq (d. 149/766) is also particularly considered by the Shi`ah to be of this category. He was one of Imam Abu Hanifah's teachers. By the end of the third century after the death of the Prophet, there were as many as thirteen individuals who were considered by the Sunni scholars as *mujtahids* of this class.[35] Each of

---

[34] Dates are Hijri dates (AH) followed by the Common Era (CE).

[35] In chronological order, they were:

1. Imam al-Ḥasan al-Baṣri, who lived in Madina and then in Baṣrah (d. 110/729).

2. Imam Abu Ḥanīfah who lived in Kūfah and Baghdad (d. 150/767).

these thirteen *mujtahids* developed a circle of devoted disciples and followers; however, only four Sunni *madhhabs* among these thirteen have survived and flourished till this day. This should not be seen as a loss, for the differences among these thirteen *madhhabs* were often not greater than the differences which existed among some of the followers of a school and its founder. In fact, had some of the prominent followers of some of the existing schools, like Imam Ghazali in the Shāfi`i school or Abu Yūsuf in the Ḥanafi school, been alive at an earlier time, they probably would have developed into *mujtahids muṭlaq* because of their deep understanding and probing analysis.

2. *Mujtahid madhhab*: interpreters of the school. These were the interpreters who did not establish independent schools but followed one of the founders of the well-known schools. They differed from the founders on fundamentals as well as on subsidiary points. Examples are Imam Abu Yūsuf (d. 182/798) and Muḥammad ibn Hasan al-Shaybāni (d. 189/805) in the Ḥanafi school; Isma`il b. Yahya al-Muzanī (d. 264/878) and Jalāl ad-Din as Suyūṭi (d. 911/1505) in the Shāfi`i school; and Ibn Taymiyah (d. 728/1328) and his disciple Ibn al-Qayyim al-Jawziyyah (751/1308) in the Hanbali school. The role of these *mu-*

---

3. Imam `Abd ar-Raḥmān al-Awza`i of Syria (d. 157/774).

4. Imam Sufyān ath-Thawri of Kūfah and Baṣrah (d. 161/778).

5. Imam al-Layth Ibn Sa`d of Egypt (d. 175/791).

6. Imam Mālik Ibn Anas of Madinah (d. 179/795).

7. Imam Sufyān Ibn `Uyaynah of Makkah (d. 198/814).

8. Imam Muḥammad Ibn Idrīs Ash-Shāfi`i (d. in Egypt 204/820).

9. Imam Isḥāq Ibn Ibrāhīm, better known as Ibn Rahawaihi, of Nisapur (d. 238/853).

10. Imam Ibrāhīm Ibn Khālid, better known as Abu Thawr, of Baghdad (d. 240/855).

11. Imam Ahmad Ibn Ḥanbal (d. in Baghdad in 241/855).

12. Imam Dawud Ibn `Alī az-Zahiri (d. in Baghdad in 270/883).

13. Imam Muḥammad Ibn Jarīr at-Tabarī, (d. in Baghdad in 310/922).

*jtahids* was no less important in the development of Islamic law than that of the founders, for they not only developed the law further, but tempered the differences between the founders and contributed to the growth of a consensus of opinion.

3. *Mujtahid masā'il*: These were the interpreters of specific issues, who issued *fatwas*. Examples are Imam at-Taḥāwī (d. 321/933) and Imam as-Sarakhsi (d. 490/1097) in the Ḥanafi school, and Imam al-Ghazali (d. 505/1111) and Imam Zakariyya al-Anṣāri in the Shāfi`i school. (These would be analogous to engineers, who apply the knowledge discovered by scientists.)

4. Finally comes the category of the limited interpreters. They were the people who restricted themselves to the views of predecessors but who had insight into the aims of the various rules and their connotations. They were well qualified for the task of evaluating the various opinions in their school, and of distinguishing between them according to their authenticity. Examples are Abu Hasan al-Karkhi (d. 340/952), and the author of *al-Hidāyah*, Burhan al-Din al-Marghināni (d. 593/1197). (These would be analogous to professors of engineering, who understand pure and applied science but who may not be in the business of building bridges and buildings.)

We should not think of these scholars in some descending order of intellectual illumination, for they all contributed to our understanding of the *Sharī'ah* as well as to its development. Ash-Shāfi`i, for example, learned from Mālik, and you will note that the succeeding scholars of law came in different periods of time, and therefore their contributions added to the crystallization and consolidation of many of the then nascent ideas, and gave them form. These scholars did not always agree with the founders' opinions, but were instrumental in developing the law and a growing consensus of respected opinion. They sought the deepest level of understanding of the *Sharī'ah*, and applied this knowledge courageously in dealing with the needs of Muslim society.

5. After them comes the category of imitators (*Muqallidūn*), who follow others without understanding. Most Muslims, no matter how qualified we might be as scientists, engineers and

doctors, or in any other area of human intellectual endeavor, usually fall into this category. However, if we are able to understand the arguments given to us on a matter that is relevant to us, this puts us at the slightly higher level of a *muttabi`* (follower), defined as someone who follows his *madhhab* while being aware of the Qur'ānic and Ḥadīth texts and the reasoning underlying its positions. This is about as exalted a position as most of us busy professionals can hope to attain.[36]

## B. The Qualified Mujtahid of Today

Given the complexity of most new and modern issues, it is almost impossible to find the full range of required qualifications in one person. A qualified medical doctor or economist is not generally a qualified Islamic jurist. Contemporary scholars are therefore in agreement that the modern mujtahid or qualified mujtahid of our time, in order to deal effectively and gratifyingly with contemporary issues, needs to be a *committee* of people who altogether have the requisite qualifications to render a judgment on the issue at hand.

The role of Islamic lawyers, if they were to fulfill their religious duty as they saw it, was to search their consciences in order to know what good Muslims were allowed or forbidden to do, which acts of the administration they ought to accept or to reject, which institutions of the customary practice they were entitled to use and which they ought to avoid. A Muslim lawyer should have God as his primary client, and his objective at all times is to fulfil God's will, and balance those with the needs of his human client whose personal self-interest is the highest moral objective. But because human beings are concerned with their personal interest, Muslim

[36] Mohammad Hashim Kamali, in his excellent book *Principles of Islamic Jurisprudence* (Islamic Texts Society, Cambridge, 1991) pp. 387–389, expands this to seven categories instead of five, by expanding the fourth group into three sub-groups. We highly recommend this book to any reader who is interested in a more scholarly and detailed study of *uṣūl al-fiqh*.

jurists were not always able to keep themselves above the personal interest of their clients, especially when the client was the Caliph or Sultan.

## C. Following A Decision Rendered By A Mujtahid (Taqlīd)

Many Muslims today are under the impression that being a *muqallid* (emulator, i.e., someone following *taqlīd*) is a bad or shameful thing. *Taqlīd* has been used as a pejorative. This is unfortunate, because in almost every other field of human endeavor, we *follow* the advice of experts. So we will use the better term *muttabi`*, meaning a well-informed follower as opposed to an uninformed follower. The challenge is to find the best expert—the best architect, the best doctor, the best tailor, etc.,—and to follow their advice. If we refused to listen to the advice of doctors and tried to be our own doctors, quack medicine would be the order of the day.[37] If you are

---

[37] Abdul Hakim Murad, in his highly recommended monograph *Understanding the Four Madhhabs* (Wise Muslim Publications, Wembley 1995), p.15, laments the situation in Britain, much like we have in the United States, where it "is common now to see activists prowling the mosques, criticising other worshippers for what they believe to be defects in their worship, even when their victims are following the verdicts of some of the leading Imams of *fiqh*." He writes,

"In a Western-influenced global culture in which people are urged from early childhood to 'think for themselves' and to challenge established authority, it can sometimes be difficult to muster enough humility to recognize one's own limitations" [probably because of an underlying insecurity, many young Muslim activists cannot bear to admit that they might not know something about their religion. And this despite the example of Imam Mālik, who, when asked forty questions about *fiqh*, answered, 'I do not know' (*lā adrī*) to thirty-six of them; quoted in Āmidi, IV,221.]

He adds,

"Today in some Arab capitals, especially where the tradition of orthodox scholarship has been weakened, it is common to see young Arabs filling their homes with every ḥadīth collection they can lay their hands upon, poring over them in the apparent belief that they are less likely to misinterpret this vast and complex literature than Imam ash-Shāfi`i, Imam Ahmad, and the other great Imams. This irresponsible approach, now increasingly widespread, is predictably opening the door to sharply divergent opinions which have seriously damaged the unity, credibility and effectiveness of the Islamic movement, and provoked sharp arguments over issues settled by the great Imams over a thousand years ago.....The fact that all the great scholars of the religion,

not embarrassed to admit that you have no medical qualifications whatsoever, you should suffer no embarrassment at all to say that you are a *muqallid* in the sense of an intelligent follower (*muttabi`*). Otherwise, quack Muslim law becomes the order of the day. Intelligent *taqlīd* is nothing more than recognizing our own professional limitations, and the more time we spend on understanding the field of *fiqh*, the more we get to realize our own limitations. Neither does *taqlīd* necessarily mean that you are ignorant of your religion. When a modern day physicist uses Newton's formulas, he is a "*muqallid*" of Newton, and there is great wisdom and understanding in that unless he applies it where it doesn't apply *Mujtahids* like Imam Ghazali and Imam Abu Yūsuf were *muqallids* in that they followed the principles established by their prior Imams, ash-Shāfi`i and Abu Hanifah, although they also disagreed in certain instances. The idea then is to become a smart *muqallid*.

Being a *muttabi`* is like having your car fixed by a mechanic even though you know how to do it yourself; there is nothing wrong in that. However, you would never allow him to replace the alternator if there was nothing wrong with it, and certainly you wouldn't pay him were he to do so. You would be excused if you were ignorant of what makes a car work, but even then you would be expected to ask that car-savvy neighbor of yours to recommend a trusted mechanic. Similarly, you are not permitted to blindly imitate (in the sense of following the *ijtihād* of others without understanding or critical evaluation) if you are capable of making the original judgment or interpretation yourself. If the mujtahid explains it to you, and you understand and follow his reasoning, and agree with it, that's fine. But if you disagree, you can't follow the conclusion of his *ijtihād*. God expects you to take your religion at least as seriously as you would your car. *Taqlīd* is only permissible regarding a matter for those who are incapable of *ijtihād*, such as the lay common person or the educated in other fields who are

---

including the ḥadīth experts, themselves belonged to *madhhabs*, and required their students to belong to *madhhabs*, seems to have been forgotten. Self-esteem has won a major victory here over common sense and Islamic responsibility."

not qualified for the task of *ijtihād*. But even then, you're expected to ask that religious friend of yours whom should you entrust with your *ijtihād*. You're responsible if you know enough.[38] And if you assert that because you don't understand how cars work you are going to reject riding in cars, and use the same logic to refuse letting your *Sharī'ah* carry you as the expression of your religion, then you are not going to get anywhere, spiritually speaking, and stand the very real danger of not being able to escape the major calamity when it hits upon your unavoidable death.

The jurists describe this common sense approach in a fancy way using some technical jargon; they say that *ijtihād* is a religious duty (*farḍ*), and is in fact a religious and collective obligation (*farḍ kifāyah*) upon all qualified persons in the event where an issue arises but no urgency is encountered over its ruling. In urgent cases, *ijtihād* becomes a personal obligation (*farḍ `ayni*) upon all the qualified *mujtahid*s. It is also a *wājib `ayni* (a personal duty, "slightly less but still binding" obligation) upon the *mujtahid* if the issue affects him personally. *Taqlīd* (in the sense of blind imitation) is forbidden to a *mujtahid* who is competent to deduce the ruling (*hukm*) directly from its sources. The 'ulamā'[39] (learned scholars) are in agreement that a *mujtahid* is bound by the result of his *ijtihād*; once he has deduced his ruling, he may not imitate other *mujtahid*s—whether they agree or not. The conclusion he reaches is

---

[38] Here in America, the land of the free, we have a lot of "wannabees" (want-to-be's), usually less-informed people who "want to be" a *mujtahid* at any price. Peddling all kinds of half-baked statements about Islām, they not only scare the Islām right out of your wits, but thereby present it as a religion that no right-minded person would want to follow. Beware of the wannabees. You've got to watch out for those in this category, for they can be dangerous to your spiritual health. Although they are so meek with their car mechanics and promptly pay up when the latter gives an incorrect explanation to the problem with their car, they argue relentlessly with their better-informed Imams and have no fear regarding their own *fatwas* based on ignorance.

[39] The singular is *'ālim*. The term means a scholar, a learned person, and not necessarily in religious knowledge, although as Islām grew after the death of the Prophet, the primary emphasis was on knowledge that pertained to what we now call "Islamic Studies." And just as a person can be a scientist or engineer *and* a scholar, with the term scholar covering all kinds of related disciplines, one can be a *faqīh* or a *mujtahid* and a *'ālim*, with the term *'ālim* covering all disciplines.

tantamount to a Divine command which he must observe. Thus if you have studied enough astronomy to become sufficiently qualified to determine that tomorrow is the start of Ramadan, you must render your own opinion accordingly and follow it. If you are absolutely convinced that tomorrow is the start of Ramadan, you've got to start fasting tomorrow even if the whole community does not. (Now you know why Muslims sometimes celebrate the *`Id ul-fitr*, concluding the fast of Ramadan, on different days in the New York metropolitan area!)

## D. Can A Muslim Follow Any School Of Law He Likes?

Muslims in America come from all over the Muslim world. If I'm a Malay student, following the *madhhab* of Imam ash-Shāfi`i, and I live in a community where the mosque is run by Pakistanis who practice Ḥanafi law, what do I do? Can I shift from one school to another and follow the Ḥanafi way of thinking on a particular subject? (This is called *takhayyur*, which literally means "selection.")

The dominant opinion among scholars is that if a person follows the rules of a specific school in a particular case, he may not shift to another school in the same case, but may do so in a different and unrelated case. For example, you can follow the Shāfi`i *madhhab* regarding the performance of prayers and pray the shortened travelling prayer of two *rak`ats* of *ẓuhr* and *`aṣr* when you are on a journey, and the Ḥanafi *madhhab* regarding marrying the boss's 21-year-old daughter without *requiring* her father's permission,[40] for these are totally unrelated matters; but you should not dispense different portions of your will in accordance with different schools.

---

[40] This opinion has been practiced in the Muslim world. For example, an Indian court recognized as valid the marriage of a girl who had been brought up as a Shāfi`i and who had married without her father's consent, based on the girl's assertion that she had become a Ḥanafi and had married as such. The Ḥanafi ruling that an adult woman may conclude her own marriage contract had been upheld in this case. Many decisions in Islamic countries have been based on such *takhayyur*. (Quoted in N.J. Coulson, *A History of Islamic Law*, Edinburgh University Press, 1964, p. 183)

So if someone asks whether modern day Muslims are "no longer obliged" to follow a *madhhab* in its entirety, the answer is that Muslims were *never obliged* to do so. What they were obliged to do was to abide by certain principles of consistency, which *uṣūl al-fiqh* explains. These principles, as we shall see, allow maximum flexibility to the Muslim while adhering to the spirit of the faith.

As many of us know, in the category of individual religious practice we can have personal choice, for such differences of opinion can coexist. It's not such a big deal if the Muslims in New York disagree on which day to celebrate the *`Id*. But on matters that involve the interests of others, especially financial matters like contracts and inheritances, resolution of disagreement requires us to follow the rules of one *madhhab*. Thus you find that Turkey may follow the *madhhab* of Imam Abu Hanifah, whereas Moroccans follow the *madhhab* of Imam Mālik. We do this in the United States as well; when companies doing business sign a contract between them, you will generally find a clause stating which state's laws will govern the contract. Even within the United States we have variation between the laws of one state and another: Minnesota franchise laws may be more advantageous to the franchisor than Texas laws. But this does not mean that Texas laws are generally more or less just than Minnesota laws, for these differences are generally in areas of choices equally just, or that evolved out of certain needs and situations that arose in Minnesota and had to be dealt with by its courts. Such are the differences between the *madhhabs*.

In interacting with members of other *madhhab*s, there are certain types of additional courtesies to be followed. For example, if you are a Hanbali lady, and merely shaking hands with a man doesn't break your *wuḍū'* under your school of law, but it does under the Shāfi`i school of law, then when your Shāfi`i lady friends invite you to lead them in *`aṣr* prayer after your tea gathering, you've got to renew your *wuḍū'* if you shook hands with her husband. Otherwise you are technically not in a state of *wuḍū'* in accordance with their *madhhab* when you lead them. Or if renewing your *wuḍū'* will mess up your makeup and you have made an *ijtihād* that you can perform *tayammum* using your clean facial dust powder, an opinion which you suspect your host may not share, then be gracious and just have someone else lead the prayer.

We may ask the related question, "Is it possible for the Sunnis to imitate other than the Imams of the four Sunni schools?" The plausible answer is that because an imitator is presumably ignorant of the rules, it is safer that he adhere to the better known schools because they have become widespread and the problems addressed by these *madhhabs* have been systematically investigated and verified.[41]

So Islām requires us to be responsible. You can't just say: I saw my father do this. You've got to understand why. So even to imitate, you've got to understand how to follow. But don't get discouraged. This degree of effort isn't any more, or different, than being an expert on knowing where to service your car best, which store sells the best clothing, or where to buy the best basmati rice to cook your *biryani* with. You spend a lot of time talking with your friends on these matters, and the effort you expend in going all the way to Little India is your *ijtihād* to get the right ingredients for your *biryani* because the rice sold in the local Shoprite supermarket just doesn't do it. Some degree of effort (*ijtihād*) is naturally required. But know your limits; you may know how to bake a Kashmiri leg of lamb but not to make Madras lamb *biryani*. So you can learn how to make a good *biryani*, and read books and try out different recipes, check with your mother, aunts and others till you perfect your skill. Similarly, understanding the requirements on being a *mujtahid* informs you as to your standing. It also gives you a recipe if you need to be a *mujtahid* regarding one particular issue

---

[41] The most attractive reason for a Sunni to follow the Ja`fari (Shi`ah) school of law is in order to engage in temporary marriage (*mut`ah*), sanctioned by Shi`i law but prohibited by all the schools of Sunni law. Some American Muslims believe, for example, that proposing *mut`ah* may be a way to deal with the issue of Western dating, whereby it would be deemed better that a Muslim student studying for a few years in a Western university, contract a temporary marriage during the period of his student years rather than date. The advantages here are that the parties take each other more seriously and respectfully, and the rights of any issue are protected by law.

for which you have received unsatisfactory answers. You may return to the Imams who advised you to discuss the matter further in light of the new information you possess. Furthermore, understanding the rules of *ijtihād* guides you in your seeking to follow the argument of legal decisions rendered by others.

In many instances, especially those occurring on the *boundaries* of what is clear, and those areas we call the *gray areas*, more than one approach is acceptable to God. The differences in opinion among jurists is considered a blessing. This plurality of legitimate avenues towards Allāh is corroborated by the Qur'ān, verses 29:69, in which Allāh declares: *Walladhīna jāhadū fīnā lanahdiyannahum subulanā; wa innallāha la-ma`a-l-muḥsinīn,* which means: "And those who strive in Us (our cause), We shall surely guide them on Our *ways* (in the plural), and Allāh is surely with the doers of good." The scholars have interpreted this verse to mean that there is more than one way to approach God, all equally valid and acceptable to God. Also the ḥadīth that "whoever does *ijtihād* and gives a right judgment will have two rewards; but if he errs in his judgment, he will have earned one reward,"[42] shows Allāh's generosity and leniency in making the effort worthy, and never sinful. Thus the *fuqahā'* (plural of *faqīh*) have agreed that when the necessary requirements of *ijtihād* are present, and exercised conscientiously and sincerely, the result is always meritorious, never blameworthy or sinful. This is also a reminder to us to be courteous and non-judgmental of others who may differ in their opinions, based upon their proper, sincere and conscientious *ijtihād.* Be kind to others, and don't attack them for their sincere differences in opinion. There are many ways to cook *biryani,* and they are all equally acceptable in the culinary world. If you are sincere and make your best effort, your *biryani* will always be accepted by God for at least the minimum reward, no matter how peculiar it might taste to others.

---

42 Muslim, *Saḥīḥ*, V, 131.

Some readers may wisely stop at this point. They have neither the time nor the need to become even a *muttabi`* (intelligent follower), much less the lowest level *mujtahid.* Not all want to stop here, though, and for therse, more needs to be said.

First, just as in learning how to cook, you have to know your way around the kitchen. You have to know the different knives, mixers, blenders, etc., and their uses. You don't use a cleaver to core an apple, for example. You also have to learn the names of spices and to differentiate between them. Some names are not at all logical. For example, allspice does not mean "all the spices"; it is really only one spice. We saw this earlier when we pointed out that heartburn is not a heart problem. If you don't know these things, you will commit some very funny culinary errors, like thinking that peppercorns are only black, because you didn't know that there is green peppercorn, white peppercorn, and red (Szechuan) peppercorn, all with different colors and flavorings.

Why am I taking your time telling you about cooking mistakes that you know so well? This may sound funny to you, but it's because many Muslims make the same kinds of errors when they talk about Islām, the Qur'ān, Ḥadīth, *Sunnah*, etc. When you ask the average Muslims if they realize that there are different kinds of Ḥadīth and *Sunnah*, they look at you with puzzlement. But as with understanding the definitions of the names of spices, if you don't clearly understand the usages of Islamic terms, the following question will stump you: If we are obliged to perform the *farḍ* prayer and not the *sunnah* prayer, because *sunnah* means "non-obligatory," how come we are *obliged* to follow the Prophet's *sunnah*? How can we be *obliged* to follow something which is *non-obligatory?* Surely just doing the *farḍ* acts should be enough! Is there a paradox here? The mistake in this statement is that the same term *sunnah* is used to refer to different things, just as we use the word pepper sometimes to mean the black pepper that you grind, or the sweet green pepper that is a green vegetable, or the hot chili peppers that make your mouth burn. The same word may be used, but the reality that it refers to in each case is totally different.

The vocabulary of *Sharī'ah* and *fiqh* has some "pepper-and-allspice" type situations. And if you don't learn this vocabulary and understand it well, you are guaranteed to make similar types of funny and sometimes illogical statements that can burn your soul just as badly as mistaking jabanero peppers for bell peppers can burn your stomach. A little knowledge is always a dangerous thing.

For this we refer you to Appendix I on fathoming the subtleties of some Islamic terms. You don't really have to know this part completely to be a perfectly functional Muslim, but if you want your thinking to be clearer, and if you want to avoid committing the kinds of logical mistakes that many Muslims do, it's not such a bad idea. Better yet, you will smile knowingly when you hear others making these types of funny statements.

# CHAPTER V

## WHAT HAVE BEEN ALL THE DE FACTO SOURCES OF ISLAMIC LAW?

As an aspiring student of Islamic law, you must seek guidance from its sources. There are two ways in which you will see the sources of law categorized by the jurists. The first categorization is by the *identity* of the lawgiver; the sources are therefore prioritized as being first that of God (the Qur'ān), then that of the Prophet (the Ḥadīth) and finally that of mankind (*ijtihād*). The Prophet is the link between God and humankind, for although he engaged in *ijtihād*, his *ijtihād* was inspired by God Who also guided him by direct Divine revelation. This categorization is based on the following ḥadīth of Mu`adh ibn Jabal:

> *When the Messenger of Allāh desired to send Mu`adh ibn Jabal to the Yemen, he asked: 'How will you judge a case?' He answered: 'I will judge in accordance with what is in the Book of Allāh.' The Prophet asked: 'And if you do not find it in the Book of Allāh?' 'Then by the* sunnah *of the Messenger of Allāh.' 'And if it is not in the* sunnah *of the Messenger of Allāh?' He [Mu`ādh] answered: 'I will exercise my opinion and not flag [in so doing]* (ajtahidu ra'yi wa la 'alu)*.' The Prophet tapped his chest and exclaimed: 'Praise be to Allāh Who harmonized the messenger of the Messenger of Allāh to what pleases the Messenger of Allāh.'*[43]

Writers who follow this line state that there are therefore three sources of Islamic law: Divine, Prophetic and purely human (without the aid of Divine revelation). Because the Qur'ān and the

---

[43] Abū Dāwūd, *Sunan, Kitāb al-Aqdiyah,* ch. 1348, ḥadīth no. 3585.

corpus of Ḥadīth are wholly contained between the covers of books, they are also often referred to as the "texts," or "textual sources." *Ijtihād*, however, is not a "closed book" but a process of human activity, continual and never-ending. The Prophet exercised his effort in rendering legal judgments; thus the initiative of *ijtihād*, as an exercise of human effort, can be rightly said to have begun with the Prophet himself, and is the precedent he established.

The second way you will see the sources categorized is based on the order of priority of the *sources* themselves, and differs from the first categorization in that it reveals the historical development of those sources that resulted from *ijtihād*. Writers who list the sources this way do so because *ijtihād* was applied as well to the Qur'ān and Ḥadīth texts in order to interpret and understand them, and to extract the rules of the *Sharī'ah* from them.[44] According to this listing, the Qur'ān, followed by the Ḥadīth, are the two primary sources of Islamic Law. They are primary because the Qur'ān is Divine in origin, and the Prophet was guided, informed and protected by God; if God did not agree with an action of the Prophet, the Qur'ānic revelation came down to correct him.[45]

---

[44] In other words, *ijtihād* in their opinion is not so much a third source of law as much as it is an activity that embraces all the sources: *ijtihād* has to be applied to the Qur'ān to understand and interpret it. The collection, collation and establishing of the Texts of Ḥadīth were the result of a major effort of *ijtihād* by a host of scholars spanning several centuries. The subsidiary sources of law are additionally the result of human *ijtihād*.

[45] As for example in the first eleven verses of Surah 80. While the Prophet was explaining the doctrines of Islām to an assembly of the unbelieving leaders of Quraysh, in the hope that he might win them over to Islām, a blind Muslim, Ibn Umm Maktum, came to the Prophet and, interrupting the Prophet, asked to be taught something. The Prophet was deeply irked by this untimely interruption, frowned, and did not pay sufficient attention to his question. These verses were then revealed in which Allāh gently chides the Prophet with the words: "He (the Prophet) frowned and turned away when the blind man came to him! And how do you know that he may purify himself, or be mindful, so that the Reminder would benefit him? As for the one who regards himself as beyond (your) need, you are solicitous towards, even though you are not responsible for his lack of self-purification; whereas regarding the one who comes striving to you, fearful (of Allāh), you pay him no regard." Although the Prophet acted in a way that is natural to us, he is advised by God that his primary responsibility is to his flock, and not to those who have yet to decide if they are part of his flock.

What authentically emanated from the Prophet's *ijtihād*, and was not corrected by God, is therefore considered to have been endorsed by God. Following and continuing this logic, human *ijtihād* which is consistent with the Qur'ān and Ḥadīth can therefore be considered "to be endorsed" by the Qur'ān and Ḥadīth (thus "endorsed" by God and His Prophet), and therefore an extension of them. This is the rationale behind the development of the science of the *Sharī'ah* as a human effort.

If we list the secondary sources in this second way, jurists came up with a total of usually four, and sometimes five, six or seven sources. The reasons why they didn't quite agree were varied, but invariably because they disagreed as to whether the source was "legitimate" or not. But we all know that even when a child is illegitimate it does not mean that the child "is not real," that he does not exist and has no rights. So I'm going to give you all the *de facto* sources of *Sharī'ah*, whether considered legitimate or illegitimate by some or others, not only as developed and discussed, but more importantly as actually *used*, by the sum total of all jurists in Islamic countries at some time or another down to this day and age. We will concern ourselves with what they did, and the reasons that impelled them to do what they did. On doing this, we discover that eleven methods were used for the derivation of laws, and we therefore may say that there have been a sum total of *eleven* sources of Islamic law. These were:

1. The Qur'ān.
2. The Ḥadīth.
3. Consensus of opinion (*Ijmā'*).
4. Analogy (*Qiyās*).
5. Judicial preference (*Istiḥsān*).
6. Public interest (*Al-maṣāliḥ al-mursalah*: sometimes just called *maṣlaḥah* or *istiṣlaḥ*).
7. Reason and logic as sources of law (*Istidlāl* and *istiṣḥāb*).
8. Social customs (*'Urf*, literally, "what is known," or Common law.)

9. Direct positive legislation by the State (Caliph, Sultan, King, Dictator, Parliament or whoever the ruling power was).
10. Creative Means or Legal Fictions (*Ḥiyal*).[46]
11. Preventing the Means (*Sadd adh-dharā'i'*).

The first two sources are the Texts; these two, plus *ijmā'* and *qiyās*, are almost unanimously agreed upon by the major schools of law as comprising the *Sharī'ah* sources. In other words, everyone agrees that these are "legitimate" sources. Not all have agreed that the remainder are.

We cannot deny that the rest of the sources, historically, as well as in our lives today, operated and continue to operate as dynamic structures and de facto sources of law. They could not be separated from the first four sources. Life is driven by real need and the reality of the human condition; to deny the existence of state legislative bodies, whether democratic or dictatorial, and judicial preference, for example, as sources of law, flies in the face of

[46] Before you get excited and accuse me of justifying legal fiction as a source of law, I wish to repeat what I said above: I am listing all the sources of law, especially when "looked at from the other side." If I were writing from a strict Shāfi`i or Maliki position, for example, I would not have included *istihsān* or legal fiction as a source of law: Imam Shāfi`i was violently opposed to them and considered them illegitimate. Many Muslims regard modern Islamic banking to be a legal fiction, while those who defend it consider it an extremely valuable effort aimed at "Islamizing" banking, a phenomenon that no society today can do without. Many Muslims regard State legislation to be illegitimate if not enacted by an Islamic state, while others feel it falls within the domain of public interest. But while the state may legislate a given law benefitting some, others (especially those hurt by this law) will consider such a law as immoral and illegitimate. Writing from an "objective" viewpoint, meaning without taking sides, and in order to have a comprehensive macroscopic view of the whole, it is necessary to include all these "sources" and define them in a nonjudgmental manner, while examining them critically. As important as the question of legitimacy is, it is a separate question that is best discussed separately.

The notion of a "fiction" does not necessarily connote an immoral thing. It is more properly thought of as a device. For example, the notion of a corporation being a "person" in the United States (or a limited company in the British system), with attending rights and responsibilites, is an example of a very useful fiction. If the fiction is used for an unjust end, then it is bad; if not, then it is good.

reality.[47] And Muslims know how difficult it is to fight the power of local customs. In time, even an innocuous thing like Thanksgiving turkey dinner with cranberry sauce eaten with family members becomes a matter of custom. Neither are the sources cleanly separated and independent of each other; they often overlap. As we learn and clarify the definitions of the terms Qur'ān, Ḥadīth and *Sunnah* (see Appendix I), these terms are phenomenally and intricately linked; the Prophet would not have been a Prophet if not for the revelation of the Qur'ān. *Ijtihād* began with the Prophet's effort and his exercise of analogy and doing things in the public interest. As chief executive, the Prophet did promulgate laws, thereby establishing the precedent for direct state legislation by the political powers; and he also adopted pre-Islamic customs that were not in conflict with the Qur'ān. The Prophet and his successors sought the public interest in many of their rulings, and exercised their reason as best as they could. Reason is not the exclusive tool of *istidlāl*, for instance; it is used in comprehending all the other sources.

In contemporary times, our human needs are such that governments and their legislative bodies have to respond to rapidly occurring circumstances by enacting laws in the public interest. Such laws are neither intrinsically outside the *Sharī'ah*, nor can we simply declare that state legislative bodies are rejected by the *Sharī'ah*, and are therefore an invalid source of law. The key to admitting them within the embrace of the *Sharī'ah*, and rendering them obeyable by Muslims, is that they do not conflict with the Qur'ān and Ḥadīth. So as long as the laws are consonant with the spirit of the Qur'ān and Ḥadīth, it becomes hard to exclude any of the above eleven sources of law.

As we look at this list, we note that what differentiates "*Shar'ī*" from "non-*Shar'ī*" law is the attempt to bring human actions in accord with the Divine preference. The *Sharī'ah* is defined

---

[47] We are not saying that unjust laws must be accepted and not fought against; what we are saying is merely that the state is in fact undeniably a source of law, and to deny any of the sources of law is to shut one's eyes to the reality of the human social condition.

by the qualifying presence of the Qur'ān and the Ḥadīth. In other words, what distinguishes the *Sharī'ah* from other laws is not that it *excludes* any aspect of human actions or sources of law, but that it directs humankind to worship God, and having done so, attempts to ensure that the rest of human laws do not conflict with this intent. Even when situations arose that violated either the spirit or the letter of the *Sharī'ah*, some jurists attempted to reconcile these differences by the use of some of the other subsidiary sources such as judicial preference in the public interest or by the use of legal fictions.

A modern-day example of this is banking. It is clear that it is in the public interest to have banks. No Islamic nation can avoid it and be part of the world economy. But the issue of usury (*ribā*) vis-a-vis banking is so pervasive that Muslims have been forced on one hand to apply the principles of judicial preference (*istiḥsān*) and the need for the public interest (*maṣlaḥa*) to justify banking, and on the other have attempted to devise a concept of Islamic banking that is *ribā*-free. Even accepting the premise that we cannot do without banking, some Muslims consider "Islamic banking" to be a legal fiction to get around the various definitions of *ribā*, which all boil down to the issue of whether it is permissible or not to give money (or capital) a market value.[48]

Because the *Sharī'ah* is defined by the Qur'ān and Ḥadīth, some modern Muslims who believe that the separation of church and state is a sign of modernity, believe that the *Sharī'ah* consists only of religious law in the ritual sense (covering prayers, fasting, pilgrimage, etc.), the prohibition of major crimes like murder, theft, and the prescription of ethical values like kindness to neighbors, charity to the poor, etc. But all law, sacred or secular, is in

---

[48] Phrasing the question this way, there are then two ways to look at this question: (I) Does Islām prohibit capital from having any market value, thus forbidding interest, no matter how small? or (II) Does Islām recognize a market value for capital, with any rate above the "market interest rate" being usury (*ribā*)? See appendix IV.

the last analysis based on the principle of justice and equity, and the pursuit of the good, whether its source is custom, state legislation, or Divine scripture. But justice and equity, and the concepts of right and wrong, can only be an extension of an attachment to God and abiding by His dictates. And since a *Sharī'ah* is understood as a law with God at its center, it is not possible in principle to limit the *Sharī'ah* to some aspects of human life and leave out others.

Although the Qur'ān and Ḥadīth covered human interests in general, it left some details of human life without commenting on, and in verse 5:101 the Qur'ān reads, "O you who believe, ask not about things if made known to you would give you trouble; and if you ask about them when the Qur'ān is being revealed, they will be made known to you. Allāh has overlooked it . . ." *(yā 'ayyuha-lladhīna āmanū, lā tas'alū `an ashyā'a in-tubda lakum tasu'kum. Wa in tas'alū `anha ḥīna yunazzalu-l-Qur'ānu tubda lakum; `afa-llāhu `anha).* God excludes nothing from His judgment, and implicitly accepts the goodness of our free choice in matters lying outside His prescriptions and prohibitions.

It is true that the primary focus of the *Sharī'ah* is on the set of rules by which a human being should behave towards God. These are the religious rules (*`ibādāt)* governing belief in God, prayer, ritual purity and taxes/almsgiving (*zakāh*), fasting, the pilgrimage (*ḥajj*) and affairs of the hereafter. But because God as Creator of the universe has placed the human being as his *khalīfah* (viceroy) on earth, humankind's responsibility towards God also has a horizontal dimension, that is, a responsibility towards the rest of humanity and towards the rest of creation. This is as it must be, for Islām does not intend to be a religion whose values are practiced one day of the week—the Sabbath day—and ignored or violated the next six days of the week. The values of *`ibādāt*, the values of godliness, spill over into the area normally labeled the worldly, which is to say, its values have to color the rules governing what may be called the secular. And in reading a typical compendium on Islamic law, you will notice that, having discussed the list of credal and specifically religious ritual topics given above, it goes on to deal with family or personal law (i.e., marriage, divorce, paternity, guardianship and succession and inheritance), then with the law of contracts, of civil wrongs and criminal law; followed by the law of evidence and of procedure, and with a multitude of other subjects, to a degree of detail that it covers even the rules of social etiquette, called *ādāb*. Even "Emily Post" issues are under the umbrella of the *Sharī'ah*. The *Sharī'ah* thus covers every field of law—public and private, national and international—together with enormous amounts of material that Westerners would not regard as law at all, because the basis of the *Sharī'ah* is the worship of, and obedience to, God through good works and moral behavior. Following the Sacred Law thus *defines* the Muslim's belief in God.

Going back to the list of eleven *Sharī'ah* sources, note that the subsidiary sources are all the result of human effort; they have a distinctly secondary position to the Qur'ān and to that portion of the Ḥadīth where the Prophet was Divinely inspired.[49] As a Muslim you are free to peruse the Qur'ān and Ḥadīth and come up with your own sincere and conscientious opinion on some matter. However, you will find that as you become more informed about *uṣūl al-fiqh* as it has been collectively developed over the centuries by the brilliant minds of the jurists, you will discover a formidably powerful and intellectually beautiful system of analytic tools that is organically rooted in the Qur'ān and Ḥadīth. With the aid of this analytic system, the results of your effort will be greatly enhanced. It may or may not change your opinion on your question, but it will certainly push you way ahead in refining and strengthening your conclusion.

A question that arises at this point is, if the *Sharī'ah* includes laws from sources other than the Qur'ān and Ḥadīth, *does one sin against God if one violates a law from one of these other sources?* An example will clarify this point.

---

[49] In addition to the above list of sources of law, a host of general maxims have also been developed, like the rule of "necessity and need," "that actions are determined by their intentions," that when necessity conflicts with some other interest, "the lesser of two evils is preferred," which are applied to render judgments.

If a state decides to establish a law that it is illegal to drive at a speed greater than 55 mph, is it a *sin against God* if one drives at 65 mph? The answer that Muslims are ordered to be obedient to the government authorities is subject to the authorities acting in accordance with righteousness. This leads to the condition that the reasoning behind the law be ethically sensible. If the law's intent is to protect people from the danger of speeding cars, and if by speeding you are putting both your life or the life of others at risk, then you are sinning, for you are jeopardizing one of the objectives (*maqāṣid*) of the *Sharī'ah* (the protection of life). But if speeding does not jeopardize your life or that of others, then there is no sin in driving at 65 mph. Therefore the general question, "Is it a sin against God if one violates a law established by the State?" cannot be given a general answer, for if a state establishes a law that makes no sense, then it clearly is not a sin to violate it. States are known to revoke laws that no longer make any sense, or that were wrong to begin with.[50]

We see here how this question highlights the relationship between the concept of sin and the intent of any law. This is why the jurists differentiated between religious observances and nonreligious observances, and pointed out the importance of reason in understanding the objectives (*maqāṣid*) of the *Sharī'ah* (see Chapter I on the Objectives of the *Sharī'ah*).

---

50 A classic example from American history is the law prohibiting blacks from sitting in the front area of a bus and mixing with whites. Such a law based on ethnic prejudice violates the Qur'ānic teaching on equality of the races. This need to check the excesses of governmental authority is supported by the ḥadīth of Abu Bakr, who, on becoming the successor to the Prophet, announced, "I have been given the authority over you, and I am not the best of you. If I do well, help me; and if I do wrong, set me right. Sincere regard for truth is loyalty and disregard for truth is treachery. The weak amongst you shall be strong with me until I have secured his rights, if God will; and the strong amongst you shall be weak with me until I have wrested from him the rights of others, if God will. Obey me so long as I obey God and His Messenger. But if I disobey God and His Messsenger, you owe me no obedience. Arise from your prayer, God have mercy upon you!" Ibn Ishaq, *Sirat rasulallah*, 1017.

Having stated the purposes and aims of the *Sharī'ah*, we now review all these sources of Islamic jurisprudence.[51]

## A. The Qur'ān

The Qur'ān is Allāh's Word, Decree, Commandments and Guidance to humanity, and thus takes precedence over everything else. All the Imams of the schools of law, whether Sunni or *Shi`i*, are in agreement on this and differ only in the interpretation of some verses. In verses 5:44, 45 and 47—three times—God unequivocally asserts:

> *And whoever judges not by what Allāh has sent down (revealed), these are the disbelievers . . . And whoever judges not by what Allāh has sent down, these are the wrongdoers . . . And whoever judges not by what Allāh has sent down, these are the depraved.*

So if you don't want to be accused by God of being a depraved, disbelieving wrongdoer, you've got to abide by "what Allāh has sent down"; and the absolute importance of judging by what Allāh has sent down gives primary precedence to the Qur'ān over the Ḥadīth and subsidiary sources.

## B. The Sunnah

This refers to the normative practice and teachings of the Prophet. His teaching is embodied in the Ḥadīth (called Traditions or Sayings), which inform us of his practices and precedents. They are

---

51 A Muslim is free, in principle, to read the Qur'ān and Ḥadīth and come up with his or her own interpretation on a given matter. This is because there is no ordained priesthood in Islām that is solely qualified to read and interpret Scripture. But just as a knowledge of grammar and syntax helps you in understanding a piece of writing, *uṣūl al-fiqh* is a tool that helps strengthen, clarify and further your understanding of the Qur'ān and the Ḥadīth, and it keeps your understanding within the boundaries of the *Sharī'ah*. This freedom is just like your freedom to treat your sickness any way you think is right for you. But a knowledge of medicine and pharmacology would help you a lot in knowing how to treat yourself, for you would know what things to avoid and what to specifically do so as to speed your convalescence.

considered as supplementing and explaining the Qur'ān. Adherence to the *sunnah* is obligatory in all the schools by authority of the following verses and others like them:

> *"And whatever the Prophet gives you, take it. And whatever he forbids you, abstain (from it)." ( 59:7)*
>
> *"Obey God and obey the Prophet and be cautious." (5:92)*
>
> *"He who obeys the Prophet obeys God" (4:80)*

And since what God sent down was via the Prophet, we have to adhere to the clear commands of the Prophet. Differences of opinion arose over the Ḥadīth between the various schools starting first between the Sunnis and the Shi`ah. The latter accepted only those traditions or, as they called them, *akhbār* (narratives), which have as their authority members of the Prophet's family.

Differences also arose amongst the Sunnis themselves who were divided into two groups, the People of Opinion (*ahl ar-ra'y*), who were the followers of Abu Hanifah in Iraq, and the People of Tradition (*ahl al-ḥadīth*), who were the followers of Mālik in the Hejaz (the Western part of the Arabian peninsula, where Mecca and Medina are located). The first rejected certain traditions accepted by the second, and it also differed with the second group concerning some of the prerequisites for acceptance of traditions.

Having covered the textual sources, those that Muslim scholars define as "those contained between the covers of books," namely the Qur'ān and Ḥadīth, we now move on to the subsidiary sources of the *Sharī'ah.* As we shall see below, these subsidiary sources are defined by a descriptive activity.

## C. Ijmā` (Consensus of Opinion)

*Ajma`a* (the verb from which the noun *ijmā'* is derived) means to agree upon something, from a root that encompasses the meanings of gather, collecting, rounding up, assembling. (The cognate word *Jumu`ah*, for Friday, refers to the day of congregating for the Friday prayer). *Ijmā'* here refers to a ruling on a matter, not fully explicated in the Qur'ān or the Ḥadīth, and embracing the consensus of "those in authority." Before we explain who "those in authority" are, the Qur'ānic basis for consensus comes from verses like the following:

> *Surely Allāh commands you to turn over the trusts to their owners; and that when you judge between people, you judge equitably. . .O you who believe! Obey Allāh and obey the Messenger and those in authority from among you.*[52] *Then if you are at variance (or dispute) regarding a matter, then refer it to Allāh and the Messenger if you believe in Allāh and the Last Day. That is goodness and the best derivation (wa ahsana ta'wilan)." (4:58–9).*

This verse places the Qur'ān and Ḥadīth as the primary and secondary sources of *Sharī'ah*, followed by "those in authority." This verse is construed to mean that consensus by those in authority is acceptable if there is no conflict with the Qur'ān and the Ḥadīth. Imam Ibn Ḥanbal, for example, defined consensus (used here in the sense equivalent to "those in authority") as the opinions and decisions of the Companions of the Prophet, among whom of course were the first four (also known as the Orthodox) Caliphs. The predominant view, however, is that "those in author-

---

[52] Some Muslims take this to mean obedience to those in political power, whether right or wrong. It does mean obedience to the state, but not if it forces the Muslim to violate the Qur'ān or Ḥadīth. This point is proven by the following:

a. The Caliph Abu Bakr, in his acceptance speech, requested the community to support him if he was right, and to correct him if wrong. (See footnote 50.)

b. The Imams al-Hasan and al-Husayn, the grandsons of the Prophet, sacrificed their lives because they did not agree with those who wielded political power.

c. The Imams Mālik, Abu Hanifah and Ibn Ḥanbal, all founders of *madhahib*, were beaten, whipped, persecuted or imprisoned because they did not agree with the political powers of the time. If this verse means obedience to the political authorities whether they were right or wrong, they would certainly not have disobeyed and suffered punishment. This confirms that it is not a sin to violate a subsidiary source of law.

ity" also includes the qualified scholars of law of later periods. Implicit here is that "those in authority" would procedurally refer first to Allāh and the Messenger (i.e., the Qur'ān and the Ḥadīth) then seek a consensus based on their understanding of these two primary sources.

Muslims have used the term *ijmā'* to refer to slightly different things. We'll list for you the various ways in which you might see the term *ijmā'* being used, but it's worth remembering that one reason why there exist these ways in which the term was used is that as time went on, the circle of people to whom authority could be ascribed widened; the term evolved as it embraced a wider spectrum of meanings. We list the evolution of it as follows:

a. The agreement of the Companions of the Prophet, which naturally includes the opinions and consensus of the first four Orthodox Caliphs (Ibn Ḥanbal and Dawud az-Zahiri's view).

b. The agreement of the first four (Orthodox) Caliphs only.

c. The agreement of the family of the Prophet, or when the jurisconsults were endorsed in their consensus by the infallible *Shi`ah* Imam. That is, consensus which embodies the views of the infallible Imam and not merely the agreement of the 'ulamā' on an opinion (The *Shi`ah* view).[53]

---

[53] The major philosophical difference between Sunni and Shi`i law rests on the Shi`i doctrine of the Imamate. Sunni law postulates a system that is basically immutable and represents the attempt by human reason to discern the Divine command, whereas Shi`i law purports to express the direct and living expression of that Divine command. The Sunni head of state (Caliph, for example) is as much bound by the law as his subjects, and his administrative powers must always be exercised within the limits set by the law. The Shi`i Imam, on the other hand, exercises legal sovereignty, and speaks with the supreme authority of the Divine Lawgiver himself. His authority therefore supersedes that of agreed practice. From a legal standpoint, the three most important branches of the Shi`is are the small minority of the Zaydis, the Isma`ilis and the overwhelmingly most numerous group, the Ithna`asharis (literally, "the Twelvers") or Imamiyyah. For the Zaydis the authority of the Imam is that of a human being; he is elected by the community on the basis of his personal abilities and has no closer link with Allāh than that of being generally "guided on the right path." The Isma`ilis and Ithna`asharis hold that the Imam, although he may be formally designated by his predecessor, is in fact appointed by God and possesses something of the Divine essence; but while the Isma`ili Imams have continued in unbroken line from the time of Imam `Alī down to the present day, the Ithna`asharis are so called because they recog-

d. The explicit and unanimous agreement of *all* qualified Muslim jurisconsults in any particular age on a matter, and that in general this ruling stands for succeeding generations. This was Imam ash-Shāfi`i's view, and because unanimous agreement was maintained only on matters of fundamental belief and acts of worship and the basics (like prohibition of murder, adultery, etc.), he was therefore forced to conclude that consensus applied only to these matters and not on others. From this we arrive at the general conclusion that it is not a sin against God to disobey a ruling emanating from a subsidiary source of law.

e. The same as meaning "d" above, but where consensus may be had either by an overt and explicit expression of opinion or by acquiescence and silence. The latter takes place when one of the jurists gives a ruling on a certain matter and the other jurists of his day hear of it and do not challenge it. Most of the companions of Abu Hanifah have regarded silence as conclusive and evidence of agreement. If you're quiet, this may not necessarily mean that you're for the ruling, but neither does it mean that you're against it.

f. An intermediate position, where consensus by silence constitutes a presumption which is not absolute. This was al-Āmidi's position.

For those of us living in a democracy, we all know how difficult it is to achieve a quorum. To decide an issue, do we need a unanimous vote, a two-thirds majority, a simple majority, or the highest percentage of votes? And for what issues do we attach the various percentages? The problems associated with *ijmā'* and how it is achieved are just as hair-raising as trying to determine which spectrum of issues you need a quorum for in our democratic republic. A key thing about *ijmā'*, though, is that it introduced a level of democracy into Islām, and no less importantly, it prevented a formation of a concept of papacy in Islām. There was no one person who could assume the mantle of the Prophet and claim Divine inspiration, and whom we all have to follow. Even the Shi`i

---

nize only twelve Imams, the last of whom retired from this world in 874 AD and is destined to reappear in the fullness of time.

concept of the infallibility of the Imam was attenuated by their application of their definition of the concept of *ijmā'*.

There exists a reciprocal relationship between the *number* of issues that can be resolved by *ijmā'* and the *degree* of agreement of the *mujtahids*; the higher degree of agreement you insist upon, the less the number of issues you will get agreement on. Also, if you insist on unanimity in arriving at a legal decision on a particular issue (not covered by the Qur'ān and *Sunnah*) that is also unanimously accepted by future generations, which was ash-Shāfi`ī's position, then it is impossible to demonstrate that *ijmā'* historically occurred as an ongoing source of specific decisions of law. And you'll also understand why others had to coin different definitions of *ijmā'*, otherwise *ijmā'* could not effectively give us any new laws.

If you look long enough at the above ways that *ijmā'* has been defined, you may notice an evolution and growth in the very definition of the term *ijmā'* itself, from a relatively limited definition of legal decisions by the immediate Companions of the Prophet, to one that embraces the acceptance over time by the community of an evolving collective body of knowledge, including *fiqh*, as the product of a continual process of *ijtihād*, including those ideas, conceptions and formulations that have achieved acceptance in the life of the community. Thus, for example, *ijmā'* in this expanded definition has contributed to the following:

a. Ensuring the correct collection, recitation and interpretation of the Qur'ān.

b. Ensuring the faithful understanding of the *Sunnah*. In fact, the need to develop the science of *fiqh* fueled and accelerated the need to compile authentic compilations of Ḥadīth, and especially fueled the critical study of the Ḥadīth, resulting in rules of the determination of the authentic hadiths. Ijmā' has therefore led to the collective recognition by the Muslim community of the canonical collections of Ḥadīth.

c. The development of the science of jurisprudence *(uṣūl al-fiqh)*, and the rules for the legitimate use of *ijtihād*, *qiyās*, etc., insofar as they have been accepted by the bulk of the Muslim community (arguably one of the most important results of *ijmā'*).

Over time, *ijmā'* has reduced the differences of opinion among Muslims over a given specific issue. *Ijmā'* refers therefore to those aspects of our understanding and knowledge that have withstood collective criticism and the test of time, and have become generally accepted by the Muslim community. We can even call it the "center of gravity" or "the mainstream Islamic thinking" or "the collective public opinion," over time, of the Islamic ideas and ideals of the community, especially as it relates to issues of law and jurisprudence. It is this notion that lies at the hub of the term *ahl as-sunnah wal-jama`ah* (those following the norm of the Prophet and the collective consensus).

*Ijmā'* has made a worthy contribution to the *Sharī'ah* inasmuch as it has made possible changes to suit the needs of evolving times and usages. *Ijmā'* is also the best evidence that the authority in Islām lies not in one individual with papal authority within a church-type organization, but in the Muslim community as a whole. Perhaps this aspect of *ijmā'* contributed to the dilution over time of the *Shi`i* concept of the Imamate as an operational reality, although the original intent was fully credible and justified. More than anything else, *ijmā'* has been the dynamic that has kept the Islamic creed intact for fifteen centuries, and has effectively contributed to the relatively remarkable sense of unity among Muslims in the face of all the kinds of fragmentary conflict that could possibly occur, and did occur, in Muslim society.

## D. Qiyās (Analogy):

With the expansion of the Islamic state and its sphere of influence, and as centuries went by, new cases occurred which were not categorically provided for in the Qur'ān, the *sunnah*, and the consensus of opinion of the Orthodox caliphs and the Companions of the Prophet. The jurists found themselves compelled, in seeking solutions, to have recourse to reason, logic and opinion. In this pursuit, however, they were not entirely free or unrestrained; they had to adhere to scientific rules and premises which they classified in a new category known as *qiyās,* or analogy. Analogy thus became the fourth source of the Islamic *Sharī'ah.*

You may wonder why *ijmā'* often precedes *qiyās* as a measure of importance, when operationally people have to exercise some level of thinking like analogy before they can vote and arrive at a consensus. For this precedence there are several reasons, among which are that different people can use analogy and arrive at differing conclusions; some may be inspired, or have a dream as to what we should do; some people may be governed by ulterior motives like personal or public interest. Your opinion on a matter is not determined solely by analogy to another situation. Just look at Congress here in the United States debating an issue, and see how different representatives sincerely and passionately argue for opposing points of view. At the end of the day, the only way they can resolve this is to take a vote. That's why *ijmā'* is third on the list. All these motives, as you put them together, make *ijmā'* more important in the long run. It is also hard to maintain your point of view if everybody thinks otherwise. You'll begin to wonder why, and perhaps you will see the larger picture.

That the Prophet practiced *qiyās* is demonstrated by several *aḥādīth,* of which the following is an example: A woman from the Juhaynah tribe came to the Prophet one day and stated: "My mother had vowed that she would perform the pilgrimage but passed away before fulfilling this vow. Should I perform the pilgrimage on her behalf?" The Prophet answered: "Yes, perform the pilgrimage for her. If your mother had passed away with debts outstanding would you not have settled them? Repay God's debts, for God is more entitled to repayment."[54] The Prophet regarded

---

[54] Although the pilgrimage is an obligation upon all Muslims, this case does not mean that every child is obliged to perform the pilgrimage on behalf of a parent who did not get to do it, although because of this ḥadīth, it has become highly popular among Muslims to do so. The case here is that the deceased woman *vowed* to perform the pilgrimage, and died before fulfilling her vow. To a Western reader, this example may also raise the issue of children being saddled with the debts of their parents. Without going into it in great detail, we may point out that even under American law, the debts of the

the deceased woman's vow of performing the pilgrimage as a debt owed to God, and therefore analogous to a debt of money owed by the deceased to a human being. In another tradition the Prophet says, "I adjudicate amongst you by opinion in what has not been dealt with by revelation."[55] And since the Prophet's adjudicating by his opinion was not rejected by the Qur'ān, *qiyās* in particular, and the use of opinion in general, as a subsidiary source of law is therefore considered to have been endorsed by God.

The classic example in Islamic legal history which introduced *qiyās* on the scene after the Prophet's death was the following. The Caliph `Umar Ibn al-Khaṭṭāb consulted with the Companions regarding the punishment which should be meted out to those who drink wine. `Alī b. Abī[56] Talib is reported to have advised: "We apply the punishment for slander," namely eighty lashes of the whip, because "if a person drinks he becomes intoxicated, and if he is intoxicated he does not restrain his speech, and in such a state he (is likely to) commit slander." Thus through analogy (*qiyās*), drinking of wine was likened to slander insofar as its punishment was concerned.

The jurists, in following the procedural precedent of the Prophet and his Companions, thus derived this new source from the fundamental juridical premise that all rules are based upon objectives and interests, and that such objectives and interests are the causes for the rules. Hence, from the rules they deduced their causes. Having done so in reference to a particular problem, they

---

deceased are to be paid by the estate of the deceased, which is considered as a separate entity, quite like a corporation is considered an entity under American law. Only if the net worth of the estate is positive do the heirs inherit something, otherwise the estate would be bankrupt. At the time of the Prophet, the concept of an independent estate did not exist as a practical matter, and the executors of the deceased's estate were generally the beneficiaries-to-be.

[55] Quoted by S. Mahmassani, *Falsatah al-Tashrī' fi al-Islām*, translated by Farhat Ziadeh, Senerbitan Hizbi, 1987, p. 81.

[56] For the benefit of non-Arab readers, Abu is the nominative case, Aba the accusative case, and Abī the genitive case. `Alī bin Abī Talib means `Alī son of Abī Talib, and the Abu becomes Abī. Although it sounds technical, an Arab ear finds it sometimes difficult to ignore grammatical correctness.

were able to apply the same rule to another problem whenever the cause for both was identical.

Let's walk through this example: wine is explicitly prohibited by Qur'ānic decree. Let's say we want to know what the ruling would be for whiskey. The cause for the prohibition of wine is the intoxicating effect. Thus by analogy, all intoxicating drinks are prohibited.

The logic of analogy proceeds as follows (we are also giving you the four pillars of analogy):

1. The original subject, *aṣl*, for which there is a decision (in our example wine, prohibited by Qur'ānic decree).
2. The new subject which is the object of the analogy, *far`* (in our example, whiskey).
3. The rule arrived at by analogy, *`illah*[57] (the cause or link which brings together the original subject and the new subject and which is the reason for the analogy; here it is the intoxicating effect).
4. The *shar`i* ruling, *hukm* (the conclusion, prohibition).

In Imam `Alī b. Abī Talib's application of the rules of *qiyās* for seeking the punishment for drinking wine, the original subject would be the punishment for slander, whose punishment we know as eighty lashes of the whip. The new subject (or question) would be "What is the punishment for drinking wine?" (the object of the analogy). The rule arrived at by analogy (the cause that brings together the original and the new subject) would be the fact that a

---

[57] The term *`illah* has several meanings. Here it means the cause, reason, plea. It also means weakness, defect, illness, which is how we see it used in the section on Ḥadīth. It should not be confused with the word *ilah* meaning "god." This should not confuse the reader any more than that the English word "bore" embraces several meanings: a boring person, the caliber or diameter of a gun barrel or tube, an instrument used for making holes by boring or turning, and in physical geography, a roaring, high-crested and destructive wave or flood caused by the rushing of a floodtide up the estuaries of certain rivers. Homonyms are not the exclusive province of English.

drunk person commits slander, and the *shar`i* ruling would be the punishment for slander (eighty lashes of the whip).

According to the prevalent view of the jurists, the prerequisites of analogy are:

1. The cause, or reason for the analogy, (*`illah*) must be the compelling factor, the idea intended by the *shar`i* ruling. It should also be apparent, complete in itself, and not ambiguous or hidden.

2. The cause should be identical in both the original subject and the subject of the analogy. The mere similarities in attributes are not sufficient to justify analogy as analogy may only be resorted to if both subjects are equal in every respect.

3. The rule in the original case should be generally applicable. Thus analogy is not permissible in case of a rule which already has a specific reference. For example, the sale of a non-existent thing, a thing not in existence at the time of the concluding of the contract, is void. Since benefits and services, according to the Ḥanafi school, are not considered in existence at the time of the contract, the contract of hire was considered as the sale of a thing which is not in existence and therefore, by analogy, void. However, the contract of hire was sanctioned by the Qur'ān, the *sunnah* and consensus. Therefore, analogy cannot supersede these more substantial bases. (The Ḥanafi school set analogy aside by use of *istihsān*, i.e. "judicial preference.")[58]

It is clear that analogy may not be considered as a valid source of law, except when it conforms to certain conditions, and is based upon logical and scientific principles and is different from opinion based upon mere whim.

If we ask, "Why is analogy so difficult to do?" we find that one of the main reasons for the difficulties and controversies arising from analogy are because *analogies are imperfect by definition.* An analogy is never an identity, thus analogy cannot be a *perfect* source of laws. A caveat will always pertain in proportion to the degree of

---

[58] This raises the relevant question as to whether trading in futures on the stock market is permissible, a matter that is beyond the scope of this section, for it takes us into a required analysis of the economic values expounded in the Qur'ān and the Ḥadīth.

lack of identity between the new subject and the original subject. This is why, for example, the punishment for drinking—on which the Qur'ān and Ḥadīth are silent—has varied; although the punishment by analogy to calumny was 80 lashes, ʿUmar b. al-Khaṭṭāb once meted out a reduced punishment of 40 lashes. We may also interpret the Qur'ān's and Ḥadīth's silence on this as demonstrating Divine recognition of the need for, and acceptance of, flexibility on these issues.

One can argue that the decision to equate the punishment for drinking to slander is arbitrary. In a state of drunkenness the drunk may steal, rape, or commit murder, or may just feel depressed and commit no crime at all. It is then correct to mete a punsihment for drinking that more correctly belongs to another crime that may be committed under the influence of alcohol? Especially when the Qur'ān and Ḥadīth have not specified a punishment?

This interpretation is further substantiated by the Qur'ānic verse 5:101 quoted earlier, which advises the believers not to ask about things that Allāh has overlooked, and which if made known would give us trouble. Allāh has knowingly and deliberately injected that flexibility so as to provide us the option to rule according to our judgment based on time and circumstance. God doesn't want to trouble you, so don't ask about things that would bother you. If you ask for trouble, God will give you trouble. And we all have enough problems as it is.

Note that although we have spoken of analogy as another "source" of law, it cannot conceptually and organically be totally separated from the Ḥadīth or *ijmā'*. The Prophet himself practiced analogy, and *ijmā'* is often the consensus of opinion based upon the individual exercise of analogy (*qiyās*), or in other words, a statistical average or a vote of those who are qualified to perform (*qiyās*), based on their own individual arguments, but invariably in favor of their recognition of the superiority of a particular *mujtahid*'s argument. Conceptually, therefore, these sources are organically cross-linked and to a large extent are nested in each other. And they are not sources like different wells are sources of water; dip your bucket into it as needed and you will draw up water. They are "sources" in the sense that you've got to dip the bucket of sometimes complex *ijtihād* into it and draw out what your *ijtihād* pulls up, often enough in the shape of your *ijtihād.*

Muslims are commonly taught about the four sources of Islamic law outlined above: the Qur'ān, the Ḥadīth, *ijmā'* (consensus) and *qiyās* (analogy). As said earlier, on these four sources there is universal agreement, primarily because these sources are centered on the Qur'ān and Ḥadīth. The Texts, defined as the Qur'ān and the *Sunnah*, are given priority over the other sources and all the schools are in agreement on this. Priority is then given to that opinion unanimously agreed upon by jurists in a particular period, which is *ijmā'.* Next is opinion based upon analogy within the limits and the conditions which we have outlined.

Historically, situations occurred which were not categorically provided for in the four sources already mentioned. The jurists discussed, and some accepted, other and sometimes new sources such as *istiḥsān*, judicial preference (literally "the seeking after what is good"); *masāliḥ mursalah*, public interest; *istiṣḥāb*, the continuation of a rule for a certain situation in a circumstance where it is not known whether or not the original situation still exists; *`urf*, (pre- and post-Islamic) laws and customs; and direct positive legislation by the ruling powers. All these sources are justified when they do not violate the principles of the Qur'ān and Ḥadīth. By the study of the reasons behind the rules and fulfilling the interests of the people in their social life, the intention was always to abide as closely as possible with absolute good and with the dictates of justice and equity. We've seen how those who thought deeply about the *Sharī'ah* recognized that real justice and equity are the basis of the *Sharī'ah*, for as God declares in verse 16:90 of the Qur'ān "Certainly Allāh enjoins justice (*`adl*) and goodness (*iḥsān*)." We now turn to the discussion of these additional subsidiary sources.

## E. Istiḥsān (Equity, or Judicial Preference):

*Istiḥsān*, which may be translated as equity under Western law, was a source of law developed by the Ḥanafi jurists. Those who did not agree with this as a source of law accused the Ḥanafis of resorting to judicial activism. The Ḥanafi school represented the People of Opinion (*Ahl ar-Ra'y*), those who more often resorted to logic and reason, as opposed to the People of Tradition (*Ahl al-Ḥadīth*) represented by the Maliki school. This was more the result of local conditions. Baghdad, being a cosmopolitan city far from the Hejaz, the home of Ḥadīth scholars, had more challenges to the traditional way of thinking and prompted resorting to greater use of the intellectual faculty. The Maliki school, being in an environment centered around a simpler way of life in Madinah, the home of prominent and resourceful Ḥadīth authorities, preferred to depend on the authority of traditions. Life is always more complex around Chicago's beltway and New York than in Des Moines or Oshkosh, and more *ijtihād* effort is required to arrive at a consensus among the federal House and Senate than at a local Town Hall assembly. Consensus in the City Hall of New York, a city with a population of several million, requires greater effort than in the City Hall of Teterboro, New Jersey, whose population is no more than a few hundred.

This difference in labelling did not mean that the Ḥanafis did not recognize the importance of Ḥadīth, or that the Malikis did not resort to reason. It was more a difference of emphasis in what the school saw as its role. The Malikis saw their objective as *preserving* an established tradition, whereas the Ḥanafis saw their role as extending tradition, although some may argue that they were creating a tradition of their own. Another difference was that the Maliki system represented a moralistic approach to legal problems in contrast to the Ḥanafis' formalistic approach; thus the Malikis placed great emphasis on the intention of a person as affecting the validity of his conduct, whereas the Ḥanafis paid greater attention to the external conduct itself.

For example, an impediment to marriage exists between a husband and his former wife whom he repudiated in a triple form[59] which can only be removed by the marriage of the woman to a third party, the consummation of this intervening marriage, and its subsequent termination. Maliki law maintains that the intention of the parties to the intervening marriage is of paramount importance, and that, if the court discovers that the purpose of such a marriage was simply to enable the wife subsequently to remarry her former husband, it will not have this effect. Ḥanafi law, on the contrary, deems any enquiry into the intention of the parties to be outside the province of the courts, and the intervening marriage will always be effective in removing the impediment, unless it is known that its express purpose was merely strategic. This technical formalism of Ḥanafi law is particularly evident in its endorsement of legal fictions (*ḥiyal*), as we shall see later. It is this kind of difference that made the Malikis be labelled as *Ahl al-Ḥadīth,* and the Hanafis as *Ahl ar-Ra'y.*

*Istiḥsān* was not a source of controversy when the Ḥanafis used it to set aside decisions based on analogy in favor of rulings based on the Qur'ān, the *sunnah* or consensus, since all jurists favored these stronger bases. The cause of controversy was when the Ḥanafis used *istihsān* as a source of laws which set aside a certain source of law (be it analogy or another source of law) on account of custom, public interest, necessity, or mitigating hardship. For example, *bay` bil-wafā'* (a type of mortgage consisting of a sale subject to future redemption) was allowed in view of the people's need for it.[60] Rules were given a wide scope under the plea of necessity and mitigation of hardships. Life is tough, so go easy on the believers.

---

[59] A divorced Muslim couple may remarry, divorce again and remarry, and divorce again. But after the third divorce, may not remarry unless the wife marries another man, consummates this marriage, and be divorced by him. Only then may the previous husband marry the woman again. This is what a triple divorce or repudiation means.

[60] Under the Ḥanafi *madhhab,* a long lease on orchards was prohibited. They therefore resorted to this recourse of selling the orchard with the right of the seller to redeem it.

A number of Maliki jurists however accepted preference in this sense and defined it as "the attention to public interest and justice."[61] Imam Ahmad b. Ḥanbal was said to have subscribed to this view. Imam ash-Shāfi`i, however, rejected it, saying, "He who practices *istihsān* (preference) assumes unto himself the power of law-making."[62] The controversy revolved around a matter of opposing principles: Do we determine what limitations religious principles set upon social conduct, or do we bend the laws to meet the needs of society?

It is clear, however, that the Caliph `Umar b. al-Khaṭṭāb was a resolute practitioner of *istihsān,* as when he suspended the punishment prescribed for theft during a time of famine (although at that time the expression itself had not yet come into being). As the second successor of the growing Islamic state, he distinguished himself for justice, firmness and courage. The caliphate of `Umar was full of conquests and dynamic changes. Consequently, new situations arose and old customs changed, requiring changes in some of the fresh *fatwas* and rules which had prevailed in the era of the Prophet or of the Caliph Abu Bakr. The Caliph `Umar faced the new situations firmly and resolutely and did not shrink from going deeply into the meaning of the texts, and overruling old interpretations of texts, if the *shar`i* policy or the interests of the Muslims made that imperative. The following are a few examples that can be juridically embraced and reconciled via the principle of juristic preference based upon equity, the public interest, or on necessity and need:

a. "Those whose hearts are to be induced." The Qur'ān made provisions for the spending of alms:

> *"The alms are only for the poor and the needy and those employed to administer it and for those whose hearts are to be induced (to Islām), and to free the captives and the debtors, and for the cause of God and*

---

[61] Shatibi, *I'tiṣām,* II, 116–129.

[62] Ghazali, *Mustaṣfā,* I, 137.

*the wayfarer, a duty imposed by Allāh. And Allāh is Knowing, Wise" (Qur'ān 9:60).*

"Those whose hearts were to be induced" were the group of waverers whom the Prophet included among the recipients of the proceeds of alms to win them over to Islām on account of their weak faith or in order to avoid their mischief or because of the high esteem in which they were held by their tribe. This is comparable to a company giving someone they really want to hire an employment bonus so he will leave his current position and come to work for them. The Qur'ān sets aside in the *zakāh* budget an allowance for paying bonuses in order to recruit converts to Islām.

In spite of this express Qur'ānic text, the Caliph `Umar discontinued this practice. He turned new converts away saying, "These were payments from the Prophet to you in order to win you over for Islām. Now, God has given power to Islām and it no longer needs to pay you." He is also reported to have added: "We do not pay anyone anything for embracing Islām. He who wishes to believe, let him believe; and he who wishes to remain infidel, let him do so." (In other words, we're a great company with the very best benefits. Everybody wants to work here, so no more employment bonuses are necessary for applying here.)

b. The sale of *ummahāt al-awlād* or slave mothers; these are slave girls who give birth to children as a result of voluntary physical intimacy with their masters. `Umar prohibited their sale saying, "Our blood has been mixed with their blood."

c. Theft, for which the punishment according to the Qur'ānic rule is: "As for the male thief and the female thief, cut off their hands, as a punishment for what they have earned, an exemplary punishment from Allāh. And Allāh is Mighty, Wise" (Qur'ān 5:38). The *sunnah* of the Prophet endorsed this rule in word and deed. `Umar, however, suspended this punishment in the Year of Famine because of necessity and in order that people may survive.[63]

---

[63] This punishment cannot be invoked for petty theft, only for grand larceny, where the value of the theft is substantial.

The consensus of jurists followed this rule. (`Umar was not always harsh.)

d. The punishment for a fornicator, not bound by marriage, is according to the majority of jurists one hundred lashes of the whip and exile for one year. The punishment by exile is established by the *sunnah.* However, when `Umar exiled Rabi`ah ibn Umayyah ibn Khalaf and the latter joined the Byzantines, `Umar said, "I shall never send anyone to exile again." His suspension of the rule, though embodied in an explicit ḥadīth text, was motivated by his desire to make sure that no Muslim would desert to the enemy. The rule didn't make *sense* any more. Why observe a rule that helps the enemy?

`Umar was always *sensible.* We might even describe *istihsān* as *juridical sensibility*, which is what I like to call it. I often wonder, if all Muslims nowadays were to exercise "sensibility," what an easier time we would have!

`Umar's action lends support not only to the Ḥanafi principle of *istihsān* as a source of law, but also to the additional sources of law we will describe below: public interest in cases (a) and (d), and the rule of necessity and need in case (c). It also lends support to the notion of the evolution of laws so that they be sensible and just.

## F. Al- Maṣālīh Al-Mursalah (Public Interest):

Jurists, with the exception of the Zahiriyyah (the followers of Dawud al-Zahiri), were in agreement that the *Sharī'ah* has rational connotations and is based ultimately upon the interests of, and the benefits to, the people.

Thus if the *Sharī'ah*, through a Text, consensus or analogy, should refer to interests as being a determining factor (in a particular case) or otherwise, such reference is decisive. But should the *Sharī'ah* make no comment regarding interests in any particular matter, it becomes legitimate to inquire about them and to make interpretations. It makes sense to enquire into the wisdom behind this rule.[64]

Thus the Imam Mālik approved the plea of public interest as one of the sources of the *Sharī'ah,* and named this new source *al-maṣālīh al-mursalah.* These interests have not been covered by any text of the *Sharī'ah* and therefore are considered *mursal,* set loose from the texts. (In the science of Ḥadīth, a *mursal* ḥadīth means one whose chain of authorities stops short of the Prophet by one narrator from the Companions' generation.) So a *msṣlaḥah mursalah* means a kind of public interest that does not rely on an interest determined by the Qur'ān or Ḥadīth. For example, there were no speed limits on the caravan highway for the camels and horses. You could travel as fast as you wished. Today, however, we have crazy drivers on the road who can kill others by their speeding, so we have speed limits. This is an example of a *maṣlaḥah mursalah,* a law based upon public interest that is not based on any notion of speed limits set at the Prophet's time by a Qur'ān or Ḥadīth quotation.

The meaning of interpretation by means of this method is to relate a particular rule to the appropriate meaning which is consonant with the general practices of the *Sharī'ah*; in other words, to consider the reasonable meaning which conforms to the public interest and to the intent of the *Sharī'ah,* and then to formulate a rule that such meaning requires. You don't want people to be endangered; this is a reasonable motive in conformance to the *Sharī'ah*; because of this we formulate a rule that you can't drive more than 55 mph on the highway, and 20 mph around the public school where our kids go.

Three conditions are attached to the adoption of this new source:

---

[64]The punishment for theft, as in 5:38 quoted above, does not explain the public interest involved. It is therefore reasonable to ask what the reason for this rule is. It is clearly done in the public interest, and sensitivity to the public interest leads us to `Umar's position where he suspended this rule under circumstances he deemed made the rule inapplicable.

- That the case under review should not be one pertaining to matters of religious observances. It can only pertain to matters of worldly transactions so that the interests involved in the case may be construed on the grounds of reason. Reason is not a ***basis*** for construing religious observances. You can't say the reason why we pray five times daily is for physical exercise, and because you swim twenty laps in your swimming pool every day, you are exempt from the five daily prayers. Or better yet, "I am always thinking about God, so why should I pray and distract myself?" You couldn't think of God more or better than the Prophet, and *he* prayed five times a day. This is a perverse example of being "holier than the Prophet."
- The interest should be in harmony with the spirit of the *Sharī'ah* and should not be in conflict with any one of its sources.
- The interest should be of the essential and the necessary, and not of the luxury (or perfectionist) type. The essential type includes the **preservation of religion, life, reason, off-spring, and property.** The necessary type pertains to the **betterment of living.** The luxury (perfectionist) type refers to **"decoration and improvement."**

Some examples based on public interest:

1. The imposition of taxes in order to meet the costs of government public services.
2. The punishment of the criminal by depriving him of property if his crime was perpetrated over that property or its equivalent.
3. In modern times, laws like the imposition of licensing for drivers and speed limits to assure public safety.

## G. Istidlāl (Deduction) and Istiṣḥāb (Extension)

*Istidlāl* or deduction is the seeking of a basis for a rule. In addition to this sense, the term has been used to connote a special source of law derived from reason and logic. "It is a source which is not a Text, consensus or analogy." The most important categories of deduction are:

1. Deduction by logical processes. For example: a sale is a contract; the basis of every contract is mutual consent; therefore it is necessary that such mutual consent be the basis of the sale.
2. Deduction by presumption of continuity or extension (*istiṣḥāb*): the literal meaning of *istiṣḥāb* is extension. It is used to denote that the state of a thing should be presumed to remain the same, either going forward or backward in time, in the absence of any established change. A few examples:

   - A missing person (for example, a Vietnam veteran missing in action, commonly known as an "MIA" ) is presumed to be alive until his death is established, either in fact or by a judicial decree of his assumed death based on the fact that the time that elapsed since his disappearance would complete his normal life span. Only then may his estate be probated, and his entitled heirs be determined.[65] The Shāfi`i

---

[65] A relevant question that arises here is, is the wife of a missing person free to remarry? The answer to this question varies according to the different schools, and is a function of several variables, among which the primary one is whether his whereabouts are known and news about him is received, or whether there is no more news of him and his whereabouts. In the first case, the wife is not entitled to remarry. In the second case, there is further variation among the schools, again a function of whether the wife is supported by the missing husband's assets or has no means of support whatsoever. In any case, the wife of a missing husband has the right to sue the court for termination of the marriage on the basis of her need for male companionship, usually after an absence of at least three to six months. A wife also has the right to sue for annulment of her marriage (to a non-missing husband) on the basis of her paying a consideration to her husband. A detailed analysis of this is beyond the scope of this book, as financial issues get intertwined. For further details the English reader may refer to the *Encyclopedia of Islamic Law, A Compendium of the Major Schools*, adapted by Laleh Bakhtiar (Chicago, ABC International Group, 1996), Section on Divorce. Also *The Five*

*madhhab* moreover applies this same principle of *istiṣḥāb* to assert that the missing person survives any relative who dies prior to the date of his presumed death, and therefore gives the missing person the right to inherit from the estate of a relative who dies during his absence.

- Presumption of original freedom from liability (unless the contrary is proved). Thus no person may be compelled to perform any obligation save on authority of a *shar`i* provision. No one can make you responsible for something, and blame you for it unless they have a strong reason to do so which is recognized by the *Sharī'ah.*
- Presumption of generality until a limitation is placed thereon. This means that a general provision should be generally applicable until it is made limited to certain situations.
- Continually regarding a text as a source of law until it is repealed. Thus a text should be respected until it is supplanted by another text or some other source of law.
- Continuity of a legally established fact until the contrary is proved. For example, if it is established that you own a given property, your ownership shall *continue* to be valid until some circumstance arises which invalidates your ownership.

## H. `Urf (Custom And Pre-Islamic Laws)

Has the *Sharī'ah* supplanted all legal systems which preceded it?

A group of jurists has maintained that the *Sharī'ah* has supplanted all previous legal systems except those parts that have been preserved by a textual provision. Others have maintained that "the laws of our predecessors are laws unto us." That is, all laws pre-

---

*Schools of Islamic Law*, n.d., ed. by Muḥammad Jawad Maghniyyah, Qum, Iran, Section on Divorce.

ceding the *Sharī'ah* should remain operative unless specifically supplanted, considering that "things which have been in existence from time immemorial shall be left as they were."

It is clear, however, that as Islām spread into countries, the *Sharī'ah* supplanted what was inconsistent with it, while it honored and left standing laws that were not inconsistent with it. Most of such laws were customary in these societies, and they have been classified into four types:

1. Those relating to transactions and rights.
2. Those relating to mores and behavior.
3. Those relating to clothing and social conduct.
4. Those relating to amusement and entertainment.

Customs differ with different regions, countries and times, and they assume peculiar forms. For example, under the third category of clothing and social conduct, the practice of not covering your head was regarded as a bad habit and a flaw in trustworthiness by the people of the Eastern countries at one time (besides, you were crazy to walk around in the heat of the desert sun with your head uncovered), while it is not so considered by people today, as customs have changed as a result of the influence of modern Western customs and the rapid mixing of cultures. The same applies to men's facial hair. At the time of the Prophet, men grew their beards but trimmed or shaved their mustaches. Shaving the beard and growing the mustache, or being clean-shaven altogether, was a sign of untrustworthiness at that time. Why was this? Just ask yourself how you think a judge in a U.S. Federal court would feel if on the day you went to court, your lawyer representing you wore red plaid shorts, dyed his hair a flaming red and cut it in a Mohawk hair style, wore a ring in one ear and another in his nose? If that is the agreed-upon costume for lawyers, then it would be fine, but until then, you had better stick to a lawyer who dresses in the garb expected of lawyers.

To the pre-Islamic Arabs, traditions and customs were the basis of their entire social life, including religion, morality, trade and transactions. With the rise of Islām, texts based on the Qur'ān and Ḥadīth became the basis of legislation while custom took a subsidiary place. Although not strictly rated as one of the sources of *Sharī'ah*, custom infiltrated the *Sharī'ah* in several ways, the most important of which were:

1. A number of texts, particularly of Ḥadīth, were based upon customary usages. This is illustrated by the following example: Barley and wheat were measured by volume in the days of the Prophet in accordance with the tradition of the Prophet which says: "Wheat by wheat and barley by barley, and measure of capacity for a measure of capacity."[66]
2. That part of the *Sunnah* based upon the tacit approval of the Prophet comprises many of the Arab customs. The Arab dress code, especially regarding the amount and type of facial hair required of a proper witness, is one example.
3. In the opinion of Imam Mālik the customary conduct of the citizens of Madina was regarded as a sufficient source of law in the absence of an explicit text. The conduct of the citizens of Madina was in most cases based upon customs and usages, old and contemporary, which had predominated in that commercial city.
4. When customs came into being through necessity, or when the Muslims in their conquests came into contact with customs hitherto unknown to them which were not in conflict with any *Sharī'ah* Texts, such customs made inroads into the *Sharī'ah* by means of the consensus of jurists or other sources of law such as preference (*istiḥsān*) or public interest.

Customs, whether general and of universal acceptance or belonging to a particular country, or a particular generation, or a particular profession, have legal effect. One of the general maxims is

---

[66] Ibn Ḥanbal, Musnad, II, 232; Abū Dāwūd, Sunan, *Kitāb al-Buyu'*, 12.

that custom is authoritative, or that it ranks as a stipulation. To be legally binding, a custom must satisfy a number of conditions:

1. It must be reasonable, and be compatible with good sense and public sentiment.
2. It must be of frequent and common recurrence. For example, if in a contract of sale, the price was not quoted in a particular currency, it would be taken to mean the currency normally in use in the territory in question, or for the commodity in question. Crude oil today, for example, is internationally quoted in US dollars; one may not negotiate a contract and then argue after its consummation that one took it to mean Hong Kong dollars and insist on paying in that currency.

It is valid only if it is not in conflict with a *Sharī'ah* text, because a text overrides custom except where the text itself is based upon a general custom. Thus if part of the definition of a good and proper male witness at the time of the Prophet was that he have a beard (a condition *based* upon the general custom during the Prophet's time), we may override this condition in societies (or in times) where having a beard is not part of the social custom.

Customs which are regarded as a subsidiary source of law are those which are in conformance to the established legal sources. Those in conflict, or in opposition, to the spirit of the *Sharī'ah* are unequivocally rejected by the *Sharī'ah*. Examples of illegal customs are the pre-Islamic practice of female genital mutilation, the Bedouin practice of disinheriting female heirs, and the indiscriminate use of declarations of divorce. Although these practices may still exist in certain parts of the Muslim world, they are not at all sanctioned by the *Sharī'ah*.

## I. Direct Positive Legislation

When social life necessitates modification of certain laws and conciliation between theory and practice, there are three methods by which this modification and conciliation have taken place:

1. Judicial preference.
2. Direct positive state legislation.
3. Legal fiction.

We have discussed under the heading of preference (*istihsān*) the argument for judicial preference, supposedly and usually exercised in the public interest. State legislation is also based on the principle that it is—and ought to be—exercised in the public interest. The history of Islamic states proves that the caliphs or sultans did not hesitate to enact laws either directly or by way of interpretation whenever public interest called for such action. The legality of such action and its linkage with the *Sharī'ah* as a source of law endorsed by the Divine will is based upon the Qur'ān, the Prophet's practice and consensus of opinion. The Qur'ān reads: "O you who have believed! Obey Allāh and obey the Prophet and those of you who are in authority" (4:59). Among "those in authority" are obviously those who wield political authority and power.

The bulk of the legislation, when there was no provision in the texts, was in connection with new problems arising from social needs and development, and particularly in issues of administration of markets and public morals (known as *hisbah*), the imposition of taxes, the organization of prisons, and the organization of government departments. The caliphs did not hesitate to change the interpretation of rules embodied in the texts if the needs of *Sharī'ah* policy or the public interest required that such changes be effected. Examples of such changes have already been mentioned in the precedents of the Caliph `Umar, such as the suspension of the punishment meted out to thieves in a year of famine, and the suspension of the payment of part of the alms to "those whose hearts are to be induced."

The caliph was in a position to exercise influence upon the *Sharī'ah* by decreeing adherence to one specific school or interpretation. The`Abbāṣid Caliphs al-Mansūr and ar-Rashīd strove to make all their subjects conform to the school of Imam Mālik but were foiled in their plans by Imam Mālik's opposition. The Fatimids sided with the Isma`ili school, the Ayyubids with the Shāfi`i school, the Iranians with the Imamiyah Shi`ah school (see footnote 53), the Yemenis with the Zaydiyyah Shi`ah school, the Wahhābis with the Hanbali school and the Ottomans with the Ḥanafi school. (Intellectually speaking, and for political purposes, you can see how the "state" joined forces with and tried to get the "church" on its side. It is not only in the United States that political candidates try to get the Christian and what is known as the Moral Majority on their side so they can win the public's heart and the elections. Yet the Caliph very rarely took decisions on his own without consultation. He was careful to abide by the rules of the *Sharī'ah* and justice, consulting with jurists and men of learning in matters not covered by the Texts.)

Respect for and adherence to the rules of the *Sharī'ah* and justice by those in authority are essential prerequisites for the claim to obedience from their subjects, according to Islamic law. There are many *aḥādīth* in support of this. Examples are: "Obedience is due only in righteous deeds"; "Obedience is a duty unless the thing commanded violates a command by God, in which case there is to be no obedience."[67]

The Qur'ān also endorses such legislation and also the method of such legislation as the result of consultation (*shura*) in the following verses: "And consult with them upon the conduct of affairs. And when you are resolved then put your trust in God" (3:159) and ". . . and those whose affairs are a matter of counsel, . . . that is great resolve" (42:38–43). The Prophet accorded with

[67] Muslim, *Saḥīḥ*, VI, 15.

these verses, and used to consult his companions in certain matters, and they often did likewise, consulting with people of learning concerning matters not explicitly provided for in the Qur'ān and Ḥadīth. It is also reported that the Caliph `Umar was among the foremost of those who followed the practice of consultation in arriving at his rulings and interpretations.

Although it is possible to argue that state legislation and customs fall under the rational classification of judicial preference (*istiḥsān*) or public interest and equity (*maṣlaḥah*) and are thereby *logical* extension of these sources, they are considered as separate subsidiary sources of *Sharī'ah* because they *operationally* originate from the political power base in one case, and from the cultural traditions in the other. Moreover, their basis is supported by the texts (for issues not answered by the texts and with the proviso that such legislation should not be in conflict with the texts).

Among the observations we wish to draw the reader's attention to is that legislation by the state is not therefore considered to be *intrinsically* "anti-*Sharī'ah*," as some may believe. As a class of law, it is deemed to be a legitimate source of law.

## J. Creative Means and Legal Fictions (Ḥiyal)

The word *ḥilah* (singular of *ḥiyal*) designates "a means to accomplish an end, a stratagem, artifice, maneuver, expedient," and in law, a legal stratagem or fiction.

In general, legal fictions are of two types:

a. those that are permissible;
b. those whose permissibility has been in dispute.

The first category represents an attempt to utilize a legal device laid down for a specific purpose to attain another purpose aiming at upholding a right, preventing an injury or easing a situation because of necessity. Such legal fictions do not destroy any *Sharī'ah* precept and are therefore recognized and accepted by all schools. For example, the inhabitants of Bukhara had been accustomed to long-term leases of land. But as the Ḥanafi school did not approve long-lease contracts for orchards, recourse was made to a legal fiction whereby the orchard was sold and the vendor retained the right to redeem it. This form of sale, *bay` bil-wafā'*, was obviously a legal fiction to circumvent the Ḥanafi prohibition of long-lease contracts and to "allow" something already allowed by the Qur'ān and Ḥadīth.

The second category of legal fictions is intended to change well-established *shar`i* rules into other different rules through an action which is ostensibly correct but implicitly void. A controversy arose among the various schools concerning the legitimacy of this type of legal fiction. Some examples of these fictions which occurred in the various realms of jurisprudence follow.

1. It is not legitimate to obtain interest or compensation on a loan because of the prohibition of usury. The legal fiction resorted to in order to make payment of compensation or interest on the loan is for the borrower to sell to the lender the commodity at a price below its value, or to buy from the lender the commodity at a price higher than its actual value, or to present to the lender in the guise of a gift a sum equivalent to the interest on the loan.
2. It is an established principle of the *Sharī'ah* that no legacy *(waṣiyyah)* is to be bequeathed to an heir except with the consent of the other heirs, in accordance with the ḥadīth Text *la waṣiyyatu li-wārith.*[68] Accordingly, the Ḥanafi school did not approve of an admission by a person on his death-bed of indebtedness to one of his heirs except with the consent of the other heirs, because such an admission would be tantamount to a legacy. The legal fiction resorted to was that a person on a death-bed admits his indebtedness to a non-heir in whom

[68] This is because the heir already inherits according to a set formula, and a bequest to an heir is tantamount to getting more than the set share. Tirmidhi, Kitāb al-Waṣāyā, hadith no. 3581.

he trusts, so that the latter obtains the sum admitted from the estate and pays it to the heir in question.

The Imam Abu Hanifah is reported to have said, "It is prohibited to intend to suspend rules overtly but the suspension of such rules implicitly is not prohibited."[69] The Ḥanafi jurists, and a number of Shāfi`i jurists also, were quite liberal in accepting legal fictions of the second or controversial type. Imam ash-Shāfi`i didn't like it: he was reported to have objected to legal fictions. Anyone acquainted with his life and integrity is aware of his aversion to fictions. Most of the fictions which the later generations of Shāfi`i jurists incorporated in their works have actually been derived from the "Easterners" or Ḥanafi jurists.[70]

The Imams Mālik and Ibn Ḥanbal and their followers prohibited legal fictions of this type. Ibn al-Qayyim al-Jawziyyah wrote lengthy chapters in which he recounted the arguments against legal fictions and replied to those who had argued in favor of endorsing them. And yet, he too had to draw a distinction between permissible and impermissible legal fictions, giving many examples illustrating his views.[71] For example, the laws of pre-emption (*ash-shuf`ah*, i.e., the act or right of buying land in preference, or before, others) have been designed to safeguard against injury or harm.[72] The approval of fictions which seek to circumvent the laws of pre-emption is in effect a disregard of the intent

---

[69] Shāṭibi, *Muwafaqat*, II, 380.

[70] Ibn al-Qayyim, *I`lām*, III, 247.

[71] Ibn al-Qayyim, *I`lām*, III, 119–352 and all vol. IV, particularly 1–40.

[72] For example, in the Ḥanafi *madhhab*, if Ahmad owns farmland adjacent to farmland owned by Alī, and Ahmad wishes to sell his farm to a third person, Uthman, Alī is entitled to claim ownership by pre-emption provided he pays a price equal to that offered by Uthman (what we call in the US the right of first refusal). One legal fiction to defeat Alī's claim of pre-emption is for Ahmad to offer the farm as an outright gift to Uthman, who would then pay Ahmad a sum of money in consideration of his gift. Thus Alī would have no right of pre-emption because there is no claim of pre-emption concerning a gift.

of the *Sharī'ah* and an acquiescence to the injury that was to be averted."[73]

The prohibition of legal fictions by these jurists is based upon the fundamental *Sharī'ah* rule that legislation is founded upon clearly intended interests and that it is necessary to avoid including provisions of the law which defeat those interests. "If the law-maker were to lay down a ruling based upon an intended interest and then to approve a legal fiction that would negate the ruling, such action would amount to repeal and would constitute pure contradiction. Those who contend otherwise violate the spirit of the *Sharī'ah* and depart from its true meaning. Again, such an action cannot be tolerated by the law-maker nor by policy of the kings of this world. . . . No ruler would prohibit his army, his subjects or his household from doing certain things and then allow them the ways and means of evading his prohibitions. If he were to do so, his action would be contradictory, and his army and subjects would have acted contrary to his intentions. Similarly, when doctors treat an ailment they prohibit the patient from following the practices which led to contracting that ailment; otherwise, their efforts would have been in vain. And how much more should this be true of the perfect *Sharī'ah* which stands at the summit of wisdom, public interest and perfection?"[74]

There are a number of bases in *Sharī'ah* which point to the prohibition of such fictions:

1. The *Sharī'ah* texts are not aimed at the deeds themselves but rather at the interests which those deeds are intended to serve. Therefore all acts should be interpreted in the light of their spirit and intent and not merely by their appearances. This precludes all legal fictions that may be outwardly correct but in reality hide within themselves forbidden acts or motives.

---

[73] *Op. cit.*, 120 and 260.

[74] Ibid.

2. For example, when the Qur'ān says "Revile not those unto whom they pray beside Allāh lest they wrongfully revile Allāh through ignorance" (6:109), Muslims are thereby constrained from reviling the idols lest the worshippers of idols make this an excuse for reviling Allāh. According to a tradition, the Prophet once said, "One of the most heinous acts is for a person to curse his parents." Some asked, "O Messenger of God, how can a person curse his parents?" He replied: "He curses the father of another man and in retort the other person curses his own father and mother."[75]
3. Attempts at by-passing the law are tantamount to deceit, and deceit is prohibited by the *Sharī'ah* as evidenced by the Qur'ān and the Ḥadīth. The Qur'ān says: "Do not ridicule Allāh's verses" (2:231). A tradition of the Prophet says, "A Muslim is prohibited from engaging in deceit."[76] Another is, "Allāh looks not at your forms and bodies but at your hearts and deeds."[77]

The two maxims, "All matters are determined according to intention[78]" and "In contracts, effect is given to intention and meaning and not to words and forms," describe the dominant view that legal fictions, though approved by Ḥanafi jurists as well as by later generations of Shāfi`i jurists, were *disapproved* of by Muḥammad ibn al-Hasan ash-Shaybāni, the disciple of Imam Abu Hanifah, while the Imams ash-Shāfi`i, Mālik and Ibn Ḥanbal and their followers *prohibited* it altogether. Other than the Ḥanafi school, which came under the influence of foreign culture and strong political pressure from its rulers to seek ways to accommodate certain ends desired by them, the other schools prohibited le-

---

[75] `Ayni, *`Umdat*, XXII, 83.

[76] Ibn al-Qayyim, *I`lām*, III, 261.

[77] Muslim, *Saḥīḥ*, *Kitāb al-Birr*, 40, 41.

[78] This is the very first ḥadīth quoted in Bukhāri's collection.

gal fiction from the start before coming under any influence of any foreign culture.

## K. Sadd adh-Dharā'i` (Preventing the Means)

The Ḥanafi school, largely because of the formalism which was one of its distinctive characteristics, was able to endorse legal fictions, and all the major treatises supporting *hiyal* were the work of Ḥanafi lawyers. Although Imam Shāfi`i was strongly against legal fictions, some later Shāfi`i scholars recognized *hiyal*. The Maliki school, with its concern for the real intention behind overt acts, consistently repudiated them, while the Hanbalis, because of their extreme moralistic approach to law, were probably the most hostile opponents of *hiyal*. This led to a counter-doctrine to *hiyal* formulated by Maliki jurists, called *sadd adh- dharā'i'*, literally meaning "preventing the means," to prohibit a generally lawful means that will lead to an unlawful end.

Authority for this principle is Qur'ānically obtained from verse 6:109 quoted in the previous section on legal fiction, which reads:

> *wa la tasubbu-lladhīna yad`ūna min dūni-llāhi, fa-yasubbu-llāha `adwan bi-ghayri `ilm;*
>
> *Do not curse the gods of those who worship other than Allāh lest they curse Allāh without knowing;*

Authority can also be drawn from the ḥadīth of the Prophet prohibiting insulting a person's parents for it leads to one's own parents being insulted, the net result in this case being equal to your having insulted your own parents. Although your act may have been justified, it is prohibited because it will lead to an evil.

Another example is the following: deferred sales are generally permissible. If you agree to buy my house for $100,000, with payment to be made in one year, such a transaction is permissible.

However, because such a deferred sale transaction is a potential means to obtaining interest, and thus a usurious transaction, it waves a red flag.[79] Imam Mālik and Ahmad b. Ḥanbal therefore consider such a sale as one that ought to be obstructed, on the grounds that it opens the door to *ribā*, although they acknowledge that *ribā* may not actually materialize. Abu Hanifah and Shāfi`i maintain that in the absence of positive knowledge (*`ilm*) or a strong suspicion (*ẓann*) that a deferred sale will lead to *ribā*, deferred sales are allowable.

This doctrine of "obstructing the means," however, developed into a source of law. The objective of *sadd adh-dharā'i'* is preventing an evil before it arises by preventing its highly probable cause, although the cause may not *necessarily* result in the evil outcome. Variations of this source of law are the encouragement of an undesirable means that leads to a desirable end, or the allowance of a lesser evil so as to prevent a greater one.[80] However, it is more usually applied to preventing a means that leads to an undesirable end, than in allowing a negative means that leads to a more desirable outcome.

Legal scholars have divided the *dharā'i'* into four categories depending on the degree of probability that the means will lead to the undesirable end. Classical examples of each are:

1. A means that will *definitely* lead to an evil. For example, digging a well on your property but so close to the neighbor's wall that the wall collapses as a result. Your right to dig a well on your property is perfectly lawful, but because it leads to a bad result it is forbidden.

[79] The means by which this is accomplished is as follows: let's say you buy my house for $100,000 right now, and hand over to me the $100,000 purchase price today. I simultaneously contract to buy back the house from you for $110,000, with the price payable to you in one year. Both transactions are independently legal, but since this is a common *means* to effectuate a loan resulting in interest of $10,000, this *means* (called *dhari`ah*) is prohibited under Maliki law.

[80] For example, lying to effectuate reconciliation among estranged family members.

2. A means that will *most likely* lead to an evil. For example, selling weapons is allowed. But selling weapons to people having an argument; although not forbidden, can result in unnecessary killing of innocents.
2. A means that might lead to evil. For example, prohibiting privacy between members of the opposite sex because it may lead to unlawful intimacy.
3. A means that rarely leads to an evil. An example is prohibiting growing grapes on one's property because it may lead one to ferment wine.

The thrust of this principle is clearly intended to maintain a sense of morality within the law. Just as we would recuse ourselves from a situation where there is a potential conflict of interest, *sadd adh-dharā'i'* is the Islamic legal principle which "generalizes" the concept of recusing, so that the Muslim is taught to refrain from a permissible action that can open a can of worms.

The Ḥanafi and Shāfi`i jurists do not recognize *sadd adh-dharā'i'* as a jurisprudential principle on the grounds that the necessary rulings on the means can be derived from other principles such as *qiyās*, *istihsān* and *`urf*. But the Maliki and Hanbali jurists regard it as a separate source.

# CHAPTER VI

## MAXIMS AND PRINCIPLES

The jurists have defined a maxim as a general rule constructed upon primary and eternal principles of pure justice and genuine goodness. Although a number of these maxims admit of exceptions and limitations, these exceptions and limitations do not undermine the general character of the rules.

The advantage to be gained from the maxims is to facilitate the understanding of problems and principles. We shall describe two maxims that are especially useful.

### A. The Rule Of Necessity And Need

Al-Ghazali said, "Everything that exceeds its limit changes into its opposite."[81] Excessive cold burns as badly as excessive heat. Thus it becomes necessary to lighten the people's burden and to disregard general rules in certain exceptional circumstances if their application were to result in injury and hardship.

The Ḥanafi jurists expressed this principle in their plea for judicial preference *(istihsān)*, while the Malikis adopted the plea of public interest *(maṣlaḥa)*. There were jurists who opposed recourse to public interest, but the majority of them accepted it, basing their acceptance upon the Qur'ān, the *sunnah* and the precedents of the Caliph `Umar ibn al-Khaṭṭāb, of which we mentioned a few in the section above on *istihsān*. Others are:

The Qur'ān says:

---

[81] *Māẓāda `an ḥaddihī inqalaba ilā-ḍiddihi.*

*And strive for Allāh as is His due; He has chosen you and has not laid upon you in religion any hardship—the faith of your father Abraham. (22:78).*

Verses 16:114 through 117 permit and forbid as follows:

*So eat of what Allāh has given you, lawful and good, . . . . He has forbidden you only what dies of itself and blood and the flesh of swine and that over which any other name than that of Allāh has been invoked;*

Yet, in spite of the prohibition, God adds as the verse continues:

*but whoever is driven thereto neither craving (i.e., not doing it out of enjoyment) nor transgressing, then surely Allāh is Forgiving, Merciful. And utter not, for what your tongues describe, the lie: that this is lawful and that that is unlawful, forging lies against Allāh. Surely those who forge lies against Allāh will not prosper—a little enjoyment, then for them is a painful chastisement.*

Allāh understands that if you were about to die from starvation and had nothing else to eat, it's okay to eat pork under these extenuating circumstances. However, you should do this only to fulfil the extent of your need, and should not eat pork because you enjoy it, claiming you need the nutritional value of amino acids while avoiding permissible sources like beef or lamb. But don't claim that what you're doing is all right. It's still not all right; it's acceptable only because you went through extenuating circumstances which drove you to do it. Once your circumstances go back to normal, and you can find rice and lamb and beef and vegetables, then eating pork goes back to being forbidden. That's what God is saying in the above verse, as the jurists like to explain with more complex terminology.

The above verses justify the maxim of necessity and need as a means of justifying a rule, and point out the significant difference between suspending a text based on necessity and need, as the Caliph `Umar did when he suspended the penalty for theft in a time of famine, and using legal fiction to justify the same rule, for then we subject ourselves to the criticism of the above verse for uttering a lie, saying that "one thing is lawful and the other not."[82]

Taking cognizance of these illustrations, the jurists established the maxim that "hardship begets facility" (*al-ḍarūrah tabīḥ al-maḥẓūrāt*). Facility means legal mitigation on account of hardship as an exception to the general rule. Hardships refer to necessity and need and not to a nonessential interest (a luxury). A situation of **necessity** refers to a person's striving to **safeguard** his **religion, life, property, mind** or **offspring** from perdition. A **need** refers to what is essential for the attainment of a good life. **Nonessentials** refer to such things as decoration or amelioration.

So if you stole a loaf of bread because you were about to die from starvation, that may be permissible, a justifiable sin because you are trying to save your life which is a situation of necessity; but if you stole some Levolor blinds because your cloth curtains are dirty and you wanted to replace them with the new blinds, that's not permissible and definitely a sin; blinds are a nonessential.

Many legal rules, such as those covering loans, transfer of debts, and incapacity, are derived from this principle; thus the leniency and indulgence shown by jurists in their rulings are all based upon this rule.

Al-Ghazali said, "All prohibited things become permissible by necessity."[83] The examples which jurists use to illustrate the application of this principle are numerous. They include legal excuses which exempt one from legal duties, such as still being a minor, (you're not obliged to pray if you're only five years old); lunacy; illness (you're exempt from fasting if you're sick); duress (you're excused if somebody put a gun to your head and said I'll blow your

---

[82] Another example is the issue of *ribā*, interest or usury. Some have argued that if one engages in it out of necessity, for example to buy a house, and to the extent of one's need, and pay off the loan once we can do so, then the circumstance of this verse may be applied. This does not mean that interest is permitted (*ḥalāl*), but just that the extenuating circumstances push us into doing it, and we do it only to the extent of our need. Such a position is better than forging a lie against God and saying that usury is *ḥalāl*.

[83] Abu Hamid Muḥammad al-Ghazali, *al-Wajiz* (Cairo, 1317 AH), vol. II, 216.

brains out unless you say that there is no god but Marilyn Monroe and you do say that); forgetfulness (your fast is still valid if you forgot that you were fasting and you accidentally drank some water). A final example we'll give is ignorance; it's acceptable if you *really* didn't know that you have to pay *zakāh* on your wife's jewelry. Muslim jurists have given particular attention to the various excuses in their treatises on the sources of law.

Other examples of permission for necessity are: eating the meat of a dead animal by a starving person,[84]and consumption of medication containing alcohol by the sick.[85]

Another example is leniency with a debtor who is in financial straits; the Qur'ān instructs as follows: "And if the debtor is in straitened circumstances then let there be postponement until (he is in) ease." (2: 280)

***Limitations to the rule:*** Although necessities render prohibited things permissible, this rule is not absolute but is subject to many limitations. Permissibility is limited by the extent of the necessity and by the time of the necessity. For example, if you drank Nyquil cold medication to help you get rid of your cold, the necessity to protect your health makes permissible the act of consuming medication containing alcohol.

However, necessity is estimated by the time and extent of the need. It is better to say "that which became permissible by necessity is estimated by the extent of the need,"[86] because what is estimated is not the necessity itself (the protection of your health in the above example) but what became permissible (the consumption of a few teaspoons of alcohol-containing medicine) on ac-

---

[84] This makes us think about the infamous plane crash in South America, where the survivors cannibalized the carcasses of those who died in the crash in order to survive. Strange circumstances make people do strange things. This is the thrust of the rule of necessity and need.

[85] Ibn Rushd, Abu al-Walid Muḥammad ibn Ahmad, *Bidayat al-Mujtahid wa Nihayat al-Muqtasid* (Cairo, n.d.), vol. I, 381.

[86] *Ibid.*, 34.

count of the necessity. Thus any license that may be deemed necessary should not be absolute but should be to the extent required for meeting the hardship. For example, if the theft of a loaf of bread be tolerated because of hunger, the theft of one ton of flour would not be so under any circumstance.

The limitation by time applies because the license by necessity, or the exceptional rule based on it, remains valid only as long as the excuse or the cause of the urgency exists. If this exceptional circumstance ceases, the license also ceases and there would be a return to the original principle. Thus in the above example, if the theft of food is tolerated during a time of famine, it is not if there is no famine. Or if consumption of alcohol-based medication is acceptable while ill, it is not after the illness is over and you are recovered.

***The question of compensation:*** If necessity renders the prohibited permissible, does this justify the trespassing upon another person's rights?

There have been differences of opinion among the different schools, but the best maxim to apply is that of Ibn Rajab which says: "A person who destroys a thing to ward off an impending injury from it is not liable to compensation. If he destroys it while using it to ward off an injury from elsewhere, then he is obligated to make good the loss."[87] So if you destroy a shipment of bread from the baker because the bread contained some poisonous bacteria that would make you sick with Legionnaire's disease, you owe the baker no compensation. (If anything, you did him the favor.) But if you used a shipment of bread to protect yourself from some crazy guy shooting at you, and all the bread got destroyed in the process, then you really owe the baker out of gratitude that his

---

[87] Ibn Rajab, Abu al-Faraj `Abd ar-Raḥmān, *Al-Qawa`id fi al-Fiqh al-Islami* (Cairo, 1933), No. 26, p.36. See also Subhi Mahmasani, *Al-Nazariyyah al-`Ammah li-al-Mujibat wa al-`Uqud fi ash-Shari'ah al-Islamiyyah* (Beirut, 1948), vol. I, 178–79. For example, if a man is attacked by a mad camel, and he kills it in self-defense, he may not be obliged to compensate its owner for his loss. But if he uses the camel to protect himself from some danger, and the camel dies in protecting the man from this danger, then he may be obliged to compensate its owner for its loss.

bread saved your life. This rule is downright sensible, and you can observe the application of sensibility.

Should allowance be given to necessity when it conflicts with some other interest? The answer is that the lesser of two evils is preferred. Of a similar meaning is a tradition ascribed to `A'ishah, "Whenever the Messenger of Allāh was asked to choose between two things he chose the easier." He also said, "Make things easy, do not make things difficult. Give good tidings, and do not frighten people away by inspiring pessimism."[88] Many corollaries stem from this maxim, such as tolerating a private injury to ward off a public injury (e.g., pulling down a house to prevent a fire from spreading), warding off evil instead of securing a benefit, and preference for the lesser injury. (Some of these may also be obtained by applying the Maliki principle of *sadd adh-dharā'i'*.)

## B. Intention in Actions

Matters are determined in accordance with intention, stemming from the will of the human being. The first ḥadīth in Bukhāri's *Saḥīḥ* reads: "Deeds are judged by intentions and every person shall have only what he intended. Thus he whose *hijrah* (migration) was for Allāh and His Messenger, his *hijrah* was for Allāh and His Messenger, and he whose *hijrah* was to achieve some worldly benefit or to take some woman in marriage, his *hijrah* was for that for which he made *hijrah*." Imam ash-Shāfi`i said, "This ḥadīth is a third of all knowledge."

Other *aḥādīth* of the Prophet inform us that intentions to do good are registered as pious deeds, while intentions to commit evil are registered as a good deed if the person changes his mind and

[88] Ahmad ibn Ḥanbal, *al-Musnad*, vol. VI, pp. 125, 420 and 423. A prime example of the Prophet's making things easier was his combining the performance of the *ḥajj* and the *`umrah* rituals together simultaneously with one intention (*niyyah*) during his Farewell pilgrimage (this method of doing the *ḥajj* and *`umrah* together is called *qiran*). This was revolutionary, and even the future Caliph `Umar initially had difficulty accepting this decision of the Prophet.

does not commit the evil, and are only registered as an evil deed when actually committed.

So if you find anything on the road with the intention of restoring it to its owner, your conduct is in order; but if you intend to keep the thing as your own, you are considered, in polite circles, to be a person who "wrongfully appropriated property." The physical act is identical in both cases, but the judgment of it differs according to the intention. Another example is that of a man who came to the Prophet and asked, "What of a man who joined us in *jihād* (fighting), his intention being for fame and booty?" The Prophet answered, "He receives nothing." The man asked the question three times and each time the Prophet said, "He receives nothing." Then he said, "Allāh only accepts actions that are intended for His pleasure."[89]

The types of issues where the jurists had to focus on gauging intentions are situations in which you have to decide guilt and liability in a court. If you lost control of your car while negotiating a corner on a rainy day, and it spun, skidded and hit a pedestrian and killed him, it is clear that you did not intend to kill him. Your guilt, and therefore your liability, is not the same as intent to kill; and even here there is a difference between killing someone in self-defense because he physically threatened you, and premeditated malicious murder of your husband to collect on his life insurance policy. The degree and nature of the intent differs. And that is why in Western law we differentiate between murder in the first degree and murder in the second degree, which is another way of saying that intention counts a lot in determining the value of your action. These examples demonstrate why it was necessary for jurists to explore the means of determining intent.

The importance of intention in determining the valuation of an act is such a major issue that further refinement in the determination of intent has been considered in detail by the jurists, such as the difference between outward expression and intention, real and

[89] *Saḥīḥ*, an-Nisa'i, *Kitāb al-Jihād*, 6 and 25.

metaphorical meanings as affecting intention, and gauging speech, such as explicit and implicit meanings in speech, its contexts, etc. People understand these points in real life very well; your son cannot take you to court because you tell him you'll "break his neck" if he didn't clean his room, because everyone knows that you don't really mean to break his neck. Neither do they suspect you of anything but kind and altruistic motives when they hear you say "sweetheart" to your 70-year-old secretary—but say it to your 20-year-old gorgeous secretary, and they are not as likely to perceive your motives as being so innocent. So watch your intentions! God is not the only being who sees them.

We are encouraged to imbue our actions with good intentions, and in our spiritual growth we are taught to take extremely careful measure of our intentions in the performance of our actions. And as you spiritually mature and advance, you learn to see, witness and act with the eye of intention, and become blessed in being given a powerful tool to measure the quality of your own actions. Even if others' intentions are bothersome, it often helps you in seeing through your own intentions more clearly. And although we can often witness others' intentions, we are advised to give them a positive spin.[90] Such situations are not what we are responsible for judging anyhow; you are never advised to go around to the mosques telling people their prayer wasn't valid because you could clearly see they weren't really concentrating on their prayers.

---

90 An experienced teacher can often tell if a student is asking a question because he really wants to know the answer, or because he wants to test the teacher to see if he knows the answer, or he wants to show off to the rest of the class how smart and probing he is. It is also apparent if more than one motive exists. The point here is that motives are quite visible and apparent. This does not mean that our "motive eye" always sees clearly, as my friend Yūsuf likes to point out. When it comes to interaction with members of the opposite sex, many find it downright impossible to gauge the other's intentions, usually because the situation is highly charged with emotion and differing implications. Very few of us detect others' intentions with 20/20 vision, some of us are totally blind to others' intentions, while the majority of us fall somewhere in between.

## C. Additional Maxims: Number Of Witnesses Required For Adequate Testimony

There are additional maxims, such as those that deal with the principles of proof and evaluation of evidence, the principles of admission and confession, of testimony and oaths. Another group of maxims pertains to obligations and contracts. Although they make interesting reading, they are of concern to you only if you wish to study Islamic law in greater detail.

But we ought to touch upon an area which arouses some passion today, namely the issue of testimony. Many Muslims simplistically think that in all cases two male witnessses, or one male and two female, are "always required." Many women are justifiably annoyed by the chauvinistic assertion that a woman's testimony is "Islamically intrinsically half of a man's," an understanding that needs to be corrected.

First, it is helpful to point out that in ancient times, the testimony of women was not accepted at all. Such was the case in Jewish law and in pre-Islamic Arabian law. Until the beginning of the 19th century, the legal codes of some of the Swiss cantons regarded the testimony of two women as equivalent to the testimony of one man. And before it was amended in the latter part of the 19th century, the Code of Napoleon excluded the testimony of women in testamentary dispositions and in a number of transactions pertaining to personal status. This historical sketch gives us a clue into the spirit of the *Sharī'ah*, which was revolutionary in that it advanced women's rights in the seventh century far beyond that in other societies. Specifically, Islām granted women the right of possession of material property, the right of inheritance, and the right to give evidence, in a society that had deprived women of any of these rights, and this in a society in which the Arab woman was customarily secluded from the men. If we extend this *spirit* of the *Sharī'ah*, it is not unreasonable to accept the testimony of a woman as being intrinsically equal to that of a man, especially in today's world, where the differentiation between the sexes has become significantly less, and where women are professionally the equal of men. The following reasons, based on a deeper understanding of the *Shar`i* rules of testimony, can be adduced to provide the basis to evolve this rule further:

In Islamic jurisprudence, the number of witnesses differs according to the different schools and types of cases. It also depends on the trustworthiness of the witnesses and not merely upon their number. A witness may be disqualified due to forgetfulness, suppression of evidence or wilful distortion of the facts resulting from partiality, incitement or bribery. He or she may also be disqualified if there is enmity between the witness and the party against whom the testimony is to be given. Neither is it accepted where prospective benefit or avoiding of loss may be involved, such as in situations where there is a blood relationship, or a relationship of employment, partnership, and the like. For example, the testimony of a father in favor of his son, or a spouse in favor of the other, is not admissible, although it may be utilized if the testimony of the one is *against* the other. The integrity, experience and level of expertise of the witness, male or female, is always a factor in assessing the witness's trustworthiness. In general, the testimony of two just men is the minimum required according to all jurists in all penal matters with an unalterable fixed punishment(*ḥudūd*) except for adultery, which requires four. Testimony in cases involving property such as sale, loan, wrongful appropriation, debts, can be as little as one man plus the oath of the plaintiff; this is accepted in all schools except the Ḥanafi and the followers of Imam al-Awza`i. This is based on a ḥadīth where the Prophet gave judgment on the basis of testimony of one witness endorsed by the oath of the plaintiff in support of his claim.[91]

The Ḥanafi school amongst others accepts the testimony of one man in some exceptional cases. For example, the testimony of the teacher alone is sufficient in cases of juvenile delinquency. The testimony of one expert is permissible for the assessment of dam-

[91] Reported by Muslim in *Saḥīḥ*, V, 128.

age to property, and for purposes of informing about the defects in the object of a sale, and other similar matters.

There were also Muslim jurists who were satisfied with the testimony of only one truthful witness. One of them was Ibn al-Qayyim al-Jawziyyah who said,

> *Everything which brings out the truth constitutes evidence. Neither God nor His Prophet disregarded a right after it had been established by any means. That which was prescribed by God and His Prophet is that once truth has come out by whatever method, it should be implemented and endorsed and may not be annulled or suspended.*[92]

Following up on this argument he adds,

> *A judge may give judgment in cases other than those involving the rights of God on the testimony of one man whose integrity is established. God did not make it a duty for judges not to give judgment save on the testimony of two witnesses, but merely ordered the owner of a right to safeguard his rights by two male witnesses or one man and two women. This does not mean that a judge may not give judgment on any lesser testimony. In fact the Prophet gave judgment on the basis of one witness and an oath and even on the basis of one testimony only.*[93]

Thus we note that the methods by which a judge gives judgment are of greater latitude than those through which God has guided the owner of a right to safeguard it.

Ibn al-Qayyim bases his contention on the fact that the Qur'ān does not mention the testimony of two male witnesses or one male and two female witnesses as the procedure by which a judge arrives at a judgment, but it mentions this procedure in connection with a person's endeavor to safeguard his right. He also bases his contention on a ḥadīth in which the Prophet approved

---

[92] Ibn Qayyim, I'lam al-Mawaqqi'īn'an Rabb al-'Alamīn (Cairo, n.d.) vol. 1, 192-193

[93] Ibn Qayyim, Al-Turuq al-Humiyyah fi's-Siyāsah ash-Shar'iyyah (Cairo, 1317 AH), pp 96-97.

the sole testimony of a Bedouin regarding his sighting of the crescent moon which signalled the beginning of the fast of Ramadan. He was also reported to have accepted the sole testimony in a case of robbery, and to have accepted the sole testimony of a woman in a case where only women are able to have knowledge of the necessary information. He was also reported to have considered the testimony of Khuzaymah, a man of unassailable integrity, as equivalent to two witnesses, saying, "It is sufficient unto a person to have Khuzaymah as a witness."[94] Ibn al-Qayyim interprets this ḥadīth as being based on a cause, namely the integrity and truthfulness of Khuzaymah. Therefore, a judge may, by analogy, accept the testimony of a single witness if his truthfulness is established. This ḥadīth does not conflict with the Qur'ān, and like other parts of the *sunnah*, serves to "interpret it, explain it, and qualify its absolutes."

A number of famous Muslim judges such as Shurayḥ and Zurārah b. Abī Awfā accepted this interpretation and gave effect to it in their rulings.

We have furnished this bit of detail to demonstrate that the Islamic rules regarding testimony are quite refined, and not in the least simplistic. There are formulas involved in the determination of the validity of the witness, and if these rules are applied, the witness' gender will be found to bear less weight in evaluating the witness's reliability than other factors. And given the Prophet's revolutionary act of advancing women's rights far beyond what existed in the Middle East and in Europe at that time, we may rightfully ask the question, if the Prophet were alive today, would he not advance them further?

---

[94] Sunan, Abū Dāwūd, Kitāb al-Aqdiyah, 20.

# CHAPTER VII

## CAN THE *SHARĪ'AH* EVOLVE?

In the late '60s I attended ecumenical and interfaith meetings with representatives of other religions, usually Judaism and Christianity, and they were curious as to how Islām dealt with the modern age. Modernity was deemed a real challenge to religiosity and spirituality. Vatican II had just been released, allowing Catholics no longer to restrict their diet to fish on Fridays, and to conduct mass in the vernacular rather than in Latin. These and some other changes were adopted to make Catholicism "keep up with the times." Since I needed God and God did not quite need me, I felt that *I was the one who had to adapt* to God's eternal dictates and not the other way around. But I do confess that some things puzzled me then, like having to keep a beard if I was going to be serious about my faith, especially since I lived in the West and at that time beards were politically loaded and not a mere fashion statement. My friend Amin Walker worked as a loan officer during those times, and had a hard time understanding why interest was *ḥarām* when it was eminently *sensible* and everybody was benefiting from it. It wasn't until I studied *uṣūl al-fiqh* that I was able to think about problems like these satisfactorily. Before this I just wasn't equipped to grapple with these issues.

In verse 42:13, the Qur'ān states that the *Sharī'ah* that God revealed to the Prophet Muḥammad contained the same commendations which were the substance of His *Sharī'ah* to the Prophets Noah, Abraham, Moses and Jesus, even though the details of worship may have differed. From a Qur'ānic point of view, the differences between the *Sharī'ahs* that were revealed through the different Prophets would be analogous to the different *madhāhib* within the Islamic faith. As we examine the common denominator of all the messages conveyed through the Prophets, we see that we are to recognize God as our Creator, that He is One, and that our purpose in life is to worship Him. This involves centering our lives on our relationship with God, and living a life that continually brings us closer to God. This is the primary objective or intent (*qasd*), which we may even label as the *spirit* of the *Sharī'ah*. All that brings us closer to God is good, and whatever distances us from God is bad.

As you look at the eleven sources of law that we listed, you will notice that the Qur'ān and the Ḥadīth are the primary and determining sources. All the rest are subsidiary and mutable because they are totally human endeavors without any direct Divine revelation, and are intended to maintain the spirit and/or the letter of the Qur'ān and Ḥadīth. When you read the Qur'ān and compare it with the contents of the Ḥadīth, you will realize that "essential Islām" is the religion of God. Thus the ritual prayer, for example, defined by the term *ṣalāh*, is a command that God gave to prior Prophets. But the format obviously was different. Every Prophet before Muḥammad was commanded to perform *ṣalāh*. So while the inner content was identical, the outer manifestation of Moses' *ṣalāh* was obviously different than Abraham's. We can regard this "differentiation" as an "evolution" of a kind. What evolved was not the eternally mandated practice of ritual prayer in its inner sense and dimension, but the outer manifestation (language, movements, etc.) to suit the language and the reality of the time. That is perhaps why the specific formula, and even the number, of the daily ritual Islamic prayer is not described in detail in the Qur'ān but in the Ḥadīth. This gives us a picture of the "relative degree of immutability" of each source of law.

As you go down the sources and examine the totality of Islamic laws and trace them back to any of the eleven sources from which they originated, it is sensible to consider those that originated from custom "more subject to evolution" than those that originated from the Qur'ān. An instruction of the Prophet based upon custom would be, therefore, more subject to evolution than an instruction based upon a Qur'ānic command. This was the opinion of the great Ḥanafi jurist Abu Yūsuf. And because the central source of Islamic law, the Qur'ān, is Divine, we've got to be meticulously careful in dealing with the problem of "changing its rules" to suit varying times, places and needs.

## A. The Principle Of The Evolution Of Laws

What was the attitude of the Muslim jurists towards the principle of the evolution of laws?

Ibn al-Qayyim al-Jawziyyah said "legal interpretation should change with the change in times, places, conditions, intentions and customs." He added: "Ignorance of this fact has resulted in grievous injustice to the *Sharī'ah*, and has caused many difficulties, hardships, and sheer impossibilities, although it is known that the noble *Sharī'ah*, which serves the highest interests of mankind, would not sanction such results."[95]

The point here is not that the law changes, but that we are required to investigate the interests upon which *Shar`i* rules are based. Because *interests* are the cause and the basis of rules, another principle necessarily follows: If the causes change or disappear, rules based upon them must change or cease to be in effect. Thus one of the **maxims** of the science of sources says, "A *Shar`i* rule based upon a cause survives or ceases with it." Thus, a *Shar`i* rule is based upon its cause; when the cause ceases the rule ceases.

No one can deny the effect of this principle of evolution upon the vacillation of opinions and the rise of the various schools of law. Imam ash-Shāfi`i changed some of the opinions he maintained in Iraq when he moved to Egypt because of the difference of social circumstances. Similarly, taxes on land decreased in the days of Abu Yūsuf from what they had been in the days of the Caliph `Umar because of a change in locale and conditions. Examples of changing *fatwa*s and rules with regard to positive legal matters are beyond enumeration.

---

[95] Ibn al-Qayyim, *I`lam*, vol. III, 1.

The majority of jurists have accepted the principle of change in legal rules. They differed, however, as to the legality of such change if the rule is based upon a text in the Qur'ān or the Ḥadīth. The difficulty stems from the particular character of the *Sharī'ah* and its Divine origin.

Repeal or supersession has in fact occurred in the Qur'ān and the *sunnah*. There is no doubt also that repeal is legal as evidenced by its occurrence and because it is the modification of a text by a later text. But is it legal to modify a text by something other than a text, for example, by interpretation, man-made legislation, custom or some other way?

The answer to this question falls into two parts. If the text is related to matters of religious observance and worship, then it is firmly fixed and unchangeable. This is because the fundamentals of religion, the principles of belief in the unity of God, and faith are eternal and immemorial truths which demand submission and adherence to the text. They are timeless and based on time-independent human conditions and circumstance. Further, religion

> *is essential to every living being and to everyone who may be born until the Day of Judgment, anywhere on earth. Thus the change in time, place or condition is of no matter. What has been established is established for eternity in every time, place and condition.*[96]

Because religion deals with your spiritual reality, and your relationship with your Lord is timeless, that part of your existence doesn't change with time.

If, however, a text relates to matters of worldly transactions, the rule therein would be to consider the meaning and to understand the causes upon which such text is based (as explained above in the section on the aims and wisdom of the *Sharī'ah*). This is the view of the majority of jurists. They differed, however, concerning the changing of rules embodied in the texts. Some forbade such change while others accepted it in certain circumstances.

---

[96] Ibn Hazm, `Alī, *Al-Ihkam li-Uṣūl al-Aḥkām* (Cairo, 1345–48 AH), vol. V, 5.

The dominant view of jurists would not accept any violation of a Qur'ānic or *Sunnah* text, and would not justify any change therein on account of a change in circumstances. This view, in fact, prohibited *fatwa*s contrary to the texts and restricted the admissibility of customs, and the concession to hardships, only to matters not provided for in the texts. Imams Abu Hanifah, ash-Shāfi`i , az-Zahiri and others adhered to this view.

In spite of this dominant view there have been some caliphs, Imams and jurists who endorsed the possibility of change in the *explanation* or the *interpretation* of texts, because of a change in their causes or in the customs upon which they are based, or in answer to necessity and public interest.

The first and most prominent examples of foregoing the texts due to circumstances were the decisions of the Caliph `Umar. We have cited above in the section on *istihsān* how the Caliph `Umar made decisions that differed from Qur'ānic and *Sunnah* injunctions. Specifically, we quoted his decisions on spending of alms for "those whose hearts are to be induced," the sale of slave mothers, the suspending of the punishment for theft during a year of famine, and the decision to suspend future exile for fornicators. These examples do not exhaust his list of precedents that give different readings from Qur'ānic and *Sunnah* texts. His aim was always the public interest and what was evidently *sensible.* We also note here that all these decisions are within the domain of worldly interests, and not in the area of fundamental religious beliefs and acts of worship. Would you consider his actions as "violating" the *Sharī'ah*, "evolving" the *Sharī'ah*, or consistent with its aims?

One question that was raised by the jurists was, if a *Sharī'ah* text is based upon customs and usages, and if these customs change, is it permissible to disregard that text? Phrased differently, should a new custom be followed when the text is based upon an old custom?

This is illustrated by the following example. Barley and wheat were measured by volume in the days of the Prophet in accordance with the tradition of the Prophet which says: "Wheat by wheat and barley by barley, and *measure of capacity for a measure of ca-*

*pacity*."[97] This was the custom in the earlier days; but the custom changed in later days, and sale by *weight* rather than by volume became the accepted norm in most countries for wheat and barley.

The majority of jurists, including the Imam Abu Hanifah and his disciple Muḥammad Ibn al-Hasan ash-Shaybāni, held that the text rather than the custom should be followed. The Imam Abu Yūsuf, Chief Justice of Baghdad, however, disagreed with their finding and ruled, basing his opinion on the principle of judicial preference (*istihsān*), that the text should be re-interpreted in favor of the new custom in such circumstances. He stressed that custom had been the primary consideration in the original rules. His decision was not only in line with new needs and customs, but also in conformity with the maxim that a rule is inseparable from its effective cause. (Another example is the custom of men having beards as a sign of propriety in assessing a witness. In today's times, and for different cultures, the custom of men's facial hair has no bearing on the quality of a witness.)

Upon the basis of this maxim some jurists have endorsed the ascertaining of the Muslim calendar, and particularly the beginning and end of the month of Ramadan, by means of astronomical calculation, justifying their departure from the Prophet's tradition ordering reliance upon the sighting of the new moon.[98] It is hard to imagine the Caliph `Umar, if he were alive today, relying on physical sighting of the moon when precise scientific methods are available to inform us when the new moon may be sighted in a given place months in advance. It just isn't *sensible* to do things the more difficult way when easier ways are available, any more than it is sensible to insist on travelling from Makkah to Madinah by camel when cars and planes are available today.

A trickier subject is that of inheritance. Pre-Islamic customs on inheritance varied widely in lands that later became Muslim, and these differences influenced the post-Islamic inheritance laws,

---

97 See footnote on p. 67.

98 Aḥmad Muḥammad Shākir, *Awā'il ash-Shuhur al-`Arabiyyah* (Cairo, 1939), 13.

even though the schemes of inheritance adopted by various schools of law shared the same fundamental rules detailed in the Qur'ān and the precedents of the Prophet. For example, where no Qur'ānic heir or male relative had survived the deceased, the Kufan jurists admitted relatives outside the male line (e.g. daughters' and sisters' children) to succession, whereas the Medinan jurists did not. Both these views are consistent with the Qur'ān and Ḥadīth, the Medinan view resting on the fact that such relatives were not specifically granted rights of succession by the Qur'ān, and the Kufan view on the fact that, by recognizing the rights of women relatives, the Qur'ān implied the rights of relatives connected with the deceased through them. This was the effect of custom. Kufan society was not as patrilinear as Medinan society.

The Imām Shihāb ad-Dīn abu-l-`Abbās Ahmad ibn Idrīs (d. 684AH/1285AD) known as al-Qarāfi al-Miṣrī, was asked the following question: "If customs change from what they were, would the *fatwa*s found in the books of jurists become void and be replaced by *fatwa*s based upon new customs, or would it be said that we are only imitators and cannot produce new rules because we are not qualified to interpret?" Imam al-Qarafi answered, "All rules in the *Sharī'ah* that are based upon customs change when customs change, in accordance with the requirements of the new custom. The question of competence to interpret does not arise because this process of change is not new interpretation. It is rather a rule deduced by previous interpretation of the jurists and accepted generally. We therefore follow them in this regard without dissent."[99]

This answer undoubtedly refers to rules based upon interpretation and is not related to the question of changing the Texts, but a subsequent passage was rather absolute in stating: "All categories of law based upon customs change if the customs upon which they are based change." This statement, if understood in a categorical sense, would embrace all rules without exception, and would agree with the views of Abu Yūsuf mentioned earlier.

---

[99] Qarāfi, *Al-Iḥkām fi Tamyīz al-Fatāwā `an al-Aḥkām* (Cairo, 1938), 67–68. Imam al-Qarafi was in his days the chief of the Māliki school in Egypt.

It is interesting to speculate, if Abu Yūsuf or al-Qarafi were alive today, as to whether they would construe the Qur'ānic prescription that the female receives half the inheritance of her equivalent male heir as a *concession* to the Arab pre-Islamic custom of disinheriting females altogether, and declare that this rule was predicated on custom, its objective being fairness and equity? In other words, would they assume that, had the Arabs granted females full and equal shares with the males, the Qur'ān may not have reduced the female share to half that of the male?

The Imam Najm ad-Din Abu ar-Rabi` Sulayman ibn `Abd al-Qawiy aṭ-Tūfi (d.716/1316), one of the prominent leaders of the Hanbali school, advocated placing public interest before the texts and consensus. In his explanation of the tradition of the Prophet which says, "Injury may not be tolerated," he said that if public interest ran counter to the texts or consensus, the latter two must give way to the former by explaining and making them more specific. The view of aṭ-Tūfi goes even further than that of the Imam Mālik's plea of public interest. Aṭ-Tūfi's view was that "the texts and consensus must be relied upon in questions of religious observances and rites," and that "public interest should be relied upon in all questions of transactions and other rules" because "the interest in administering the rights of people is . . . known by custom and reason, so that if a rule based on the *Sharī'ah* should prove inadequate to delineate that interest, we would implicitly know that we are to have recourse in attaining it to those matters that foster it."[100]

In other words the Imam aṭ-Tūfi's view, as expressed in his treatise *Al-masālih al-mursalah,* is that the tradition "Injury may not be tolerated," amounts to saying that each rule based upon a text holds, "unless public interest requires otherwise."[101]

---

100 Ridā, Muḥammad Rashid, *Risālat Yusr al-Islām wa Uṣūl at-Tashrī` al-`Amm* (Cairo, 1938), 72–73.

101 This is a comment on Tūfi's views by the late Shaykh Mustafa al-Ghalayini in the latter's book, *al-Islām Rūḥ al-Madaniyyah* (Beirut, 1935), 30.

So now Madrassat ul-Iman in Brooklyn (see page 18) has three approaches to borrowing money if they can't find a rich angel to just donate them the money. They can:

1. Ask an Islamic banker for an interest-free loan,
2. Engage in a legal fiction (where the bank buys the property, and agrees to deed it over to them after twenty years of payments to them for a "service charge"), or
3. They can take out a regular mortgage and pay interest and state that they did this in accordance with Imam aṭ-Tūfi's view that in order not to create injury upon themselves (and the writings explained above of Imam Qarafi and Abu Yūsuf), that their interest in the education of their children and their need to do so gives them the license to take out a standard mortgage loan.

The preceding outline on the evolution of laws shows the various opinions concerning the application of *Sharī'ah* texts to suit changes in times, places and conditions. It is imperative at this point to indicate three important factors which tend to minimize the conflict of opinions on this matter:

1. First, the scope for conflict is narrow because the texts which deal with worldly affairs are very few in comparison with the texts which deal with religious observances.[102] Other than interest on loans, abortion during the first trimester, issues relating to women and dress codes, there aren't that many legal issues that Muslims lose much sleep over.
2. Second, most of the rules that lend themselves to changes and modifications relate to questions of detail and not to the generally applicable maxims which remained, and still remain, firm and uniform throughout the various countries.

---

[102] No more than six hundred Qur'ānic verses are considered as having legal import, from a total of more than six thousand verses.

3. Third, a number of traditions which related to questions of daily life, and which emanated from the Prophet in the form of opinion, are not obligatory or binding (i.e., they are not *sunnah tashrī`iyyah*). Imam Muslim relates, the Prophet passed by a group of people pollinating their palm trees and remarked that if they were not to do so it would be better. On being informed of his remark, those people abandoned the practice of pollination. The result was that the fruit did not ripen. When the Prophet was informed of what had happened, he said,

   *I am only a human being. If I order you to do something concerning your religion, heed my order, but if I order you concerning an opinion of mine, why I am merely a human being. You are better informed on matters relating to your daily life.*[103]

The decisions made and referred to above which appear to disregard the Texts, are not in themselves alien, but in fact do conform, to the *spirit* of the *Sharī'ah* which aims at making life easier and less exacting to the people. The Qur'ān says, "God desires for you ease; He desires not hardship for you" (2:185). The traditions of the Prophet emphasize the point further: "Make things easier, not more difficult; bring good tidings to the people and don't drive them away,"[104] "Assume unto yourselves such work as you are able to perform."[105] "Refrain from doing that which I have prohibited, and carry out that which I have ordered you to do within the limits of your capabilities."[106] In other words, you sin. God knows it, the Prophet knows it, and everybody may or may not know it, but most important of all, *you* know it. But try your best to be a good and sensible believer.

---

[103] Muslim, *Saḥīḥ*, VII, 95, *Kitāb al-Faḍā'il*, 177.

[104] `Ayni, *Umdat*, II, 45. This tradition, with a slight variation, occurs also in Muslim, Saḥīḥ, V, 141.

[105] `Ayni, *Umdat*, XI, 85.

[106] Muslim, *Saḥīḥ*, VII, 91.

It is necessary to emphasize that the principle of the evolution and changeability of legal rules does not mean changing the texts themselves. The texts are Divine and cannot be changed in any case. What is meant by change is really the change in the interpretation of these texts in the light of necessity and the change in the customs or in the effective causes upon which they are based. For example, when the Caliph `Umar suspended the Qur'ānic rule to cut off the hands of thieves, this was in order for a person stealing to survive. The *text* was not changed; what "changed" was his *interpretation* of the circumstances validating the text, that is, his weighing and evaluating the context to determine if the text is applicable.

This is an important point to note, for as we have stated earlier, the value of an act cannot be determined without its circumstances; no act has intrinsic ethical value without its circumstances. It is common knowledge among Muslims that they are prohibited from fasting on the `Id days, and that Muslim women are exempted from performing *ṣalāh* during their monthly periods, actions which are generally regarded as highly meritorious.[107] The

---

[107] The prohibition of menstruating women from *entering* mosques is not explicitly stated either in the Qur'ān or in the Ḥadīth. It has been construed by analogical extension to verse 4:43. This verse prohibits those who are in a state of ritual impurity (both men and women) resulting from sexual activity from approaching prayer, and, by extension, from sitting in the mosques, although not from passing through it. And because a menstruating woman is required to have the similar full bath at the end of her period, the prohibition of approaching prayer is applied to her too. But this analogical reasoning is contradicted, and therefore overruled, by a ḥadīth reported in *Saḥiḥ* Muslim, *Kitāb al-Haiḍ*, 11, which relates the Prophet asking his wife `A'ishah to fetch him the mat from the mosque. She said: "I am menstruating," to which he answered, "Get me the mat, for the menstruation is not in your hand." So we see from this ḥadīth that the exemption from prayer does not extend to entering the mosque. Neither does the exemption from prayer emanate from the *phenomenon* of bleeding, for in another ḥadīth, the Prophet responded to a woman who suffered from prolonged flow of blood and inquired whether she should abandon prayer, "Not at all, for that is only a vein, and is not menstruation, so when menstruation comes, abandon prayer, and when it ends, wash the blood from yourself and pray." And to another woman who had the same condition he said, "Take a bath and offer the prayer." (*Ibid.*, hadiths 95 to 100.) We see the Prophet differentiating here between *menstrual* and *non-menstrual* bleeding, and between *entering a mosque* and *performing the prayer* while in the menstrual period. From these hadiths we conclude that a menstruating woman is permitted to enter a mosque, and a woman bleeding outside her normal menstrual period is not ex-

taking of a human life, which is generally a major sin, but which may be a *requirement* for a soldier fighting in a just war, or as punishment for a murderer, is another example demonstrating that the textual ruling regarding an act cannot be divorced from its context if "good" is to be done.

All the preceding quotations and provisions, which are derived from recognized *shar`i* sources, from Islamic precedents or from the opinions of the learned, exemplify a general principle; namely, that the rules governing transactions are based upon reasonable causes and are attributed to the interests, needs and customs of people. These rules stand with their reasons and fall with them; further, they change in accordance with public interest and necessity, and are modified because of a change in environments, times, conditions and customs.

The foregoing also demonstrates that the *Sharī'ah* was not viewed as a rigid, unevolving body of law, and that it was and still is deemed compatible with civilization in every time and place. It further proves that the *Sharī'ah* did not lack men like the Caliph `Umar or the Imam Abu Yūsuf, al-Qarāfi, aṭ-Tūfi and others who looked for its real aims and who, in its application, went beyond its letter or text to its true intent. The *spirit* and intent of the *Sharī'ah*, therefore, was and still is founded upon public interest, public good and the facilitation of life in general.

As an example of the evolution of thought on a particular subject, consider the existence of slavery during the Prophet's time, when it was common all over the world. The Greeks, the Romans, and all the empires in the region practiced slavery, and it was not then ethnically oriented as it was in the United States.

---

empt from praying. (An important point needs to be made here for the benefit of American readers. The "mosque" is defined under Islamic law as just that space in which the prayer is conducted, and not the whole building or building complex which includes the mosque area. In the United States, we often use the name "mosque" to refer to an Islamic Center, which may comprise more than one building, and may include offices, a meeting hall which may be in the basement of the building or above the mosque area, classrooms, toilet and bathroom facilities for making ablution, etc. Any rules applying to mosques only refers to the prayer area, and not to the rest of the complex.)

Slaves could be black, brown or white. Perusing the Qur'ān and Ḥadīth, one can make a strong argument that Islām did not *in the long run* condone slavery. Rather than outlaw it altogether, a difficult thing during the times, the Qur'ān established a pattern of laws that limited the circumstances under which one can obtain slaves on the one hand; and on the other it encouraged the freeing of slaves, limited the slave owners' rights, and gave the slaves rights, including the rights of family and property ownership. In time, slavery was gradually in practice eliminated in Muslim lands.[108] Based on this, one can also make an analogous argument with regard to the position of women. Pre-Islamically, women had no rights in Arabia, and were regarded as property (a son would inherit his father's wives). Islām gave women rights of ownership and inheritance, the right to ask for a divorce, and protection from some abusive practices. Is it time, one wonders, for the recognition of women to be advanced further? The Prophet considered the testimony of Khuzaymah, a man of great veracity, to be equal to that of two men,[109] and he rejected the testimony of a deceitful person, or of a dependent, and even of nomad Arabs because they were then fickle and untrustworthy.[110] In other words, the acceptance of a witness is a function of his or her known trustworthiness. Many of us know women whose testimony we trust more than many men. And in gynecological and obstetric situations where men were generally prohibited by tradition and custom, the testimony of women took precedence under the *Sharī'ah.* Would it be appropriate, in this day and age, no longer to regard the testimony of a woman as *intrinsically* half that of a man's; and to regard this particular example as representative of the genre of evolving

---

108 Another argument that has been made is that slavery was a humane option that saved lives. During the many and frequent wars, the winners enslaved the losers, for as slaves, they had economic value. Had Islām outlawed slavery, the probable result would have been that the victors would have summarily executed the enemy, much as what has transpired during the major wars and ethnic cleansings of this century.

109 Sunan, Abū Dāwūd, *Kitāb al-Aqḍiyah*, 20.

110 Ibid, 16 and 17.

decision-making reflected by the Caliph `Umar and Imam Abu Yūsuf? This is a genre of questions that is made all the more relevant because Muslim nations like Pakistan, Bangladesh and Turkey, have had women heads of state, even before the United States of America, with all its openness. Reality often overtakes our capacity to deal with it!

And although arguments can and are made on the other side of both the slavery and women's rights issues, the point we are making here is that a careful reading of the spirit and letter of Islamic law, and its Qur'ānic and Ḥadīth bases—especially when looked at within its historical and evolving context—directs the impulse of the Muslim community towards the elimination of slavery and the recognition of women's rights. We can either take the rulings in the static sense or accept the momentum of this impulse and carry it to its logical and just conclusion, regarding the precedents established by the Caliph `Umar and Imam Abu Yūsuf as impulses in this direction.

# CHAPTER VIII

## SOLVING DILEMMAS

Having acquainted ourselves with the collective wisdom of our precedents and our way around the juridical kitchen, can we now come back to the dilemmas that impelled us to write this book and craft an *ijtihād* recipe for their solution?

First, as we said in analyzing some of the examples at the beginning of the book, you have to find out what the issue really is. The issue is not always strictly a legal problem although it may have legal implications. For example, is the determination of the moment of death a medical/biological question or is it a legal question? Different ways of defining the moment of death have legal ramifications. Many questions thrown to the courts are driven by non-legal issues like economics, for instance, and stand to be corrected as knowledge in those fields advances. Whereas the objective of the law is justice, an accurate, fair and just legal decision is often dependent on expert professional knowledge of other fields.

In breaking down any dilemma into its components, some problems become more tractable, and we have seen how some of the dilemmas even get resolved without much application of any *Sharī'ah* sources. For those dilemmas that remain unresolved, the following formula in reviewing and searching of the *Sharī'ah* sources for any applicable statements is helpful:

1. Are there Qur'ānic verses which deal with the subject, or help portray a picture that you can put together that is consistent with all of the Qur'ān, and thereby give you an answer?
2. Are there any *aḥādīth* that do the above? Did the Prophet deal with the same or a similar situation?
3. Are there any previous precedents or a general consensus of juridical opinion?
4. Can any analogies be made to the Qur'ān, the Ḥadīth and previous precedents?
5. Is there any public interest to be served?
6. Are there any important customs to be protected and preserved, which guard the public interest?
7. Are there any maxims, like the rule of necessity and need, or mitigation of hardship, that are relevant to the issue or specific case at hand?

At all times we must bear in mind the *objectives* (*maqāṣid*) of the *Sharī'ah*, namely, the protection of life, reason, religion, lineage and property, which include the harmonious enhancement of these *maqāṣid*. And in all of the above, we must apply our reason and logic appropriately, and avoid improper legal fictions.

The dilemmas facing Muslims today are hardly in the area of their beliefs and worship. They have to do predominantly with the following subject areas:

1. Enhanced, new and rapidly developing **technology**, especially in an area like medicine where the ability exists to extend physical life, sometimes even beyond the desire of the patient to live any more. In some instances where the demand for the new medication is beyond the financial capacity of those who need it, the dilemma becomes, given finite financial resources, to whom to provide medical services from

among the numerous potentially deserving cases. Medical technology has also made organ transplants possible, abortion easier, and has also enabled us to determine certain congenital problems in a fetus. Conscientiously, do we then abort the pregnancy? And if we do so based on the argument that the quality of life of the fetus will be such that it will not be worth living, does this not then open the door to euthanasia? These dilemmas are faced not only by Muslim physicians, but by non-Muslim physicians as well. The rise of the field of medical ethics has prompted Muslim physicians to think seriously about developing some operational tools.[111]

2. The interaction of Muslims with **values** and **customs** of societies and cultures not historically Islamic, especially when minority Muslim communities are living in predominantly non-Muslim countries. This urges us to examine all laws based on custom—both those of the society we live in as well as laws considered Islamic that are based on pre-Islamic custom—and aim more for developing a consonance with the intent and spirit of the Qur'ān and Ḥadīth. Dress codes (especially women's dress codes), personal grooming such as growing a beard or mustache, and the relationship between the sexes are examples where customs play a significant role, and different cultural codes imbue a particular action with different values. Another issue is the question of meat slaughtered by non-Muslims. (It is prohibited for a Muslim to consume the meat of an animal that has been slaughtered in

[111] For an interesting and informative treatment of some of these issues, see the paper "Islamic Values and Western Science: a case study of reproductive biology," by Munawar Ahmad Anees, in *The Touch of Midas, Science, Values and Environment in Islām and the West,* ed. by Ziauddin Sardar (Manchester University Press, 1984). Also Muḥammad Abdul Rauf, "History of Medical Ethics —Contemporary Muslim Perspective," in W.T.Reich (ed.), *Encyclopaedia of Bioethics* (The Free Press, New York, 1978) vol. II, p. 894.

the name of a god *other* than the One Almighty God, but how about meat not slaughtered in the name of any God?)[112]

3. In **economics**, the Islamic prohibition of usury cuts into the heart of banking (more so when we recognize that banks provide loans on funds that they do not own based typically on a reserve of 10%. In other words, for every dollar the bank owns as assets, it can loan up to ten dollars, the remaining nine dollars coming from borrowings). It also raises questions on the definition of modern currency based on paper—and now paperless—money that is no longer based on a gold or basket-of-commodities standard, a currency that typically fluctuates widely with respect to foreign currencies.[113] And should not Muslims consider inflation of currency an indirect form of usury, one that makes market interest rates of five to twelve percent seem less of an evil than an often higher rate of inflation? How can we therefore speak of interest and its prohibition under Islamic law without taking into account the rate of inflation? And is currency truly a commodity, like gold and silver, wheat and barley, or is it more of a formula, an algorithm?[114]

---

112 Within the Islamic community, "cultural" practices have arisen even within the Islamic practice as well. We have witnessed strong disagreements within the American Muslim community on matters that are peripheral and due to norms in different parts of the Islamic world. For example, some Muslims have gotten rather upset that the *mu'ādhhin* did not stick his fingers in his ears while calling the *adhan*, or who insist that prayer is null and void unless you cover your head. Being unaware that these are peripheral and not essential practices, such individuals cause acute discomfort in our mosques, and turn away those who strive towards a closer relationship with their Creator.

113 See Appendix IV, On Riba.

114 One apparent intention in the prohibition of *ribā* is that no group should take undue advantage of another, like banks foreclosing against farms during the depression after having extended them loans that could not be repaid due to drastic and unfortunate circumstances. But then can we extend the concept of *ribā* to apply to price-fixing, especially by monopolies, arguing that it is an example of *ribā* in the conceptual sense?

4. In the area of **politics**, some articulation of what an Islamic state ought to mean is needed. Many Muslims feel that a number of Western societies have developed systems of rule, protection of human rights, and economic opportunites for employment and wealth creation that express more of the Islamic ideal than their traditional lands have. They now long to be able to change the governments peacefully in their own countries towards the development of systems of rule that are more representational and simultaneously express the highest ideals of Islamic ethics and morality.[115]

The cross-linking of these areas has accelerated both the pace of change and the complexity in trying to understand and resolve these issues. Computerized banking, medical technology and easily available travel have combined to intensify the interplay of these domains. Although peripheral to the overriding importance of the religious creed, strong passions have been aroused by the differences of opinion on these subjects because Islām embraces all areas of life.

The reason why issues like abortion and interest are controversial and difficult is because there is a demand for them. As we look at the issue of interest, for example, the convenience provided by banking and availability of credit that accords mortgages for housing that results in a monthly payment comparable to renting an equivalent home, contributes to the typical Muslim's feeling that it is the sensible thing to do. Living in a nation whose government strives to keep its economy and currency stable, with a low inflation, the immigrant Muslim invariably lives a more comfortable lifestyle than he does in his typically developing home country. The personal and public interest appears to be well served and enhanced. Although all this admittedly does not make *ribā*

---

115 See *The Principles of State and Government in Islām*, by Muḥammad Asad, for some interesting essays on some of the issues that crop up with the intersection of Western and Eastern societies and forms of government.

*ḥalāl* (permissible), it makes it very difficult for the average, working American Muslim to avoid it at the personal level.

## CHAPTER IX

# CONCLUSION: THE CHALLENGES AHEAD

In this brief essay, we have outlined for you the contours of the philosophy of the *Sharī'ah*, the Sacred Law of Islām. You have learnt what its primary focus is, and how its understanding (*fiqh*) has been developed to join seamlessly with what is contemporarily thought of as secular or non-religious law. We have also demonstrated how applying this knowledge may assist you in developing answers to some pressing issues. Because modern technology over the past century has predominantly originated from Western societies, some Muslims have identified modern technology with Western cultural values. Most Muslims, however, realize that this is not the case, and recognize that the adoption of modern technology does not necessarily equal the adopting of Western cultural values. It is nevertheless true that the rapid pace of evolution of modern technology is creating new situations that are challenging to the traditional customs and norms of human society, yet this is true not only for Muslim societies, but for all societies worldwide, Western as well as Eastern, native and traditional. This rapid pace of technological advance is forcing us to develop a deeper understanding of ourselves and of our most fundamental values. For instance, an increasingly sophisticated and often prohibitively expensive medical technology has spurred the growth of the field of medical ethics, and Muslim medical practitioners are finding themselves challenged to develop a matrix of Islamic ethical guidelines and working definitions of life and death that can be meaningfully applied to the types of dilemmas they are faced with. Working on the boundary of human life, they are continually faced with wrenching decisions. A physician who has a spiritual and logically consistent understanding of selfhood, life and death is better able to relate to the concerns of his believing patients, their families and loved ones.

But as you survey the crisp commandments of the faith of Islām, you may also have noted that of all the issues confronting us in our spiritual journey in this life, the issues where there exists some real level of controversy are quite few in number. Most of the details of worship are clear. In practicing our faith, these differences should not cause major splits. Allāh did not reveal His Sacred Law, via His prophets, in order to cause hardship and violence in this world. In the Qur'ān Allāh speaks disparagingly of those who split themselves up into groups after His Word came down to them.[116] To politicize legitimate differences of opinion is therefore to violate this Divine command and to merit the criticism of God Himself, a danger that any sensitive believer ought judiciously to avoid.

This does not mean that we should lack the courage to address the problems that life confronts us with. Ultimately, we do have to have the courage of our convictions, and decide accordingly, knowing that in the final analysis, and from the Divine point of view, Allāh our Creator has the infinite capacity to correct any well-intentioned error we commit. Our responsibility is to ensure that our decisions are predicated on purity of intention, respect, regard and an honest attempt at self-consistency with the principles of *fiqh* derived from the Qur'ān, Ḥadīth and other authentic Islamic legislative and jurisprudential sources. We should maintain as well the deepest possible sensitivity to our humanity and well-being as a single, faithful community under God. For as God declares in His noble Qur'ān:

---

[116] *inna-lladhīna farraqū dīnahum wa kānū shiya'an lasta minhum fī shay'in; innamā amruhum ila-llāhi thumma yunabbi'uhum bi-mā kānū ya'malūn.*

Surely as for those who split up their religion and became sects, you have nothing to do with them. Their affair is with Allāh, then He will inform them of what they did. (6:159)

*Qul yā `ibādi alladhīna asrafū `alā anfusihim! Lā taqnaṭū min raḥmati-llāh. Inn-allāha yaghfiru-dhdhunūba jamī`an. Innahū huwa-l-ghafūr ur-raḥim.*

*O My servants who have transgressed against their own souls! Don't despair of Allāh's Mercy; certainly Allāh forgives all sins; He is indeed Forgiving, Merciful. (39:53).*

We must hope for it and expect it.

The final revelation to humanity from the One and Only Creator, has provided us with a beautiful and most elegant road map, the Qur'ānic *Sharī'ah.* And contrary to what many who feel intimidated by the challenges of modern times believe, Islām and its *Sharī'ah* did in fact meet with challenges in its earlier history that were no less traumatic and challenging than those of the modern world. Islām not only survived the challenges posed by cosmopolitan societies with ancient cultural histories (like that of Egypt, Mesopotamia and Persia), but *developed* its science of jurisprudence during this period of challenge; and then survived the sacking of Baghdad by the Mongols in 1258 AD by wrapping itself in the protective cocoon classically known as the "closing of the door of *ijtihād*" (juridical interpretation). Opening these doors of *ijtihād* to confront the challenges of modern times will not only make our task much easier, it will also make it far more exciting.

The challenge facing Muslim jurisprudence today lies between the need to define the relationship between the standards imposed by the religious faith and the mundane forces which activate society. On one side is the solution offered by classical jurisprudence, under which religious principles were elaborated into a comprehensive scheme of duties to determine the conduct of society. The other extreme solution is that of secularism—and Ataturk's Turkey was an example of this—which relegated religious principles to the realm of individual conscience, and allowed the forces of society unfettered control over the shape of the law. Muslim nations have struggled to form themselves somewhere between these two poles, attempting to develop a concept of law as a code of behavior which is founded upon certain basic and immutable religious principles but which, within these limits, does not neglect the factor of change and allows the adoption of extraneous standards which may prove more acceptable to current Muslim opinion. Do we apply the Ḥanafi philosophy of *ahl ar-ra'y* (the People of Opinion) or Maliki viewpoint of *ahl al-ḥadīth* (the People of Tradition)? This is tantamount to asking whether our reference ought to be either, "What concessions may be demanded from Islamic law by the needs of society," or, "What are the limitations that religious principles set upon society?" For the Muslim who wishes to practice his faith at the happy medium of these two poles, the challenge becomes how to learn to recognize the essential from the nonessential within the faith, and the relative degrees of essentiality.

Devout Muslims harbor a yearning for practicing Islām as it was practiced at the time of the Prophet, with the direct and simple freshness of revelation in their hearts. The *Sharī'ah's* primary impulse is the maintaining of this quality, by equipping the believer with the tools to maintain this direct sense of freshness of worship. Any appearance of complexity is really the effort to safeguard the freshness of Divine revelation and its integrity from the onslaught of the demands and vicissitudes of human life through its varying times and cultures. Human contexts evolve with time, but the human essence and spirit continues eternally unchanged. Although the intersection between the unchanging and the evolving within the human envelope places maximum stress upon the art of practicing the Law, Islamic jurisprudence is equipped to address successfully the full spectrum of human needs. Muslims may lack the knowledge of these tools, but rarely lack the courage to apply what they know. Lay Muslims are typically not shy to express the courage of their convictions, but need to base it more on knowledge.

Presumptuousness is much of this because of a distinguishing peculiarity of Islām: the absence of formal religious leadership, or rather, that its leadership lies fairly well distributed within its population at large. Islām is a grass-roots religion; its leadership is rooted in the community, the *ummah.* The expectations that in other communities fall on the church or rabbinical authorities, settles in Islamic society upon, at best, an organizationally amorphous set of spokespeople. This is why Islām has defied all human attempts in its history to organize it under the aegis of a pontificating, formal or political, church-like structure or organization. In this sense, Islām is intrinsically democratic; power and authority lie in the *ummah*. No bureaucratic organization has ever succeeded in holding sway over Islām. To the extent that there exists an Islamic religious leadership, the leaders' principal task is to guide the community in the practical affairs of life, instead of confining themselves to considerations of ritual and beliefs in the Hereafter. The challenges facing the Muslim world in dealing with 21st-century issues will require a greater degree of worldliness on the part of their religious leadership and spokespeople. Religious scholars who have no more than a rudimentary understanding of modern economics, for example, cannot be expected to speak to the community regarding its economic concerns in a language that resonates in their hearts and wins their minds. Islām is a perennially modern religion. The charismatic power of the Prophet Muḥammad as a leader was in no small measure a function of his ability to integrate the spiritual with the worldly to the highest degree humanly possible. He was not only a Prophet, a spiritual guide concerned with matters of the hereafter; he was also a loving father and husband, an experienced businessman, a head of state who felt responsible for his nation, and a judge concerned with the justice and compassion of his decisions; in short, a socially active and perennially modern man in many human roles. He was not isolated from human society and its concerns. The Prophet as *insan kamil* (a *perfected* human) was nevertheless perfectly *human*, an identity which gives meaning to the Muslims' finding in him their perfect example.

Islām does not need us; it is we who need Islām. Muslims who function as if Islām needs them do it a disservice, and attract those who harbor enmity to religion and God. We do not do God a favor by submitting to Him, but it is He Who has favored us by guiding us to faith; so God says in verse 49:17 of the Qur'ān. If we practice our faith with this sentiment while recognizing that *we* constitute the elements of the Islamic power base—and by extension its religious leaders, thinkers and spokespeople—it becomes clear why the Muslim world needs us to think humbly, responsibly yet creatively about those fundamentals of the Islamic impulse and to lead the community effectively in the practical, social aspects of life. As soon as we understand this, we begin to realize that a spiritual, economic and socio-political revival of the Muslim community's self-definition is intimately connected with and depends upon our gaining a new and direct insight into the pristine teachings of the *Sharī'ah* of Islām. Every day, more and more Muslims are becoming conscious of the fact that the gaining of such an insight is their principal, unavoidable task, and it is to the end of raising the threshold of their knowledge of the *Sharī'ah* that this book is dedicated.

# APPENDIX I

# FATHOMING THE SUBTLETIES OF SOME ISLAMIC TERMS

Although familiar with the meanings of particular terms, Muslims need to grasp the subtle *differences* in meaning between a given term and another which has a high degree of overlap in meaning, or between the same word used in different contexts. We saw this when we examined the differences between the terms *ijtihād* and *fiqh*, and between a *mujtahid* and a *faqīh*. Muslims often use some terms interchangeably, like *ḥadīth* and *sunnah*, for example, or one term (like *sunnah*) to mean a different thing, and to do this is fine most of the time. But when they use the same word to refer not to the area of overlap, but to the area of difference without being fully aware of it, problems can arise.

## A. What is the difference between the terms *fiqh* and *Shari`ah?*

In its widest and most inclusive Qur'ānic sense, the term *Sharī'ah* refers to "Divine Ordinances." Thus it is a set of laws ordained by God, the Lawgiver/Legislator (*Sharī'*), and revealed to any one community, as declared in verse 42:13:

> *He (God) has ordained* (shara`a) *for you of religion* (dīn) *what He commended unto Noah, and that which We have revealed to you (Muḥammad), and that which We commended unto Abraham and Moses and Jesus—to establish religion* (an aqīmu-ddīna) *and not to be divided therein.*

The *Sharī'ah* revealed through the Prophet Muḥammad comprises the same contents of what was given by God to the other prophets mentioned in this verse, namely Noah, Abraham, Moses and Jesus. In the broadest sense, the *Sharī'ah* is the common denominator of the whole cluster of systems of law that God revealed to at least these five Messengers mentioned in verse 42:13; it is that eternal *Divine Law that carries and embodies the Divine Intent (or expectations) of humankind.* We may call this the *Qur'ānic* definition of the term *Sharī'ah.*[117] This definition is fleshed out further in verses like 98:5 which says that the previous generations "were not enjoined but to worship God uprightly, being religiously sincere, and to establish prayer and give charity; that is the valuable religion (*dīn ul-qayyimah*)."

This Qur'ānic definition of the term *Sharī'ah* takes us beyond any parochial colorations of our own *Sharī'ah* to what is beyond language and expressed in the eternal Divine Intent. Because what God reveals is by definition *shar'i*, differences between Judaic and Islamic law (insofar as what was revealed by God to their respective Prophets) are not so much of substance as of detail. The em-

---

[117] See my book *Islām: A Search for Meaning,* on the different categories of meaning. Verse 5:48 says,

"For every one, We made from you, a law and a program (*li-kullin ja'alna minkum shir'atan wa minhāja* )." Although some may believe that this verse contradicts verse 42:13, it actually doesn't. Verse 5:48 combines two ideas:

1. That God gave each community a law (a *Sharī'ah*), and

2. That God made this law "from the people" He ordained it to (*ja'alna minkum minhāja*), that is, the law reflects the language and culture of the people.

Just because God gives a *Sharī'ah* to different communities that may differ in some aspects, that does not mean that the ordinances differ in what defines them as a *Sharī'ah*. For example, although you can say that a black man, a white man, a red man and a yellow man are *different* men, speaking different languages, they are all equally and identically men, or human beings, because their differences are not differences in their humanness, no matter how you choose to define a human being. Analogously, although God sent *Sharī'ahs* to different communities, and there were obviously different colorations to each, they are all equally *shar'i*. Islām recognizes any and all authentic revelations from God; during the time of the Prophet, those societies that were in contact with the Prophet, namely the Jewish and Christian, were recognized under the special status *ahl al-kitāb* (People of the Book).

phasis on not giving weight to these differences is so strong in this verse that God continues with a command "*that you establish religion and not be divided therein.*" What is common is God's commandment to believe in Him: this is the first and primary determinant of any *Sharī'ah*, and defines a *Sharī'ah* as such. And since the *Sharī'ah* has one primary intent, namely that human behavior be good, with the first and defining behavior being belief in the One Almighty God without partner, the *Sharī'ah* is considered as being one organic, immutable entity.[118]

So when we say that there is only one *Sharī'ah,* and that it is immutable, this immutability belongs more to the eternal Divine intent and objectives, for it is the envelope, or the carrier, of equity, goodness and justice—concepts that all human beings in all societies generally agree upon—except that it has a "Divine spin." It is goodness focussed on God, Who is One and Eternal. This point is key in identifying any law as expressing the *Shar`iah.*

Muslims use the term "*Sharī'ah*"—meaning *their Sharī'ah*—in several ways. In the narrowest sense, Muslims define it as the Divine Intent as set in the crystallized ensemble of rules and ordinances, of prescriptions and prohibitions revealed in the Islamic scripture, the Qur'ān, and as amplified by the teachings (known as the *Ḥadīth*, or *Sunnah*) of the Prophet Muḥammad. And because thought is part of action, all the elements of the Islamic creed, that is, what a Muslim must believe in order to be a Muslim, are also included in the *Sharī'ah.* In this least inclusive sense, Muslims tend to label any thing beyond that as "not *Sharī'ah.*" Whatever is *shar`i* (the adjectival or adverbial form, meaning that something is consistent with the *Sharī'ah*) in this sense means it is consistent with the Qur'ān and Ḥadīth.

Muslims have also used the term in a looser sense, where the *Sharī'ah* refers to all that falls under the umbrella of the expression "Islamic Law," in this case defined as the whole complex of laws

---

118 It is interesting to compare this notion of an essential law that comprises the common denominator of all previous divine revelations with the Western notion of a natural law, in which Western law finds its origins.

Muslims have historically lived under in the Muslim world, even if there were additional laws promulgated that were not found in the Qur'ān and Ḥadīth, and even if there were some differences between what they practiced in one part of the Muslim world and another.[119] Muslims living in nations with large non-Muslim populations sometimes use the term to refer to their customary practice *that differs* from what non-Muslims do. This is a definition by contrast, most commonly referring to issues of personal law, like marriages and inheritance. This usage became more notable when Muslim populations came under colonial rule and European law was instituted. The colonialists generally allowed the Muslims to apply their laws under separate *Sharī'ah* courts.

Therefore, when the term *Sharī'ah* is used, some care is in order if we are to have no confusion regarding which sense of the word we mean. When Muslims say "the *Sharī'ah* is immutable," what is referred to is the Divine Intent embodied in the Qur'ān and Ḥadīth. When Muslims speak of the "sources of the *Sharī'ah*," they are referring to "sources of Islamic Law as practiced by Muslims" and that which is consonant with the spirit and letter of Divine Intent. And when they ask, "Can the *Sharī'ah* evolve?" what they mean is not "can the Divine Intent change?" but "can our *understanding* of the deepest principles of the *Sharī'ah* and their respective priorities reach such a level and degree that we can always express the unchanging eternal Divine Intent?" The question which follows is then: "Can some rulings derived from the secondary sources (other than the Qur'ān and Ḥadīth), such as analogy and consensus of the past generations, be modified to suit current needs?"

Among the followers of the Prophet Muḥammad, the differing schools (*madhāhib*) are not of the *Sharī'ah* (the Divine Law) but of *fiqh*[120] (jurisprudence). The *Sharī'ah* is "the eternal Divine In-

---

[119] For example, *mut'ah* (temporary marriage) is permitted under Shi`i law while prohibited under the Sunni schools of law. Since both opinions are part of Islamic practice, the conclusion must be that they are equally *shar`i.*

[120] The word *fiqh* is a noun derived from the verb *faqaha,* meaning to understand. It is used to mean understanding of the law, thus jurisprudence.

tent"; it is what comes down as ordinances from God. *Fiqh* (jurisprudence) is the human intellectual endeavor, or the science, of comprehending the Divine Law and Intent. Thus Muslims speak of *madhāhib of fiqh* (i.e., ways of looking at and understanding the Divine law, spoken of as "schools of jurisprudence"), not *madhāhib of Sharī'ah.* The reason why this distinction is important to Muslims is that the *Sharī'ah* (as an immutable law sent down by Divinity) is a permanent, eternal instruction to Muslims. It is what God has given humanity. God did not instruct Prophet Muḥammad to pray without giving similar instruction to Abraham, Moses and Jesus. They all had to pray, to fast, and to give charity. And they all were commanded to avoid the same sins, like murder, theft, adultery, usury, etc. That's what 42:13 and other verses like it tell us. God did not reveal *different* religions to His Prophets; it was all the same religion. The difference was in the language and in the details of worship. For example, Moses obviously prayed in Hebrew and Prophet Muḥammad prayed in Arabic. The Jewish fast is from night-time to the following sunset whereas Muslims fast from dawn to sunset; Muslims pray five times a day while the people of the Book may have had to pray three or seven times a day, etc. The difference between the details of worship among the different Prophets, seen from God's point of view, would be more or less like the difference of the *madhāhib* seen from our current Islamic point of view.

The various and collective *results* of the mutable human effort of looking at, understanding and comprehending one and the same *Sharī'ah* adds to our *fiqh* (understanding). Thus it becomes possible to understand why certain aspects of the *Sharī'ah* may be looked at differently, as a function of place and time, each and all equally valid, and each and all equally well displaying the impulse of one *Sharī'ah*, with the *madhāhib* of *fiqh* being imaged as routes by which one approaches and abides with one and the same *Sharī'ah.*

*Fiqh* has been defined by the jurists as "the *science* of the derived legal rules as acquired from their particular sources." There is similarity between the *madhāhib* on the essential *farḍ/ḥarām* (obligatory and prohibited) classes of actions, especially those dealing with matters of religious worship and observances; the differences between them are in the nonreligious categories, and even then they are few and relatively minor. This is because they conceptually originate in the domain where freedom to interpret and legislate exists. Compared to sects in other religions, the differences between the *madhāhib* are minor indeed.[121]

The link between the *Sharī'ah* and *fiqh* is the human intellectual *effort* directed towards attaining this understanding, called *ijtihād*. The *Sharī'ah* is considered to be Divinely given, partly from well-established sources handed down *(manqūl),* such as the Qur'ān and the *Sunnah,* and partly arrived at by reason *(ma`qūl),* such as consensus, analogy, judicial preference, etc. *Ijtihād* was the method for the deduction of rules from these sources and the means by which transactions and social needs were given the necessary flexibility. *Ijtihād* was therefore the essential ingredient, or tool, in the growth of the *Sharī'ah* as a humanly comprehended and applied entity.

*Mujtahids* (jurists) followed the text, if such existed regarding the resolution of a matter, but resorted to opinion in its absence. Their methods were analogy (*qiyās*), preference (*istihsān*), public interest (*maṣlaḥa, or istiṣlāḥ*), and deduction by presumption (*istidlāl and istiṣḥāb*). But the jurists followed different paths in their search for suitable rules, leading to the rise of different schools of jurisprudence (the *madhāhib* of *fiqh*). Discussions, debates and personal contact among the jurists resulted in narrowing the gaps which separated the schools during the time of their

---

121 We point this out because some Western scholars have chosen to speak of the Ḥanafi sect, the Shāfi`i sect, etc. But the differences among the *madhāhib* are much less than the differences among religious sects like Catholicism and the various denominations of Protestant Christianity. And although some speak of the Sunni and Shi`ah as "sects," Muslims prefer to avoid that terminology because the Shi`i scripture and creed is identical with the Sunni scripture and creed, and Shi`i law does not vary from any one of the four Sunni *madhāhib* any more than the Sunni *madhāhib* differ among themselves.

founders. This growing consensus of juridical opinion over time is perhaps the best definition of *ijmā'* (consensus of juridical opinion), and is analogous to the growing consensus of opinion over time in any intellectual field, such as physics for example, regarding those parts of its subject matter (like relativistic and quantum physics) that were initially subjects of great controversy but which eventually became part of the accepted body of thought.[122]

[122] A more universal example is the change in the public conception of the sun rising and setting on a flat and static earth to the currently held knowledge that the earth orbits the sun.

## B. What Does *Madhhab* Mean,

## And Why Did The Different *Madhāhib* Arise?

What is the logical basis for the rise of the different schools of jurisprudence? Historically, the schools of jurisprudence developed because of the needs that arose in different parts of the Muslim world. These schools evolved around certain individuals who responded to this felt need in accordance with their understanding and their milieu. The logic of this development is more easily explained by walking through the following example.

Let us look at verse 62:9 which commands the believers as follows: "O you who have believed, when the call is made for prayer on Friday, hasten to the remembrance of Allāh and leave off commerce. That is better for you if you knew." This verse makes the Friday prayer an obligation, and also *prohibits* the conduct of business during the time of Friday prayers. But does this prohibition also imply that a business deal consummated during this time is null? Or is it null only upon men, for whom the Friday prayer is mandatory and not upon women, for whom the Friday prayer is not mandatory but optional? And what about a business deal consummated on your behalf by your non-Muslim partner (or employee) during this time? It is clear that, while adhering to the letter of the verse's command, one state may interpret this verse in such a way that any business contract consummated during the time of Friday prayer is null for both men and women, while another state may interpret the verse to mean that it is null for men, but that a business contract consummated by women is valid. A third interpretation is that although conducting business at this time is prohibited, the contract shall still be recognized as valid, on the premise that the prohibition is not equal to nullification of the contract, that is, that the sin of not making the Friday prayer in favor of a business deal does not invalidate the deal. Another way of saying this is that, in the absence of specific wording in the Qur'ān or the *Ḥadīth* nullifying the contract, the penalty for violating the Divine command not to make a business deal at the time of Friday prayer does not have to be invalidity of the contract. And we can complicate this further by saying that the intent of the verse is not to prohibit business dealing within a given time frame, but to emphasize that the performance of the Friday prayer within the time frame of its performance is more important than the business deal. This conclusion can be reached because the verse continues by telling the believers that "when the prayer is concluded then *disperse* and seek of Allāh's grace" (a euphemism meaning that we can go back to our jobs). Otherwise we are forced to conclude that after the Friday prayer we *must* leave the mosque, the imperative verb to "disperse on the earth" (*fa-ntashirū fi-l-'ard*) amounting to a prohibition from hanging around in the mosque.[123] And you don't have to be an Imam to know how many people love to hang around in the mosque after the *Jum`ah* prayers are over. Most of us do not realize that a simple verse like this can lead to so many implications! Evidently, different interpretations of the sources of law like this are equally valid under the *Sharī'ah*, for they fall within the area of legitimate differences of juridical interpretation. This example also shows why the law of contracts of more than one *madhhab* cannot as a rule coexist in one state, which led to different countries of the Muslim world each following one *madhhab* to the exclusion of the others. (You can pray in the same *mosque* with your hands on your chest next to someone praying with his hands by his side, but it is difficult to have two different rules in the same

[123] Jurists take this as an illustrative example of a Qur'ānic command whose intent is not a command; the imperative form of the verb *fa-ntashirū* is not a commandment to perform the act of dispersing from the mosque after the termination of the Friday prayer, but a permission to do so. Otherwise we have the peculiar conclusion that it is *forbidden* to stay in the mosque after the Friday prayers.

*court* as to whether a business deal consummated during the time of Friday prayer is valid.)[124]

This example also shows us that these different interpretations, or rulings on whether a business contract is valid or not if conducted at the time of the Friday prayer, are equally *shar'i*, that is, they express the juridical impulse, and sense of equity and justice, and the letter of the law of one *Sharī'ah.* They are not expressive of different *Sharī'ahs,* but of different *fiqh*s (understandings). Understanding how one *Sharī'ah* can manifest in variant specific rulings helps us understand how the one Divine *Sharī'ah* can express itself in different revelations to different prophets in what appears to us humans as different rulings. More importantly, it helps us learn how to draw the often elusive boundary between something that is consistent with the *Sharī'ah* and something that violates it.

This example also drives home the meaning of the statement made above that there is only one Islamic *Sharī'ah*, and why Muslims apply the term *madhhab* to *fiqh*, and not to the *Sharī'ah*; so that we speak of *madhāhib* of *fiqh*, but not *madhāhib* of the *Sharī'ah.* It is a way of differentiating, in our language, between the Qur'ān and Ḥadīth as that which is "God-given," (the *Sharī'ah*) and the ensemble of varying equally possible and acceptable opinions that emanate from the human effort and perspectives (the *madhāhib* All the *madhāhib*, regardless of varying outer appearances, express the same inner ordinances of the *Sharī'ah.* It is also in recognition of, and in obedience to, verse 42:13, where we are commanded not to be divided in our religion.

Thus the need arose for deeper understanding of religion and interpretation. The first objective is in obedience to verse 9:122 which commanded the believers not to all go out together for a

---

124 As to the more general question as to whether a traveller is bound by the rules and *madhhab* of his homeland or that of the country he is visiting, the answer depends on the specifics of the situation. A traveller can maintain the rules of his *madhhab* in matters of personal ritual worship, and may be able to maintain it in matters pertaining to his marriage if he is married to someone of the same *madhhab*; but may not be able to maintain it in a matter of a business deal with a local merchant.

battle. The Qur'ān asks: "Why then does not a person from every group from among them apply themselves to the understanding in religion, *(liyatafaqqahu fi-ddin),* and that they may caution their community when they return to them, so that they may be careful?" This verse shows that each community should have a group of religious advisors who—by studying the faith more deeply—would be able to advise their people appropriately. We've got to be careful in order to be religious. The Qur'ān through this verse equates the value of this effort (of those staying behind) with fighting a just war *(jihād).* Thus we see the Qur'ānic link between the idea of *jihād*, the struggle in a just war, and *ijtihād*, the effort waged in gaining understanding (*fiqh*) in the faith.[125] The basis for the term *ijtihād* as the effort required to arrive at a legal judgment for a case is also given by several *aḥādīth*, of which legal scholars love to quote the *ḥādīth* of Mu`ādh b. Jabal (quoted on p. 56).

[125]Perhaps this is why some Muslims confuse the terms *jihād* and *ijtihād*, or *mujāhid* and *mujtahid. Jihād* means the effort applied in waging a war, and a *mujāhid* is a warrior, or fighter; *ijtihād* means the effort applied to legal rulings, and a *mujtahid* is a jurist.

## C. How Do We Differentiate Between The Terms Ḥadīth And Sunnah?[126]

Because the terms *ḥadīth* and *sunnah* are very often used interchangeably, let us get a real grip on both what *ḥadīth* and *sunnah* mean in common and, more importantly, how these words can differ in usage. You may wonder: what Muslim doesn't know what the terms *ḥadīth* and *sunnah* mean? And yet if understood as it ought to be, no one would have concluded that the *ḥadīth* must be ignored!

What some of us have forgotten is the need to factor into our computation that the Arabic language has remained substantially intact over more than 1400 years. The key word here is "substantially" and not "completely." In fact, some of these key words have developed very complex semantic fields.[127] In many instances, the words themselves were given additional new meanings, and additional new applications, or twists and spins of meaning. In this

---

[126]This note was prompted by the eruption of a controversy in Malaysia by followers of the late Dr. Rashad Khalifa, who adopted a policy of "rejecting the Ḥadīth," known in Malay as *"tolak Ḥadīth."* It is important to note that the Qur'ān is a *conceptual* subset of the Ḥadīth (in the literal sense, i.e., *ḥadīth* means all that came through the mouth of the Prophet, but not in the technical jurisprudential sense, where *ḥadīth* refers to everything the Prophet said "other than the Qur'ān.") All that Muslims know of the Qur'ān was informed and defined by the Ḥadīth (in the literal sense) since it was through the mouth of the Prophet that the Qur'ān was revealed to the Muslims. The Prophet informed his followers what belonged in the Qur'ān and what did not, as well as the order of the Qur'ānic verses and chapters. It is logically inconsistent, therefore, as some have maintained, to accept the Qur'ān and reject the Ḥadīth. We use the word *Ḥadīth* in the generally used jurisprudential sense of "what the Prophet said other than the Qur'ān," and that is complementary, supportive and descriptive to it and its message. In this section, however, we redefine it in its absolute, literal, etymological sense.

[127] By "complex semantic fields," we mean that the terms span a number of meanings, or have different meanings in different contexts, or have been used by people in many different ways, and that all these meanings interact and participate in the overall complexion of meaning and the way it is used.

section, we will examine the terms *ḥadīth*, *Qur'ān* and *sunnah*, not so much to tell you what you know already, but to point out some of these subtle shades of differential meanings where people can get really tripped up.

## i. The Ḥadīth

The expression *ḥadīth*[128] *rasulullah* means "a news report, or story, about *anything* the Prophet Muḥammad said or did, including if he saw or heard something and said something or remained silent." The word *haddatha* means "to speak" and therefore the term *ḥadīth* has an emphasis on speech, or the report about something, although the term *ḥadīth* also refers to an event, an occurrence. Thus the term *ḥadīth* is often used in this context in three senses: one is a report (also called *khabar,* a news item) about something that the Prophet said or did; the second sense is that of the speech of the Prophet; and the third the act of the Prophet. *Al-ḥadīth* in Arabic (meaning *The Ḥadīth*—often written with a capital H in English)' refers to the totality of *hadith*s (*aḥādīth* is the plural in Arabic). And it is defined as *everything* he said or did, regardless of its value as a teaching to be followed by his followers. The basis for determining the importance of various portions of the Prophet's *Ḥadīth* is itself provided by the Prophet's statements; in other words, by the *ḥadīth* itself.

The statements and actions of the Prophet were recorded by his companions from the earliest times. Unlike the Qur'ān, which was officially collected and put together by the time of the Caliph `Uthman (the project was begun during the caliphate of Abu Bakr), no official codification of the *Ḥadīth* was attempted, although the idea occurred to `Umar to do so. But he either changed his mind or felt that since the Qur'ān project had not as

[128] The word *ḥadīth* means new, and just as we ask a friend "What's new?"—from which the word *news* comes from—the Prophet's companions used to ask each other "What's (the) ḥadīth?" in the same sense as "What's (the latest) new(s) regarding the Prophet?"

yet been completed, to initiate a *Ḥadīth* project would have been premature.

Various individuals had their own personal collections of *Ḥadīth* beginning from the time of the Prophet, which really began as their own recollections of things the Prophet had said or done in their company. As time went on, various opinions surfaced as to whether the *Ḥadīth* should even be written or recorded. Because the *hadiths* were personal accounts of events, the written forms were considered merely mnemonic devices; they were more properly to be conveyed orally so that the intent of the *Ḥadīth* and its context became clear.[129] But as the Islamic empire expanded after the death of the Prophet, memories faded with the death of individuals, and the need for legal support created a growing need for the *Ḥadīth* to be collected in written form. By the third century after the death of the Prophet, the following six collections of *Ḥadīth*, named after the individuals who collected them, were considered authoritative:

1. Al-Bukhāri, (d. 256/870).
2. Muslim, (d. 261/875).
3. Abū Dāwūd, (d. 275/888).
4. At-Tirmidhī, (d. 279/892).
5. An-Nasā'ī, (d. 303/915).
6. In Mājah, (d. 273/886).

---

[129] One of my favorite stories about misunderstanding the intent of a ḥadīth because the context is misunderstood is the following. The Prophet was sitting with his companions one day and someone who had had camel's meat for dinner had broken wind. The Prophet, not wanting to embarrass him, said "Will the person who had camel's meat for dinner please go renew his *wudu*?" I suppose that had he worn a purple scarf he would have said "Will the person who is wearing a purple scarf go renew his *wudu*?" The others, not knowing the intention of the Prophet, assumed that eating camel's meat broke one's ablution (*wudu'*), and you will therefore meet people who advise you to renew your *wudu'* whenever you eat camel's meat. So you can see how important it can be to know the context of a given ḥadīth to really have a sound understanding of that to which the ḥadīth refers. Even when a ḥadīth is known to be reported by reliable sources, you can find yourself wondering about its *sensibility*. Invariably, there is probably something missing in the picture that made you feel that way, for the Prophet was always sensible.

These are not the only collections of Ḥadīth. The *Muwaṭṭa'* of Imam Mālik and the *Musnad*[130] of Imam Ahmad ibn Ḥanbal are in fact more highly regarded than the *Sunan* of Ibn Mājah. But because the hadiths quoted in the *Muwaṭṭa'* are included in the first two, it is subsumed in them as part of the six.

The two books of Imam al-Bukhāri and Imam Muslim are called *Saḥīḥ*, and these two are often called the "two *Sahih*s" (*as-Ṣaḥīḥān*), because *aḥādīth* which are considered as *saḥīḥ* (sound) are included in them. The *aḥādīth* included in the other four works deal almost exclusively with the *sunnah*s, and that is why they are called *as-Sunan.* In addition to *aḥādīth* that are *saḥīḥ*, they also contain *aḥādīth* which are not, although when one of these collectors think that a ḥadīth given by them should be rejected they usually call the reader's attention to the fact.

Among the *Shi`ah* the following five books are held in particularly high esteem:

1. *Al-Kāfī* of al-Kulīnī (d. 328/939)
2. *Man lā yastaḥḍiruhu'l-faqīh*, of al-Qummi (d. 381/991)
3. *Tahdhib al-Aḥkām* by aṭ-Tūṣī (d. 459/1067)
4. *Al-Istibṣār fī-ma'khtalafa fīhi'l-Akhbār,* also by aṭ-Tūṣī
5. *Nahj al-Balāghah* of al-Murtaḍā (d. 436/1044)

A ḥadīth quotation consists of two parts: the *text*, called *matn*, and the chain of narration, often called "chain of authorities," called *isnād,* or *sanad*, which literally means "the support." This latter part is what you see when you read that person A says "I have heard from B on the authority of C, who heard the Prophet say such and-such." It is the names of the persons who have handed the text of the ḥadīth to one another. Another thing to

130 The term *musnad* means "supported," from the term *isnād.* In a *musnad* the *aḥādīth* are grouped and classified not by subject matter but by the names of the sources. It was an intermediate stage in the collection of Ḥadīth, as the collections of various companions became put together in a compendium. Thus all the *aḥādīth* heard from one individual are grouped together, then the *aḥādīth* from another, and so forth.

bear in mind is that a ḥadīth is defined as the sum of the *isnād* (chain of authorities) and the *matn* (text). Therefore a particular text or story that is related by a different chain of authorities is considered a *separate* ḥadīth. So when you hear that Imam al-Bukhāri sifted through 100,000 *aḥādīth*, this does not mean 100,000 separate Prophetic statements or stories about the Prophet; it could be 10,000 stories, with each story related by ten different *isnāds*.

The differences between the schools are both in the text *(matn)* of a given ḥadīth as well as over the ways and means in which a ḥadīth was ascertained, and the prerequisites to the acceptance of their authenticity. This predominantly meant examining the *isnād*, for some chains of authority were faulty. For example, the person hearing the particular ḥadīth may have died before the next person on the chain was born, or that one of the people on the chain was known to be unreliable in his reporting. We know of similar situations in our own lives, for our friends or relatives don't all speak and relate stories about things that may have happened to them or other members of their family in equally truthful ways. Perhaps your aunt Fatimah is someone who always tells it like it is; whereas your aunt Fawziah likes to embellish her stories. It isn't that she is untruthful, it's just that she exaggerates the story and gives it a colorful and dramatic spin, or emphasizes that part of the story that helps her make the point. Another uncle you know says the truth, but loves to add certain untruths to his stories. Your honest grandfather never lies, but his memory is getting faulty, while a cousin of yours just cannot be trusted at all—he out and out lies. Almost everyone relates a story to drive home a point on their personal agenda that they wish us to see or adopt. These kinds of things are natural human ways of relating news and events, and we see these types of reporting even in today's news media as well. Human beings being what they are, this also happened in the reporting of *aḥādīth*. One report of an event may have quoted the Prophet word for word, whereas another report may have its reporter describe the event in his own words. While both are truthful, we cannot equate the first report's reliability as equal to the second. So just as not everything other than your aunt Fatimah's stories are false, not all *aḥādīth* other than the *saḥīḥ* ones are false.

Another way of looking at this is to consider the reasoning behind swearing in court to tell "the truth, the whole truth, and nothing but the truth." This would be analogous to a *saḥīḥ* report. While telling the truth, it is also possible to tell the truth, but not all of it, which would slant the hearer's understanding, or to tell the whole truth and add some false statements as well.

No one disputes that obedience to the Prophet is mandatory. Just as stories can have different colorations of truth, Ḥadīth scholars recognized the need to categorize the Ḥadīth into degrees of authenticity that reflect such differing colorations. This led to the rise of the Science of Ḥadīth, whose objective was the process of determination, and thereby classification, of *aḥādīth* into categories of relative authenticity. The efforts expended in this have been prodigious, and the lessons learned from this effort are multifarious. Embedded in the fruits of this effort is the full and fascinating spectrum of Islamic political history and the history of Islamic thought.

In sifting the *aḥādīth*, the scholars of Ḥadīth categorized them in several different ways:

**1. By the *strength of its isnād* and *consistency of its text*.** In this class we have the following three:

**a**. *Saḥīḥ* (sound). This name is given to the utterly faultless ḥadīth in whose text and *isnād* there is no weakness (*`illah*).

**b**. *Ḥasan* (beautiful). This is a ḥadīth that is not absolutely faultless, either because its *isnād* is not quite complete, or because there is no perfect agreement regarding the reliability of its authorities.

**c**. *Da`īf* (weak). This is a ḥadīth against which serious doubts can be raised, either by reason of its contents or because one or more of its transmitters is not noted for his accuracy, sound hearing, perfect memory, etc.

**2. By the *degree of its renown* at the time of the Prophet and the next two generations** (thus translating to the strength or weakness of its *isnād*). Here we have the following:

**a**. *Mutawātir*: universally known. This is a ḥadīth handed down on many sides, by many different *isnāds*, generally known from very early times and to which objections have never been raised. So many people heard it from the Prophet and related it that it is beyond dispute.

**b**. *Mashhūr*: this is a ḥadīth handed down by at least three different reliable authorities, or according to another view, a ḥadīth which, although widely disseminated later, was originally only transmitted by one person in the first generation. For example, Abu Bakr or `Umar may have been the only one to hear a story from the Prophet, who then related it to many people and it became widespread.

**c**. *`Azīz*: this is a ḥadīth transmitted by at least two *isnāds* and was not so generally disseminated as a *mutawātir* or *mashhūr* ḥadīth.

**d**. *āḥād*: this is a ḥadīth transmitted by only one *isnād.*

**e**. *Gharīb*: this is in general a rare ḥadīth. When in reference to its *contents* rather than its *isnād*, *gharīb* refers also to a ḥadīth that contains foreign or rare expressions.

The legal importance of this classification is that *aḥādīth* belonging to the first two classes of *mutawātir* and *mashhūr* are recognized by all the important Sunni jurists as the second source of *Sharī'ah* after the Qur'ān. The *āḥād* hadiths are accepted as taking precedence over *qiyās* (analogical deduction) by all Sunni schools except the Ḥanafi school, which gives priority to *qiyās.* The situation is not so black and white, however. Imam Mālik would go along with an *āḥād* ḥadīth if it was backed by the practices of the Companions and the Followers; otherwise, he preferred *qiyās.* Imam Abu Hanifah accepted some *āḥād* traditions and rejected others on the basis of his own criteria; in this he followed the practice of Abu Bakr and `Umar ibn al-Khaṭṭāb.[131] He accepted them in connection with ordinary matters, if he was satisfied about the legal acumen and instinct of the reporter; while in cases of intricate legal problems he rejected them unless they were supported by circumstantial evidence and fundamental Islamic principles.

**3. By its *degree of unacceptability* among the scholars of Ḥadīth**

**a**. It may happen that the value of a ḥadīth is uncertain because some remarks by the transmitter have been interpolated among the words of the Prophet and it is impossible to accurately separate these two components of the text; such a ḥadīth is called *mudraj* (interpolated). This is like your uncle who tells the truth in his stories, but loves to add certain things you just know were false or didn't happen.

**b**. If a ḥadīth is transmitted by only one informant, whose authority is also considered weak, the ḥadīth is called *matrūk* (abandoned, i.e., no longer considered or accepted).

**c**. If a ḥadīth is considered absolutely false, it is called *mawḍū`* (fabricated).

If a ḥadīth is mentioned in both the *Saḥīḥ* of Bukhāri and Muslim, it is sometimes referred to as *muttafaq `alaihi* (meaning "agreed upon"). You may also come across additional terms used by some collectors of Ḥadīth. For example, the term *majhūl* (unknown) is used by Tirmidhi to refer to an *isnād* transmitted by someone in an unrecognized manner. *Mu`allal* refers to a ḥadīth which may appear sound but has some weakness (*`illah*) not readily

---

[131] Confronted with a legal case in which a woman had miscarried following an attack from another woman, he asked an assembly of Companions: "Who heard the Prophet giving his verdict regarding miscarried fetuses?" Al-Mughirah ibn Shu`ba said: "I heard him judging that a male or female slave be given." `Umar asked him to produce a witness who would corroborrate his narration. Muḥammad ibn Maslama stepped forward and concurred that the ḥadīth was genuine. `Umar accepted this ḥadīth and gave his judgment accordingly on the case. (Bukhāri, *Saḥīḥ*, *Kitāb ad-Diyat*, hadiths nos. 42 and 43.)

apparent. *Shādhdh* (anomalous, strange) describes a ḥadīth coming from a single transmitter and contradicting another ḥadīth.

**4. By the *extent* to which the *isnād* reaches the Prophet.** In this category we have the following:

**a.** If the *isnād* is unbroken and complete, it is called *muttaṣil* (connected), otherwise it is generally called *munqaṭi`* (cut off, severed).

If the *isnād* is *muttaṣil* and the last authority is a companion of the Prophet, the ḥadīth is called *musnad* (supported). If the *isnād* is comparatively short because the last authority received the ḥadīth from the original authority via the intermediary of a few persons, the ḥadīth is called *`alī* (exalted, or high). This is considered a great advantage, because the possibility that errors have crept into this ḥadīth is very small.

If the *musnad* ḥadīth also contains special observations regarding all the authorities, for example, it is expressly mentioned that all the authorities swore an oath as they handed on the ḥadīth, the ḥadīth is called *musalsal* (chained, continuous).

**b.** The *munqaṭi`* is of several types:

(i) If the *isnād* only goes back to an authority belonging to the first generation after the Prophet (a *tābi'ī*), and the name of the companion (*ṣaḥābī*) who heard it from the Prophet is missing, that ḥadīth is called *mursal.*

(ii) If the *isnād* has two or more transmitters missing, it is called *mu'ḍal.*

(iii) If the *isnād* has one of the authorities indicated as "a man," without his name being mentioned, it is called *mubham* (vague, doubtful). In some *isnāds,* a transmitter A may not have heard the ḥadīth directly from the other authority B or may not have been personally acquainted with him, but heard the ḥadīth through the intermediary of another person C not mentioned in the *isnād.* In this case the authorities are listed as A *`an* B, which means A "from" B. Such a ḥadīth is called *mu`an`an.* This is like when your aunt Fatimah learnt that her cousin got pregnant, confided it to your sister, who then told you and you in turn tell your mother that you have come to understand "from" your aunt Fatimah that her cousin got pregnant, without revealing to her that your sister told you the information.

**5. By whom the *text* (*matn*) of the ḥadīth pertains to.** Not all *aḥādīth* deal with the sayings or doings of the Prophet. Some *aḥādīth* speak about the companions, and others about the first generation after them.

**a.** If the ḥadīth speaks about the Prophet, it is called *marfū`*.

**b.** If the text deals with the sayings or doings of the companions (*ṣaḥābīs*), the ḥadīth is called *mawqūf*.

**c.** If the text deals with the sayings or doings of the first generation after the Prophet (*tābi'ūn*) the ḥadīth is called *maqtū`*.

So now you understand when you see hadiths described by more than one adjective, such as *marfū` muttaṣil saḥīḥ āḥād*, that this means a ḥadīth that deals with the sayings or doings of the Prophet, whose *isnād* reaches a companion of the Prophet, of which the scholars of Ḥadīth are in full agreement regarding the reliability of its authorities, and which was only related by one companion.

In looking at the above categorizations of the Ḥadīth, we find that it exhibits not only a great deal of scholarship, but more importantly, the enormous *care* that these scholars exercised so as to retain all that can be of value to the Muslim community. We are very much aware in our current times that the news media of any country is subject to many pressures, political and social, to slant news in favor of a particular aim or objective. If a similar analysis were demanded of the news media of today, where a news item would be qualified by analogous criteria of accuracy (whether it was *saḥīḥ*, *ḥasan* or *da`if* our understanding of current affairs would be greatly enhanced). Political pressures existed during the first few centuries of Islām, during which the *aḥādīth* were collected, and to assume that political aims or particular intentions were absent within the Islamic community is to be unrealistic.

Thus some aḥādīth were forged towards these objectives. But even the false ḥadīth, which the compilers recognized as such, tell us a lot about the history of Islām and the various motives that governed those who felt impelled to forge ḥadīth about the Prophet. Forged *aḥādīth* do not lower the standing of the Prophet or Islām; if anything they demonstrate the importance and very high standing of the Prophet among the community. This is just like that jealous aunt of yours who cannot help spreading lies about your mother because she is jealous of her brother's love for her; it is a sign of your mother's high standing that such lies are forged against her. But just because some *aḥādīth* were forged, and the scholars refined the "degrees of authenticity" as above, it is folly to jump to the conclusion that all of the Ḥadīth should be rejected; for such a logic forces us to reject the Qur'ān as well since the Qur'ān's contents and order are well known by the same "method"—one may say—as the *mutawātir* Ḥadīth. This would be like denying the existence of your great-grandmother whom you never saw, because your jealous aunt spread some false rumours, a distinction that you would certainly take into account.

Now let us look at the term ḥadīth a little more closely. First we'll define the term ḥadīth in a global fashion and then look at the different ways people used the word ḥadīth. If we define ḥadīth as meaning the report of *every* speech or action of the Prophet, we find that we have the following different kinds of "ḥadīth," or different bands of the ḥadīth spectrum, some of which we don't even call ḥadīth:

**1. Where the Prophet was inspired (in speech) completely—that is, both the idea and the very words themselves were inspired to the Prophet.** Here is one of those situations where the Prophet functioned as God's mouthpiece. This subset of the Ḥadīth consists of two parts. One part God chose to incorporate into the Divine Scripture of Muslims. This is called the Qur'ān. However, God has a lot of things to say to a prophet, and not all of it is public information for us to know about. Therefore not all of God's communications and speech to the Prophet is included in the Qur'ān or is part of it. There are Divine communications and statements which are not Qur'ān. The Prophet shared some (not all) of these conversations and stories with his companions, some of which are prefaced by the words, "God has said," and these are popularly known as *aḥādīth qudsiyyah.* (This is a subset of the Ḥadīth in which Allāh speaks in the first person. If one were to be purely logical about this, and because Muslims generally define the Qur'ān as what was revealed to the Prophet, one might infer that this ought to be part of the Qur'ān, but it is not—again by authority of God via the authority of the Ḥadīth. So don't try to be so logical; we pointed out the danger of thinking that allspice is all the spices, or that heartburn is a heart ailment. Language isn't always so logical.)

The Qur'ān is defined as the Qur'ān not *just* because it is God's speech, but because it is His revealed *composition.* A lot of verses in the Qur'ān are quotations of human beings, like what the Prophets and their enemies said in certain situations in the past, what the good believers say when they pray to God, and what the unbelievers say in this life and will say in the next, including their screaming in Hell. It's hard to think of the Qur'ānic verses like 79:24 where Pharaoh responds to Moses by saying "I am your exalted god" as "God's speech" in the strict sense of God endorsing the truth of such a statement. The Prophet was very concerned about his followers being able to distinguish between the Qur'ān and what was not Qur'ān, and, according to some reports, in the beginning of his mission he forbade his companions from writing anything down other than the Qur'ān until it became so familiar that he rescinded this prohibition. In this capacity the Prophet was acting in the role of Messenger of God with maximum purity. No input of his own is present.

The Qur'ān is always "God speaking about things," but because the Prophet was God's mouthpiece, it is semantically correct to also call the Qur'ān part of the Prophet's speech (Ḥadīth) in the same sense as we speak of the *ḥadīth qudsiyyah.* We know of the Qur'ān only because the Prophet taught it to us, and informed us about it. To use the language of the science of the Hadīth, our chain of authority regarding the Qur'ān goes only through the

Prophet. We know that in common usage the terms Qur'ān and Ḥadīth are used to refer to different entities. But we are deliberately stating the point this way because if you understand this point you will understand why it is illogical and impossible to accept the Qur'ān and reject the Ḥadīth, as some people have done. If you accept the Qur'ān you have implicitly accepted the Ḥadīth, whether you admit it or not. This would be like saying "I'll accept purple but I absolutely reject all the colors of the rainbow," without realizing that "all the colors of the rainbow" includes purple and therefore fall into a contradiction. If you can imagine a situation where the only way you can possibly know about the color purple is through the rainbow, then you've grasped the error in logic that those who accept the Qur'ān and not the Ḥadīth have committed.[132]

**2. Where the Prophet was completely inspired with the action and the complete choreography, or movement, of the action.** Here is where the Divine revelation consisted not primarily of speech, but of a command to action. Again this category can be divided into two components. One is *tashrī`iyyah*, which implies the believers are to follow the Prophet's action. Examples of this are the form and movements of the ritual prayer (*ṣalāh*), the ablutions to be performed in preparation for it, and the rituals of pilgrimage (*`umrah* and *ḥajj*). In this capacity the Prophet was also

---

[132] Those who reject the Ḥadīth base their argument on the fact that some *aḥādīth* were false, and some were fabricated for political purposes. Such an argument does not, and cannot, deny the Ḥadīth's reality. If anything, it emphasizes the importance of the Ḥadīth. What we have tried to show in this section is that since the Qur'ān was known only through the Prophet, insofar as its contents and what was excluded, it is therefore logically an organic part of the Ḥadīth in the etymological sense of the term "ḥadīth." We would not know of the Qur'ān without the existence of the Prophet, and thus of the Ḥadīth. The Prophet (and thus "the Ḥadīth") informed his companions what was Qur'ān and what was not Qur'ān. The "boundary" of the Qur'ān is therefore given by the Ḥadīth. To reject the Ḥadīth *in toto* therefore must mean that we reject the Qur'ān if we are to be logically consistent. Another point worth remembering is that the Ḥadīth, because it was collected over a few decades after the death of the Prophet, does not have the same degree of authenticity as the Qur'ān. Therefore, it is permitted to reject a particular ḥadīth, or some ḥadīth, without rejecting the Ḥadīth in toto. At the other end of the spectrum, there is a body of ḥadīth which is just as authentic as the Qur'ān, and which cannot be summarily denied.

acting in the role of Messenger of God with maximum purity. Although this is not considered Qur'ān, it has an equivalent standing to it insofar as it is revelation of movement. Some of this category (but not all) is obligatory upon Muslims to follow. It should be clear that not all of the Divine inspirations, teachings and instructions given to the believers through the Prophet *can* be contained in the Qur'ān, for the Qur'ān is only speech. The Qur'ān is defined in the narrow sense as only those Divine inspirations where the wording and sounds were inspired to the Prophet (with some variations in pronunciation permitted due to regional differences in Arabia at the time). The revelation on how to pray the ritual prayer of *ṣalāh*, although commanded in the Qur'ān, could not possibly have been demonstrated by speech alone. God mandated the archangel Jibril, through whom on several occasions the Qur'ān was revealed to the Prophet, to personally instruct the Prophet on the choreography of *ṣalāh*, that is, on how to perform the movements of ritual ablution (*wuḍū'*) and prayer (*ṣalāh*). It is analogous to teaching someone how to dance. It is probably impossible to teach someone how to dance without demonstrating it in action and having the student follow the movements; style and rhythm of movement can only be perceived by eye and not by ear. Accepting that God commands us to perform *ṣalāh*, do you expect Allāh to say in the Qur'ān, "Stand up, recite the *fātihah,* then follow it by one or more verses of your choice," etc.? Not only would it take us forever to learn the prayer, but we would have a hundred different *tafsīrs* on how to perform it! It is much easier just to show you. Now perhaps some people think that God has only required us to think about Him in a certain way; and that our worship lies just in ideas and beliefs, and not in actions. Thought, speech and physical movement are all part of the totality of human action. And if you accept the Qur'ān as true, you will find that Allāh does command us in the Qur'ān to perform certain actions that span the spectrum of thought, speech and physical movement, among them *ṣalāh*, *`umrah* and *ḥajj*.[133] But how are we sup-

---

133 In many verses the Qur'ān commands, "And establish ṣalāh and give the zakāh"

posed to perform these? The Prophet was taught by Allāh the *choreography* of Islamic rituals, via the archangel Jibril, and on how to make the movements.[134] The Prophet in turn instructed his companions on how to perform the Divinely mandated action (like *ṣalāh* and *ḥajj*), just as he instructed his companions on a Divine revelation of speech (the Qur'ān).[135] This category of the Prophet's

---

(2:110 is just one of many). The command for ḥajj and `umrah are given in "And fulfill the ḥajj and `umrah for the sake of Allāh" (2:196); and also in 3:96 which reads, "And upon people is the obligation to make pilgrimage to the House—for whomever is able to make it."

[134] The Qur'ān was taught to the Prophet in one of two ways. One was when the archangel Gabriel (*Jibril* in Arabic) visited the Prophet and gave him the revelation. The other way was when the revelation descended directly upon him. When this happened, he would hear something like a pealing sound, perhaps like a siren, which was his cue that the revelation was about to descend upon him. He would then retire and the Qur'ānic revelation would be imprinted in his mind. This method was more difficult on the Prophet, for the enormous weight of the Divine Word desecending made him break into a sweat, even on cold days.

The five-times-daily ritual prayer was given to the Prophet on the night of *mi'rāj* (ascension). On this night, as the Prophet ascended the higher regions of heaven, he witnessed angels standing, bowing and prostrating and seated before God, glorifying and supplicating Him. The Prophet loved what he saw, and wished to be able to worship God in a similar fashion, and his wish was granted by incorporating the movements of these angels into the choreography of the Islamic prayer.

[135] Many Muslims do not realize that the formulas and prescriptions of Islamic rituals encapsulate many Qur'ānic injunctions. Take *ṣalāh*, for example. When a Muslim performs ṣalāh he is fulfilling many Qur'ānic commands, among which are the following:

> And establish prayer (*aqīmu-ṣṣalāta*) and give the *zakāh* payment (*ātu-zzakāta*) and bow with those who bow down (literally: and do *ruku`* with those who do *ruku`*) (2:43).
>
> O you who have believed! Bow down and prostrate and worship your Lord and do good so that you may succeed (literally do *ruku`* and *sujud*) (22:77).
>
> And glorify the praises of your Lord (*wa sabbiḥ bi-ḥamdi rabbika*) before the rising of the sun and before its setting; and glorify Him at night and at the end of prostration (*wa min al-layli fa-sabbiḥ-hu wa adbāra-ssujūd*) (50:39–40).
>
> . . .O you who have believed! Do *ṣalāh* upon him (the Prophet) and greet him with surrender (33:56).

How do you suppose we are to fulfill these Qur'ānic commands to do *ruku`* and *sujud*, to glorify and praise Allāh before sunrise and sunset, and at the end of the *sujud*; and

teaching is part (but not all) of the ensemble called "the precedent-setting action of the Prophet which has legal import," or in Arabic, *sunnah tashrī`iyyah.* Again, and just as we saw with the category of speech, not all action that was completely inspired to the Prophet has legal import to his followers; some action inspired in the Prophet was specifically for him to do. Examples of this are like when he threw a handful of dust at the unbelievers during the battle of Badr. God describes this event as, "And you did not throw when you threw, but it was Allāh Who threw" (8:16). This is an example of a specific action totally inspired in the Prophet; when he did this he was a mere instrument for the Divine Will into which his own will was completely effaced and submerged. But this is not an example of a *sunnah tashrī`iyyah* in the sense that we all have to go out and throw dust upon our unbelieving colleagues at work. Neither, for that matter, did the Prophet keep throwing dust on every unbeliever he met thereafter. However, the state of being completely inspired to action by the Divine Will as a result of being surrendered to it is a goal that every believer ideally seeks. (This is part of the objective of the spiritual path, identified in Islamic practice with *taṣawwuf*, and is the inner experiential meaning of the term *Muslim*—one who submits, or surrenders.)

**3. Where the Prophet was inspired with the idea, but was left to phrase the idea in his own words.** In this category come the anecdotes and verbal teachings of the Prophet to his followers. The Prophet was given to see incidents from the lives of previous peoples, and sights of heaven and hell, and he described

---

how are we to do *ṣalāh* upon the Prophet? If we were to string together all the Qur'ānic commands to perform *ṣalāh*, remembrance, *ruku`* and *sujud*, they come to quite a number, and it is actually amazing to see that many of these commands "to perform" are fulfilled by performing the five-times-daily *salahs* at their prescribed times. Our *ruku`* and *sujud*, our glorifying Allāh during *ruku`* and *sujud*, and our invoking *ṣalāh* upon Muḥammad during the *julus*, are all fulfilments of the above Divine commands. Many such ritual commandments in the Qur'ān are fulfilled by our performance of the ritual acts in accordance with the Prophet's practice and teaching, for he was inspired not only with the Qur'ān, but also with actions comprising thought, speech and movement.

these to his followers. Here the Prophet also put in his own words his understanding of how the faith was to be practiced, and taught his followers accordingly. Since the Prophet *spoke* this, we can apply some of our technical knowledge to look like experts and call this *sunnah qawliyyah*, the speech of the Prophet.

**4. Where the Prophet was inspired with the idea of the action but was left to do it his own way.** An example of this was during the interval of time before the Qur'ān came down with the new direction for prayer, that of the Ka`bah in Mecca (2:142–145). Although the form of prayer had been established and given to the Prophet, the direction of prayer had not been until this verse was revealed. During this period the Prophet chose to pray in the direction of Jerusalem.

**5. Where the Prophet was not inspired by God, but acted on his own human impulse.** These are his actions and speech conducted as an ordinary human. One example is given by the ḥadīth already quoted earlier of when the Prophet passed by a group of people pollinating their palm trees. Such *aḥādīth* which relate to questions of daily life, and which emanated from the Prophet in the form of opinion, are neither obligatory nor binding.

## ii. The Sunnah

The literal meaning of the word *sunnah* is precedent, or normative practice. Most Muslims understand the expression "*sunnah* of the Prophet" to mean "the Prophet's normative and customary practice which Muslims ought to follow." The question now becomes, what does "ought to follow" include or exclude? Since the words ḥadīth and *sunnah* are not absolutely identical, although in fact many use the terms interchangeably because there is a large overlap in meaning, we'll follow the same procedure in analyzing the term *sunnah* as we did above for the term ḥadīth.

The scholars of Ḥadīth have defined a ḥadīth of the Prophet as a report about something the Prophet said or did; it is therefore a story, or a report, about an action of the Prophet. To simplify matters, they have defined any action of the Prophet as a *sunnah*, even if the Prophet did it only once and therefore may not have any precedent value. This is wise because the decision as to what might be a source of guidance belongs to jurists, not to ḥadīth scholars (it is a jurisprudential, *fiqh*, decision, not a ḥadīth decision). Thus to them a ḥadīth is defined as a report of a *sunnah*. Loosely speaking, then, the Ḥadīth as a whole is the ensemble of stories that *inform* you about the Sunnah as a whole. The Ḥadīth scholars did not dismiss any action of the Prophet from his *sunnah*. Because of this all-inclusive definition of the term *sunnah*, the jurists now enter the picture and wisely inform us that some *sunnah* we must follow, some *sunnah* we are forbidden from following, some *sunnah* is recommended and some *sunnah* is purely neutral. So we learn that the word *sunnah* is used by Muslims, Muslim jurists and scholars in several different senses, and unless you are aware of them you can easily get confused. We now list and demonstrate these different senses and ways in which the word *sunnah* has been used.

**1. The normative practice or precedent of the Prophet Muḥammad which has to be followed.** This sense is indicated by the Prophet's advising his followers: "I have left behind for you that with which, if you hold fast to it, you will not go astray: The Book of Allāh and my *Sunnah*."[136] This is the sense in which most Muslims understand the term, especially in regard to following the Prophet's example in his practice of the religion. Basically this means the Prophet is telling us "Do as I do when it comes to these matters." But this also includes a second notion, which follows.

**2. As a defining limit of the extent to which one should perform the rituals.** This sense of *sunnah* means "don't try to be holier than the Prophet." This is indicated by the story of the three

---

[136] Imam Ahmad Ibn Ḥanbal, *Al-Musnad* (Cairo 1930), vol. II, p.26.

men who came to the Prophet's wives asking about how he performed his rituals. They thought the extent of the Prophet's worship was insufficient for them, and therefore one swore he would stay up in prayer all night, the other swore to fast every day of his life, and the third swore to avoid marriage. The Prophet overheard this, was displeased by it, and responded by saying: "Now by Allāh! Indeed I am the most fearful of Allāh and pious of you all; but I fast and I break my fast, I perform [voluntary] prayer [at night] and I also sleep, and I marry women. So whoever desires differently from my *sunnah* [practice, norm], he is not of me."[137] (In other words, if you think you can be holier than the Prophet, forget it! The Prophet is telling us here not to try to do—in the religious sense of course—what *he* wouldn't even dream of doing.) From this ḥadīth we derive an understanding of the Prophet's usage of the term *sunnah,* referring not only to his ritual acts of worship, but to an idea of the limit, or extent, of worship. Hence, it is also a part of the *Sunnah* of Muḥammad to engage in activity that may not be considered religious per se (in this context sleeping, eating and having relations with women), but considered by Muḥammad to be an act of worship because, among other reasons, it provides a sense of contrast, thus a context, that gives our acts of worship their spiritual value. (In cooking, some novices think that because adding a little salt or curry powder into the pot makes the dish taste better, they keep adding more and more salt or curry powder, believing that the dish will keep on getting better and better until it gets perfect. What the Prophet is saying here is if you do this in your religious life, your religion gets overdone, oversalted and overspiced, and may have to be thrown away.)

**3. The nonobligatory (*nāfilah*) ritual actions of the Prophet which are not obligatory to be followed, but are highly recommended.** For example, we ask someone if he has

---

[137]Imam An-Nawawī, *Riyaḍ al-Ṣāliḥīn* (Beirut, 1984), pp. 94–95. The Prophet used the expression "of, or from, me" often to mean "of my followers." In their desire to be perfected believers, many felt that they had to live a life that avoided much of the worldly. The Prophet's theme was that the perfected believer is one who is involved in life, not one who avoids it.

performed the *farḍ* (obligatory) or the *sunnah* of the *maghrib* prayer. *Sunnah* in this context is a short-hand notation for "the Prophet's *nāfilah* (nonobligatory) action of ritual worship," and does not at all mean that the *farḍ* is not part of the Prophet's *sunnah* (normative practice); it most certainly is. Muslims also commonly use this sense, often without realizing that it is quite different from sense 1 above. (The sense of *sunnah* here is the Prophet advising us, "Do what I'm doing here, if and when you feel like it.") If the Prophet regularly performed this kind of *sunnah*, it is called a *sunnah mu'akkadah* (a regular, or an always-repeated, *sunnah*); otherwise it is called a *sunnah ghayr mu'akkadah* (a not-always-repeated *sunnah*). An example of a *sunnah mu'akkadah* is the two *sunnah rak'ats* that the Prophet performed before the *farḍ* of the dawn (*fajr*) prayer; an example of a *sunnah ghayr mu'akkadah* is the four *rak'ats* before the afternoon (*`aṣr*) prayer.

**4. An action or statement of the Prophet Muḥammad that Muslims are forbidden to follow.** For example, the Prophet had as many as nine wives simultaneously, but Muslim men are forbidden from having more than four. This is an example of a *sunnah* which must not be followed. (Here the Prophet is saying "Don't do what I'm doing, or have done, here.)

**5. An act of the Prophet that is neutral whether followed or not.** One example is the cultural and technological contexts of the time; the Prophet wore Arab dress, travelled by camel and loved to eat *tharīd* (an Arab dish made of bread soaked typically in lamb soup, sometimes cooked in yoghurt). This does not mean that we must wear Arab dress, travel by camel and enjoy eating *tharīd.* Another example is in our choice of career or profession. Among the roles of the Prophet were that of military commander and judge; but this does not mean that we are obliged to become military commanders or judges in order to fulfill our religious obligation. These are examples of *sunnah* which are not normative for the believers to follow.

Because of these differences, the jurists labelled the *sunnah* as follows:

*1. Sunnah tashrī`iyyah,* i.e., the juridical *sunnah* (that which has juridical or normative value). It must be obeyed and followed. For example, the Prophet's mode of performing the ritual prayer is a *sunnah tashrī`iyyah* in the sense that Muslims are obliged to follow the Prophet in the way they perform their prayers.

*2. Sunnah ghayr tashrī`iyyah,* i.e., the nonjuridical *sunnah* (that which has no legal or normative value). This is what need not be followed or obeyed, or was an exclusive right of the Prophet and forbidden to others, and therefore it must be "disobeyed." The *sunnah* of being a military commander or a judge is a *sunnah* ghayr *tashrī`iyyah* in that a Muslim is not obliged to become a military commander or a judge to perfect his religion.

In addition, the scholars also categorized the *sunnah* according to the nature of the report, or ḥadīth, as follows:

*1. As-sunnah al-fi`liyyah*, i.e., the "*actions* of the Prophet."

*2. As-sunnah al-qawliyyah*, i.e., the "*speech* of the Prophet."

*3. As-sunnah at-taqririyyah*, i.e., the "*silence* (or tacit approval) of the Prophet." This was when an event occurred in the presence of the Prophet, or something was said in his presence, and he remained silent, or smiled, implying his tacit approval. This follows and implies the Divine endorsement (*taqrīr*); if something happened during the Prophet's time and no revelation came down to correct or change it, then that action is considered acceptable to God.

So if your Mormon friend suggests you marry five of his cousins because you would be adhering to a *sunnah* of the Prophet, or become a judge because that too was a *sunnah*, you can answer, "But the *shar`i* ruling is disobedience to the first *sunnah* (i.e., it is a *sunnah* that Muslims are forbidden to follow), and the second is not a *sunnah tashrī`iyyah* (i.e., a *sunnah* that has no binding or normative value)," and you will have displayed a subtle level of Islamic scholarship.

All these categorizations are really common-sense classifications. Even you could have come up with these classifications if you weren't so busy with other real-life matters and had the time to stare at, and think about, the Ḥadīth and *Sunnah* long enough.

The upshot of this discussion on the terms ḥadīth and *sunnah* is that you have to be careful when you hear or read these terms. You will often find these terms used in all their different senses interchangeably, and usually, as we said, that's acceptable. But sometimes it can cause peculiar conclusions. You must also recognize that to accept the Qur'ān and not the Ḥadīth creates a fundamental logical contradiction. Muḥammad became a Prophet because of Divine fiat. The demarcation lines between those moments when Muḥammad spoke or acted purely as a Prophet and when he spoke or acted purely as a normal human being with no Divine input at all is not always a sudden switch-off.

The jurists were aware of the import of the distinctions made above and they separated the roles of the Prophet into prophet (and thereby religious teacher, or Imam), head of state, military leader, chief judge, and an individual influenced by cultural norms and personal preference. In each category there was his *sunnah* (practice and precedent), and each was to be understood and placed in its context vis-à-vis its instructional value to succeeding generations of Muslims. As a Prophet, and therefore a spiritual teacher and guide, he was to be followed. But his actions as military leader, his strategies and tactics—even when Divinely inspired—constitute *sunnah* that can be superseded by later knowledge. Not all of the Prophet's actions are precedents binding on succeeding generations of Muslims. This is easy to see. But what is not so easy to see are the precedents he established as head of state and as judge. Because these areas blended values from his role as Prophet, the interplay between the roles and the social and cultural contexts in which his judgments were made need to be delineated and understood. Just as some of the Prophet's practices and decisions as a military general are now superseded by advanced military technology, some of the Prophet's decisions as a judge or head of state have become analogously superseded. This takes us into the subject of the derivation and evolution of laws. When we try to come up with modern notions of an Islamic state or Islamic economics, it takes a subtle intellect to be able to recognize where the domains of supersession have occurred.

What is perhaps more important to us at this stage is that we learn how to glean and extract from the Prophet's behavior his intention, attitudes and demeanor in dealing with situations arising from domestic, family and work-place challenges. Therefore, as an example, the fact that he brushed his teeth with a *siwāk,* a twig whose bark is partially removed to reveal a brush-like portion, does not necessarily mean that we must do precisely likewise. We can extract his intention in doing so, namely to keep his breath fresh and teeth and gums healthy. During the Prophet's time there were no commercially available toothbrushes, anti-tartar plaque-removing toothpaste and mouthwash. We can therefore render an opinion that the Prophet's intent, fulfilled by using a *siwāk,* can be fulfilled now by brushing our teeth with a toothbrush and toothpaste.

This kind of thinking was applied by the jurists when they extracted laws and juridical intent from Qur'ānic verses and rulings.

## APPENDIX II

# CATEGORIZATION OF HUMAN ACTIONS

As Islām spread, and non-Arabs who were new to Islām needed to learn the how-tos of their faith, they needed to know how to put their actions into a value system. The jurists filled this need by their recognition that all human actions (including what are usually referred to in the West as secular actions) are embraced by the *Sharī'ah*, and, for the purposes of assessment and judgment, classified *all* of human action into the following categories:

1. *Farḍ*[138]*:* compulsory and required to do; a sin if not done. An example is the five-times-daily prayer.
2. *Mustaḥab:* preferred or liked; no sin if not done, but rewarded for being done.[139] An example is praying nonobligatory prayers in the middle of the night.
3. *Mubāh:* permitted; no value is given to this class of actions. An example is drinking tea in the morning.
4. *Makrūh:* disliked, but no sin attached to committing it. An example is smoking cigarettes.
5. *Ḥarām:* forbidden. It is a sin to commit this action. An example is committing murder.

---

[138] This is divided into *farḍ `ayn*, an individual obligation which every Muslim is obliged to do and no one can do on his behalf, like the five-times daily prayer, and *farḍ kifāyah*, which is an obligation upon the whole Muslim community, but which can be fulfilled by a representative number, for example the funeral prayer (*salāt ul-janazah*) upon the corpse of a deceased Muslim.

[139] Under the *mustaḥab* class is a special subset of noncompulsory actions that were done by the Prophet, and called *sunnah*, i.e. the precedent or practice of the Prophet. The term *sunnah* means precedent, and is often used to mean *all* of the Prophet's practices, obligatory and nonobligatory, as forming the sum-total of practical guidelines for Muslims to follow. It is important to note that the use of the term *sunnah* in this context of classification of acts is very specific; it refers only to the noncompulsory acts of the Prophet that are deemed highly meritorious to emulate. (See Appendix I on the terms Ḥadīth and Sunnah for more analysis of this term.)

Abiding by these classifications is conforming to justice and good; thus avoiding forbidden actions is good behavior. And because the above five categories cover all of human actions, this underlines the comprehensive definition of the *Sharī'ah* as a body of law that includes all of human behavior, religious as well as worldly.

For Muslims, this formula is neat and nice, easy to understand, and enables us to put our actions into a value system. It should be pointed out, though, that the circumstances of an act do determine into which category it belongs. For example, taking a human life is generally forbidden (*ḥarām*), but when done in self-defense it becomes permitted (*ja'iz*, a term meaning permitted).

This is not the only way actions have been classified, although the above classification is one that describes each band of the spectrum of human actions. For example, the simple classification of all acts into the permissible and the impermissible gives us two classes: all actions that are lawful (*ḥalāl*), and those forbidden (*ḥarām*).

You will also come across the terms *wājib* (mandatory), *mandūb* (recommended), and *murakhkhaṣ* (licensed), this last term referring to the generally allowed, or *ḥalāl*). The term *wājib* (mandatory) has not been used with precisely the same connotation within different schools. The Ḥanafi *madhhab* differentiates between *wājib* which is a *farḍ* and *wājib* which is not; to them the *farḍ* is an obligation whose obligatory nature is known unambiguously and with certainty from the texts of the Qur'ān and Ḥadīth, and therefore its omission is a sin; whereas a plain or "mere" *wājib* is an action that is mandatory, but because it is known with a lesser degree of certainty from the Qur'ān and Ḥadīth, no sin is attached to not doing it. For example, the prayers of `Id are considered a *wājib* in the Ḥanafi *madhhab*, but a *sunnah* in the Shāfi`i *madhhab*. Another example of a *wājib* in the Ḥanafi school, but not in the Shāfi`i, is prostrating (*sajdah*) when one recites those verses in the Qur'ān where a prostration is indicated. The Shāfi`is, however, do not make this distinction; to them a *wājib* is a *farḍ*.

## APPENDIX III

# A LITTLE HISTORY: THE CLOSING AND OPENING OF THE GATES OF IJTIHĀD

During the first few centuries after the Prophet's death, the Muslim *ummah* (the Muslim body politic) was challenged by many potentially devastating conflicts. The schism regarding rulership after the Caliphate of Sayyiduna `Alī led to the split between the Sunnis and the Shi`is and other splinter groups like the Khārijites. As each developed their own set of political beliefs, another rationalistic group known as the Mu`tazilah sprouted who espoused doctrines that were in many instances rather logical and reasonable. The problem was not in the reasonableness of the various views of these groups but more in the intolerant and violent mode of expressing these ideas by their exponents. The Khārijis unbelievably found it joyful to have assassinated the likes of Imam `Alī and Imam An-Nasā'ī, actions that no right-minded Muslim would condone. They accused anyone who disagreed with their views to be a *kāfir* (unbeliever).

All this may sound rather familiar to many of us who attend Muslim conventions and gatherings and readily find some who are quick to accuse others of being *kāfirs* because they subscribe to a different opinion than they do on a particular matter.

What contributed to the success of Sunnism over all the other groups was that it was not exclusive; it allowed for differences of opinion. Between the third and the fifth century of the Hijrah (and we can point to Imam al-Ghazali as perhaps marking the pinnacle of this effort), the *ijtihād* of Sunni thought managed to develop the science of *uṣūl al-fiqh* to such a well worked-out system that it attracted the majority of the scholars; moreover Sunnism accepted the differences of opinion among the *madhāhib* as being equally legitimate. Even the tension that existed between the ulamā and the

Sufis was greatly attenuated by the writings of intellects like Imam al-Ghazali. This effort, together with the collection of what became accepted as canonical (*saḥīḥ*) *aḥādīth* aiding the development of the jurisprudential sciences, reduced the polarizations within the Islamic *ummah*, and the result was that the polarization created by these various movements diminished. In the long run, the best ideas win. And what was embodied in *uṣūl al-fiqh* turned out to be the most workable ideas. The four schools of Sunni thought survived the test, and the tools (including the language) of *uṣūl al-fiqh* became the norm of the majority of Muslims, Sunni as well as Shi`i, so much that the difference today between Shi`i law and Sunni law in the majority of issues is no greater than the difference among any one of the Sunni schools and another.

The role of an Imam in the Shi`i belief, as was the role of the Prophet and that of the first four "Orthodox"[140] Caliphs in Sunni belief, embraced what we in the United States would today call the powers of the chief executive, the supreme court judge, and spiritual master or guide. When Mu'āwiya fought Imam `Alī and successfully established the Umayyad dynasty in Damascus, he could seize only political power, but not the hearts and minds of the population. One neither becomes a scholar nor a spiritual teacher by force or wishful thinking. The charismatic spiritual guides were to be found in the leaders of those who later became known as Sufis, while the role of "supreme court judge" evolved upon those who contributed to the growth and development of *uṣūl al-fiqh*. Sufi masters and *fuqahā'* often functioned as counterpoises to the political influence of the Caliphs.

By the time Baghdad fell to the Mongols in the 13th century AD, the schools of law had already developed and matured as legally operative systems. Some scholars believe that as a reaction to the violent fall of Baghdad and the destruction of its libraries, the Sunni jurists evolved the by no means unanimous opinion on

---

140 This is the usual translation of the Arabic expression *al-khulafa' ar-Rashīdun*, meaning "rightly guided." It implies that those who usurped political power after Imam `Alī were not considered by the Muslim population to be of the highest spiritual caliber.

"closing the gate of *ijtihād*" for fear of persecution, further agreeing that the four Sunni schools were sufficient. Things then got somewhat petrified and ossified, because if you don't advance you regress. Gradually rigidity enveloped all phases of life, resulting in the prevalence of blind imitation (blind *taqlīd*) and the cessation of interpretation in jurisprudence, in an abundance of anomalies based upon ignorance and in the prevalence of superstitions. Ignorant imitators (*muqallids*) would cling to trivial matters wholly unrelated to jurisprudence. For example, they discussed irrelevant issues, such as "how many angels can stand on the head of a pin," or whether it was permissible to ride a camel which had drunk wine because of possible contact with the forbidden substance through the sweat of the camel, or whether melted butter into which a mouse had fallen and drowned could be used as fuel for lamps because the air would thus be polluted by the impurity of the flesh of a dead animal.

In response to this, and particularly with the dawn of the 19th century, reform movements sprang up everywhere and the school of *as-Salaf as-Salih* emerged, initiated by Sayyid Jamal ad-Din al-Afghani (1839–1897AD) and carried on after his death by his pupil, the Imam Shaykh Muḥammad `Abduh (1849–1905AD), Mufti of Egypt. This *Salafiyyah* school advocated a return to the Qur'ān and the *Sunnah* while combating rigidity, superstition and novelties incompatible with religion. They also stood for the "unification" of the various Islamic schools, to a large extent motivated by the desire to rid the Islamic world of the then burdensome yoke of colonialism of the 18th to the 20th centuries. This is partly what is intended by the oft-heard cry of "no *madhhāb* in Islām." It is not so much an argument, as that fanaticism against another *madhhāb*, or another group of Muslims, is out of order. They believed that the *Sharī'ah* is compatible with modern civilization, and issued many *fatwas* legitimizing transactions necessitated by the requirements of modern commerce. Their motto was, "in the event of a conflict between reason and authority (i.e., precedents), reason should be given the upper hand." This is in line with the statement by Ibn Taymiyah: "substantiated narratives in the *Sharī'ah* are always in conformity with the dictates of reason."[141]

Another reform movement was the *Wahhābi* movement, initiated by Shaykh Muḥammad b. `Abd al-Wahhāb (1115–1206 AH/1703–1792 AD), who was born in Najd, the central region of Saudi Arabia. As a rejuvenator of the Hanbali school he was second only to Ibn Taymiyah and Ibn al-Qayyim. He advocated a return to the religious spirit of the forefathers who, for the basic principles of their religion referred to the Qur'ān and the authentic *Sunnah* of the Prophet, and who fought against the blind imitation that "had killed among the Islamic people serious thought and the spirit of independence and had extinguished the flame of activity." He was a bitter antagonist of those who held to the excuse "we found our fathers so doing" without subjecting such a heritage to the dictates of reason. Commentaries, texts, opinions and whims containing any of these elements were repudiated.

The *Salafiyyah* school is similar to the *Wahhābi* school in that both advocated a return to the origins of the *Sharī'ah* based upon the Qur'ān and the genuine *sunnah.* Moreover they advocated the deduction of rules from these original sources and emancipation from the static views of imitator-jurists. But although these currents swept away superstitious practices, they could not in fact eliminate the sound bases of the *madhāhib.* As we have seen above, the reason why the *madhāhib* arose in the first place was based on *legitimate* differences of opinion.

We spoke earlier about *taqlīd* (blind imitation) and the need to be an intelligent imitator (a *muttabi`*). In simple words, these reform movements sought to throw out the dirty bathwater that had been (in their opinion) mistakenly kept all these centuries with the all-important baby. The danger today is that some contemporary followers who do not recognize the difference between the baby and the bathwater are close to throwing out the baby as well.

---

[141] Muḥammad `Abduh, Al-Islām wan-Nasraniyyah ma`al-`Ilm wal-Madaniyyah (Cairo, 1350 AH), 56.

These movements coincided with major shifts in the political developments of the times, and to some extent the interaction with European powers and the latter's enaction of various commercial and criminal codes. In response to felt need, the legislative movement in nations with major Muslim populations resulted in focussed attempts officially to codify and narrow the differences regarding the sources and body of jurisprudence. Towards this objective, and motivated by the contemporary needs of commerce and social evolution, Turkey, the seat of the Ottoman Empire and Caliphate, in 1876 issued *Majallat al-Aḥkām al-`Adliyah* (The Corpus of Juridical Rules). The Majallah did not go into questions of religious observances or penal matters; its scope was restricted to the rules of law in civil transactions.

On the Indian subcontinent, and up until the partition into India and Pakistan, the legislative situation was dictated by the British policy of letting the people of India conduct their lives according to their own customs and laws. In 1772, the British authorities enacted a law which provided that the *Sharī'ah* should be applicable to all cases relating to inheritance, marriage and other sectarian problems peculiar to Muslims. Those administering justice in cases involving Muslims therefore had to have recourse to the Islamic *Sharī'ah* and to Arabic books on jurisprudence. *Al-Hidāyah* was the most popular reference for the Ḥanafi school. Also well known were the collections of Indian *fatwas*, *al-`Ālamgiriyah*[142] and *as-Sirājiyah*.[143] *Sharā'i` al-Islām* was the major ref-

142 This collection was the result of Sultan Aurangzeb's interest, in the 17th century, in the collection of *fatwas*. He formed a committee of India's leading jurists with Shaykh Nizam as president to prepare a comprehensive legal reference work containing the books titled *Ẓāhir ar-Riwāyah* (*al-Mabṣut, al-Jāmi` al-Kabir, al-Jāmi` aṣ-Ṣaghir*, etc.), which had been approved by the most distinguished jurists, and the rare problems accepted by the men of learning. This they did in the book known as *al-Fatāwā al-`Ālamgiriyah* after the title of the sultan (`Ālamgir). It is a comprehensive work in six large volumes arranged on the model of *al-Hidāyah* by al-Marghināni, which discusses religious observances as well as transactions like the rest of the Islamic juridical books. It is one of the major references in Ḥanafi jurisprudence.

143 Written by Siraj Muḥammad as-Sajawandi, a Muslim jurist of the sixth century AH. This book is known for treating the subject of religious duties (*farā'id*) and inheritance (*mawarith*).

erence work in the Ja`fari *madhhab* (the major *madhhab* associated with the *Shi`ah*). In applying the rules of the *Sharī'ah*, the judges did not always stay within the confines of the doctrines and *fatwas* of the jurists, but broadened their interpretation on occasion due to the influence of their English legal training and the changing needs of modern society. The birth of Pakistan added impetus to the desire to formulate a society governed by the *Sharī'ah*.

With the above movements, a growing momentum of opinion sprouted into the 20th century, the consensus of which was that the doors of *ijtihād* needed to be, and had become, clearly and widely opened. In any time of history, the development of law has always been driven by felt need, but the areas of development, and of felt need, were—in the case of the *Sharī'ah*—never in the areas of the essential Islamic creed or practice, but predominantly in the area of worldly affairs, like marriage and divorce laws, inheritance and business transactions.

Nevertheless, the philosophy of the *Sharī'ah*, as developed by the jurists over the first few centuries of Islām, served the Muslims well in dealing with whatever issues arose. This philosophy needed less in the way of change or modification than it needed in the way of understanding and application. The opening of the door of *ijtihād* in the 19th century meant more in the way of purification, of cleaning off the anomalies based upon ignorance and superstitions, and injecting a more widespread education among the Muslim population, and of raising their mean average level of common religious knowledge. The results of the *Salafiyyah* and *Wahhābi* movements ought only be the throwing away of the dirty bathwater, and never the baby. It's easy, though not very personally enjoyable, to keep the dirty bathwater with the baby (and some Muslims practice their faith that way), and equally easy to throw the baby away with the bathwater (these are those "Muslims" who have whittled away their religion altogether). But to throw out six centuries of bathwater and keep the baby—which is the preferred position of the majority of contemporary Muslims—is the challenge.

Over the last century, laws in Islamic lands have blended what was deemed most equitable from whatever schools of law, applying the principle of *takhayyur*[144], especially in the areas of personal law (marriages and divorce) and inheritances, to eliminate abuses that had crept into practice. This selecting from different schools to achieve some sense of equity was called *talfiq* (literally, "patched up, pieced together"). One example is given by *the Syrian Law of Personal Status* of 1953, which enjoined husbands not to take additional wives unless they were financially capable of duly supporting them, and empowered the *qādī* to withhold permission for a man who is already married to marry a second wife, where it is established that he is not in a position to maintain them both.

Another example is given by the Egyptian *Law of Waqf* of 1946. Widespread dissatisfaction with the system of *waqf* settlement had made reforms in the traditional law highly desirable. Moralists criticized the evils of a system which allowed a person to deprive his legal heirs of their rights by the simple expedient of declaring all his property to be *waqf* (an endowment), reserving the use of it for himself during his lifetime and excluding from any benefit all or such of his family as he might choose. As a remedy to this, the Law of 1946 provided, first, that all such *waqfs,* other than those for specifically religious purposes, should have a maximum duration of sixty years or two successive series of beneficiaries, whichever was less; and second, that all legal heirs of the founder should have, after his death, an obligatory entitlement in the *waqf* equivalent to their rights of succession, whether they had been expressly nominated as beneficiaries or not. The limitation upon the period of the *waqf* was based on Maliki doctrine, while the rule of "obligatory entitlement" rested on the views of Ibn Hazm and certain Hanbali jurists, who regarded the exclusion of some of the deceased's heirs as oppressive and rendered the opin-

---

144 The modern process of selecting a course of legal action from the various juristic opinions of the different *madhahib.*

ion that in such cases the excluded heirs should be admitted to share in the *waqf.*

*Takhayyur* and *talfiq* (the process of patching together or combining the views of different schools and jurists, or aspects therefrom, to form a single legal rule) is a sign that *sensibility* and the removal of injustice and inequity in the practical application of the law are paramount when compared to mere logical consistency. The Ḥanafi school refers to this principle of sensible equity as *istihsān.*

# APPENDIX IV

## ON RIBA[145]

In this section we probe the complexity of the *riba* issue, and highlight some preliminary reflections and considerations.

In a forthcoming book that will go deeper into the issues involved in this subject, we will explain the nature of money and banking, inflation and deflation, and why money is no longer based on a gold standard. We will also describe some of the efforts Muslim economists have made in developing theories towards an interest-free banking system, and the real life practical challenges that stand in the way of making such a system work.

For the benefit of this book, we shall focus on how riba is defined, the economic and moral aspects of riba and interest, and how we may in the interim deal with this issue until an ideal interest free economic and banking system is established.

### How riba is defined

Riba is translated as usury, and Muslim jurists have technically defined two kinds of riba: one on money and the other on goods. The first, called *riba'n-nasī'ah,* is defined as any agreed upon *fixed* return on a monetary loan. The other kind is called *riba'l-faḍl,* defined as an exchange in kind of unequal quantities of a commodity due to a time or quality difference. For example, as when a container of dates is taken now for two containers returned at harvest time, or when two containers of low quality dry

---

[145] For the best treatment on the issue of riba and Islamic banking that I have read so far, I recommend *Islamic Banking and Interest, A Study of the Prohibition of Riba and its Contemporary Interpretation,* by Abdullah Saeed, E.J.Brill, Leiden, 1996.

dates are simultaneously exchanged for one of high quality fresh dates. The Prophet regarded these transactions as riba transactions. Instead, he recommended that the two containers of dry dates be sold, and with the money proceeds from the sale, purchase the one container of moist dates. This would be a non-riba transaction.

Why, you may ask? The answer is *we really don't know*, partly because the verses revealed on riba were among the very last to be revealed, as related on the authority of Ibn `Abbas[146], and that the Prophet did not live very long after that to give sufficient explanation to the community. In fact Ibn Kathir notes that the usury problem has been one of the most difficult and problematic for jurists. The second Caliph, `Umar b. al-Khattab, was quoted as having said, "There are three things concerning which I wish the Messenger of Allah had left us a clear injunction to follow; among these were the problems of usury."

For the sake of this discussion we will focus on *riba'n-nasī'ah*, interest on money and banking, for this is the issue that concerns Muslims the most. Unlike modern Western economies, where usury is loosely defined as an "excessive" rate of interest, the majority of Muslim authorities regard interest on a loan, no matter how small, as riba, and therefore strictly forbidden. This explicit prohibition on interest *no matter how small* makes it difficult for the contemporary Muslim to understand why even a small interest rate should be considered haram, especially in today's context of modern banking. To get to the bottom of things, especially the intractability of this issue, we need to understand the nature of money and the overall context of today's banking system, subjects that will be discussed in our future book.

While every sin has an opprobrium, where does riba's evil lie? Is it in its form, i.e. in gaining a fixed rate of interest on a loan, or in its moral content? If we define riba purely by its external form, i.e. the taking of a fixed rate of interest, then all we have to do is

---

146 Ibn Kathir, I, pp. 581-2

devise alternate ways of making capital available, like leases, that address the riba issue in its *form*. But if we define riba by its ethical opprobrium, then we need to define where this immorality lies, and address that.

## Interest: the time value or opportunity cost of money

Interest is often called the time value or opportunity cost of money. This idea comes from the notion that if you had a sum of money, you could invest it in some fashion to earn more money. For example, you could buy a shop and stock it with product and sell it to earn a profit. The argument goes somewhat along the lines that in a successful economy, if the average return of businesses is 10% to 12%, then an investor who invests his cash in a 50-50 partnership with a business person may be entitled to a return of 5% to 6%. From this the step is made to say that the opportunity cost of money is approximately 5% per year.

Because of the investment opportunities that it can provide, money has a commodity value. Just as a storefront space has a commodity value, where it can be rented to a businessman or woman who can use this space to establish a profitable business enterprise, a smart businessperson can use a sum of money to establish a profitable business enterprise. And just as we have a real estate market or a food market, we also have in today's world a capital market.

In the capital market, money rates are the rates at which money is loaned. These rates are established by the market, depending on supply and demand, the creditworthiness of the borrower, the amount of funds borrowed, the quality of the collateral, the time period of the loan (whether it is short term or long term) and other such factors.

## Why is riba forbidden? The economics argument

Stability of currency is important to people. They don't like it when their savings dwindle in value due to inflation. When this happens, their savings, which took them years to accrue and which they may have wanted to use to purchase a home, is unable to procure the home. What has happened here is that money, in its role as a store of surplus value, has lost ground against its role as a medium of exchange because of a severe shift in its role as a unit of account. When this shift is negative, i.e. when money loses value, we call it inflation, and when the shift is positive, i.e. when money increases in value, we call that deflation. Although most people abhor inflation, most are unaware of the equally destructive forces of deflation. We now explore how interest is deflationary.

Let us start with a hypothetical situation: a country where there is a zero inflation rate, a constant money supply and no growth in GDP, and where there is no such thing as a time value for money. Suddenly a new law is imposed decreeing that money will have an effective time value of 6%. What this means is that money as a store of value (surplus liquid money) now has an inherent right to increase annually by 6% against the products of labor and illiquid assets. All the owners of cash find that after one year, their money has 6% greater buying power, while the owners of illiquid assets find that their assets are worth less. This means that the *products of labor and illiquid assets have deflated against money at the rate of its opportunity cost.* So your home worth $100,000 at the beginning of the year is worth $94,000 at the end of the year.

If we extend the scenario to incorporate the kinds of rates the Qur'ân speaks of in verse 3:130 below, where annual rates reached 100% to 200%, what happens is that your asset can be reduced in value by half to one third in a year. Your house worth $100,000 is now worth somewhere between $33,000 and $50,000.

This *erosion* of wealth and assets in favor of the holder of liquid capital is the very definition of usury, and this is where its opprobrium lies, for it is a *de facto* impoverishment of the owners of illiquid assets in favor of owners of money.

When capital is invested so that labor becomes bonded and enslaved to the owners of capital, or when the collateral provided to secure the capital invested is eroded and lost by its owners, evil has occurred. High rates of interest make this a more likely event. The Qur'ân is quite explicit on the ills of predatory rates of interest:

*O you who have believed! Do not consume riba, doubling and redoubling, and fear Allah so that you may prosper. 3:130*

Some Muslim writers have used this verse to indicate that what is prohibited is this "doubling and redoubling" rates of interest, and not the modern day market rates of interest. However, this is not the opinion of the majority of Islamic scholars.

## The moral argument against riba

It is clearly immoral to loan money—*even at a zero rate of interest*—to a poor family needing the basic requirements of life such as food, shelter and clothing, *if the intention* is to then foreclose on their assets or enslave them into bonded labor when they cannot pay up on the loan. This penalty was the practice in olden times both in Europe and in pre-Islamic societies. What you have done is use your money as a hook to bait another's property to your unfair advantage. This is the sense of the following Qur'ânic verse:

*And whatever you give as riba (usury) so that it may erode*[147] *(literally, "increase within") people's property does not increase with Allah; but*

---

[147] The expression *li yarbua fi amwāli 'n-nās* literally means "grows into, or within, people's property." The sense of this is that your loan funds are injected into another's asset and grows inside of it like a metastizing cancer, which grows within healthy tissue and transforms it into its own at the expense of eroding the healthy tissue. Thus the opprobrium of usury is that it is money loaned that erodes the borrower's equity.

> *what you give in zakah (charity) desiring Allah's pleasure— these will be multiplied. 30:39*

The opprobrium of "increase in people's property" is just this use of your liquid funds that ostensibly helps, but in fact is implanted in people's property so that your share grows and erodes theirs, with their loss being your gain.

Such a family in the United States would not get a loan at a bank, but would be referred to the welfare department for assistance. The verse can also be interpreted to mean that it is wrong to make a collaterized *loan* to those needing *charitable* help.

But clearly while a well off person may give zakah to a poor family in need of food or shelter, it is hard to interpret this verse as suggesting that in a business context a capital owner ought to *charitably donate* his zakah funds so that someone else can make money on it and not at the very least want his funds back, if not to share in the expected profit.

So if someone wants to start a business, and offers me his house worth $100,000 as collateral for a $50,000 loan; *even at a zero rate of interest*, it would be wrong for me to do this if my intention is to foreclose on his asset and profit by the difference between the $50,000 put up and the $100,000 value of the collateral. This is also the sense of the above verse, where capital is used as bait to hook a much larger catch. I will have committed what the above verse says is placing my money so that it *expands (yarbu) into other people's property*, much like a cancer metastizing into healthy tissue.

However, if he freely offers to sell me his $100,000 home at a discounted price of $50,000, and I accept it, that is fine. I have purchased his home (or *traded* my $50,000 for his home) valued at $100,000, for $50,000. That is not riba, because implicit in the sale is that if he could have gotten $70,000 for his home he would have sold it to someone else. Therefore the price is presumed to be fair market price. The Qur'ân points out the difference between these two situations in verse 2:275:

*Those who consume riba do not arise except as the one whom Satan knocks down by his touch.*[148] *This is because they say, Trading (literally, selling) is like riba; but Allah has made trading (selling) lawful and riba unlawful...Allah will destroy (the value of) riba, and will cause charity to grow (in value)...O you who believe, protect yourselves from Allah and leave off what remains of riba*

These examples show that the *intentions* with which the loan is made, and that are planned in the event the loan is not paid, have a lot to do with determining the "overall sinfulness" of the act. Although the rate of interest does not yet enter the picture in these examples, capital invested with a predatory intention becomes downright rapacious when high rates of interest are additionally imposed.

## Can riba under certain specific contexts be a good?

In most sins, the evil of the sin is evident, and we are able to separate the technical definition from the rationale or moral intent. We have pointed out that the value of an act under Islamic law—as under any law—does not just lie in its outer form. The Prophet permitted lying in three circumstances, although it is considered one of the greatest sins. One of these circumstances was when it was done to bring harmony between two family disputants.[149] This does not mean that we have made lying acceptable; it means that in a set of specific circumstances, lying is rendered permissible when it generates no harm and helps people to accomplish a good. This is in keeping with the principle of Islamic

---

148 What does "do not arise except as one whom Satan knocks down by his touch" mean? Is it an economics statement or a spiritual statement? Spiritually, the Satanic effects are of heaviness and constriction. Most of the commentators agree that this relates to a "madness" that those who consume usury will exhibit on the Day of Judgment. The rest of the verse explains the analogy by saying that the equation of riba to trade is an unlawful one that God rejects. Making this equation, God asserts, is letting our thinking be knocked down by Satan.

149 *Sunan* Abu Dawud, Kitab al-Adab, hadith no. 4921.

law that all of the Shari`ah is directed towards the benefit of humankind. It is also an application of the Prophet's dictum that all acts are judged by intention.

Can we define a set of circumstances in which the opprobrium of riba is as close to being eliminated? And where the advantages of riba under such a carefully controlled licensed system far outweigh its costs, just like lying in the above circumstances that the Prophet condoned? If so, what are these circumstances?

The simple answer is that the circumstances would have to be circumscribed by an economic system that offers the following values:

1. It should encourage capital and labor to be cooperative, not adversarial.
2. The rates of interest should be as low as possible so as not to erode people's equity in their assets; such low rates would encourage capital and labor to create greater economic expansion and greater distribution of wealth. This is how poverty can be eliminated.
3. Eliminate the ills of aggressive inflation and deflation, or at the very least attenuate them to a degree that human society can reasonably tolerate.
4. More wealth is created overall, both for the owners/providers of labor or illiquid capital (the borrowers), as well as for the capital owners.

As Islam is concerned about the public interest (*istiḥsān* under Hanafi, *or al-maṣlaḥah al-mursalah* under Maliki law), and the public interest is very well served by modern banking, a strong argument can be brought in support of the position where interest rates are designed not to *erode* but to *build* borrowers' equity. We construct a form of riba, to paraphrase the words of verse 30:39, where the "riba" does not *yarbuwa fī amwāli 'n-nāsi* (expands *within and erodes* people's wealth) but *yarbuwa amwāli 'n-nāsi* (helps people's wealth grow). A form of riba that does not commit the crime of 3:130, of doubling and redoubling, but that expects a rate of return that approximates the average of all business investments. This brings the riba rate of return more in tune with business or trade, and absolves itself of the criticism of verse 2:275, so that it is more like *bay`* (trade).

We still cannot say that riba is not haram, for the same verse is explicit; "Allah has made trade lawful and forbidden riba." What we can assert is that the contextual limitations imposed upon riba fall into the category of a circumstance that mitigates and attenuates the sin, analogous to the Prophet's hadith condoning lying for the purposes of creating harmony. The good end justifies the use of a means normally sinful. Islamic banking attempts to create "riba-free" methods are indeed laudable, but with the exception of the few instances of participatory financing on a partnership basis, do not appear to escape the substantial reality of interest as placing a time or rental value on money.

In a trade or business transaction, both buyer and seller profit by the transaction. Loans often result in a mutual profit. An example is a mortgage loan, where the person buying the house pays mortgage payments approximating the value of rent payments, and instead of paying rent and not building any equity, he or she builds increasing equity in the house till the house is owned outright, usually over a period of anywhere from fifteen to thirty years. If money is loaned at a rate of interest where new or additional wealth is created for both the lenders and the borrowers, then obviously no wrong has occurred; good has occurred. Because of this reality and the legitimate needs for business capital, some Islamic jurists structured legal devices to get around riba's formal definition. This took the form of sale buy-backs and lease agreements. For example, I sell you my house today for $100,000 and agree to buy it back from you for $110,000 after one year; or where the lender buys the house you desire and rents it out to you for an agreed upon term, at the end of which term it is deeded to you. This solution is acceptable if we define riba by its form.

The reality, however, is that even at low rates of interest, loans do not always result in increase of wealth for the borrower. Economic vagaries such as deflation, shifts in the economic scene, etc., can and do result in the borrower, through no fault of his own, failing to increase his wealth through the funds borrowed. In the above example of a mortgage loan, the real estate market may drop significantly, resulting in negative equity, a situation where more is owed to the bank than the value of the home. If the lender insists on its return in such a situation, the result can be seriously damaging to the borrower. Here is where patience on the lender is encouraged in demanding payment, who is urged at the very least to postpone the loan payments and even to partially or fully write it off:

> *And if (the debtor) is in straitness, let there be postponement till (he is in ease). And if you forgo it is better for you, if you knew.* 2:280

So far we have looked at the fairness issue from the point of view of the borrower. From the lender's point of view, there also exist some fairness issues. A lending institution can also be hurt by factors beyond their control (and not only by the fraudulent acts of borrowers who borrow money with no intention of repaying). Primary among these is inflation, which lowers the value of money itself. Expected profits from a 6% to 12% rate of return can be easily wiped out by a comparable inflation rate. The Qur'ân, being concerned with justice, refers to this sense of mutual equity by saying:

But if you do not [relinquish what is left of riba] then be apprised of war from Allah and His messenger; and if you repent, your capital is due to you, *neither wronging nor being wronged.* 2:279

How can we ascertain that in a fixed interest system, both borrowers and lenders are not wronged?

Muslim jurists have generally concluded that a *sharing* of risk between the capital investor and the one needing the funds is the proper and just solution. By this they mean that the provider of funds takes an equity position. If the business fails, the investor loses his funds with no recourse against the partner.

In today's banking system, a bank sees itself in a business with real attending risk. It lends money, expecting a certain percentage of bad loans. When such happens, it writes off these bad loans. It does not take bad debtors and enslave them. Most of the time the recourse on the loans are against the mortgaged property. And if it forecloses on this collateralized property, it is required to take only the amount of principal and interest owed them, plus the costs of the foreclosure. On the plus side, the bank provides services to customers, such as safekeeping of their money and a means to pay their bills via checks. Overall, borrowers are more protected today by a number of options such as non-recourse loans and bankruptcy laws. So it is fair to say that the banking system today is not only not as predatory as the money lending systems of times past, it has also evolved into a business where risk is "more shared" than in systems of times past.

Most important, the banking system today has given us increased prosperity. It has increased financial liquidity by making the capital owned at large by people available to businesses and projects that increase a nation's wealth. Government involvement by establishing banking laws has helped in protecting people from the power of unbridled capital. Such laws protect lenders from usurious rates that were the norm when there were no banks, and when moneylenders and pawnshops were the means by which funds were raised. Today's capital markets have increased the level of partnership between capital and labor, and have resulted in greater wealth for the whole world. Because the benefits are beyond dispute, Muslims have had no choice but to develop Islamic banking norms. However, apart from the investment banking aspect that can be constructed along partnership lines, Islamic banks are discovering that it is difficult to avoid functioning according to the rules of normal banking practice. No method has yet been found to insulate the banks from the Central bank and its reliance on interest rates and reserve requirements in controlling the money supply and the inflationary/deflationary forces, issues that go to the very heart of the riba question. It is especially difficult to avoid the time value of money as determined by the capital markets.

As we explore and extend Islam's ethical concerns regarding the riba issue, especially onto the context of modern banking, we find it to be a concern about people's economic wellbeing and the protection of their asset base. A case can be made that in the larger monetary context, the prohibition on riba can be construed as a prohibition on the ills of aggressive monetary instability due to deflation. And since the Qur'ân wants neither the owner of capital nor the borrower to be wronged, inflation is also an evil to be proscribed. The prohibition on riba is a strong statement in favor of a stable currency that keeps inflationary and deflationary forces in check. In most countries today, riba within the banking system is far less a cause of economic injustice and suffering than rampant inflation or deflation and government corruption.

# APPENDIX V

## THE TRANSVAAL FATWA[150]

Shaikh Muhammad `Abduh (1849-1905) held the office of Grand Mufti in Egypt from June 3, 1899 until his death in 1905. He was in many respects a reformer, who worked to adapt an understanding of Muslim beliefs and points of view to the conditions of modern life and modern thought. A Muslim from the Transvaal in South Africa sought a fatwa on three questions, and Shaikh `Abduh answered them, thus this fatwa became known as the "Transvaal Fatwa." It created a controversy at the time, primarily because Shaikh `Abduh was charged with declaring lawful food that many Muslims believed the Shari`ah declared unlawful.

We will quote the full text of the Transvaal fatwa here, partly for its conclusions but more because it serves as a good platform to discuss this issue. We will therefore comment on this fatwa by adducing relevant Qur'ânic and Hadith texts that clarify Shaikh `Abduh's thinking process on the second question regarding eating animals slaughtered by Christians, an issue many contemporary Muslims still contend with.

The questions raised were:

1. There are individuals [Muslims] in this country who wear the hat in order to carry on their business and secure the return of profit to themselves. Is this permissible or not?

---

[150] Much of this section is quoted from *The MacDonald Presentation Volume*, "Muhammad `Abduh and the Transvaal Fatwa," transl. by Charles C. Adams pp. 11ff, Princeton University Press, 1933.

2. The manner in which they [i.e. Christians of the Transvaal] slaughter animals intended for food differs [from the manner prescribed for Muslims] because they strike cows with an axe and after that they slaughter [i.e. cut their throats], without repeating the *basmalah* [In the name of God]; and small cattle they also slaughter without repeating the *basmalah.* Is this permissible or not?
3. The Shafi`ites perform the public prayers standing behind the Hanafites, without repeating the *basmalah*, and they perform the prayers behind them on the occasion of the two feasts [`*īd ul-fiṭr* and `*īd ul-aḍḥa*]. It is well known that there is a difference of opinion between the Shafi`ites and the Hanafites, whether repeating the basmalah and the *takbīrs* of the two feasts is obligatory or not. Is it permissible to perform the prayers, the one behind the other, or not?

Shaikh Muhammad `Abduh's fatwa read as follows:

The wearing of the hat, if the one who wears it does not intend thereby to leave Islam and enter another religion, is not to be considered as constituting the wearer an unbeliever; and if wearing it is to meet some need, such as to protect from the sun or prevent some undesirable result or to make possible some advantage, it has likewise not been considered as 'disliked' [makrūh] because the idea of conformity to another religion has disappeared entirely.

As for slaughtered animals, my opinion is that the Muslims in those distant parts should follow the text of the Book of Allah [the Qur'ân], where He says: 'And the food of those who have been given the Book is lawful for you' [sura 5:5]; and that they should rely upon what the illustrious Imam Abu Bakr ibn al-`Arabi the Maliki has said, namely, that the chief point to be considered is that what is slaughtered should be intended to be eaten by the Christians, both clergy and laity, and should be regarded as food for the whole body of them. For, if it is their custom to take the life of an animal, in whatsoever manner it may be done, and after the slaughtering, the chiefs of their religion are accustomed to eat of it, it is permissible for the Muslim to eat of it, because it is then called 'the food of the People of the Book.' The Christians in the time of the Prophet were in a condition similar to their condition today; especially since the Christians of the Transvaal are among the most intolerant in their religion and the strictest in their adherence to their religious books. Therefore everything that belongs under the heading 'slaughtered' is to be considered as 'the food of the People of the Book,' so long as the slaughter has taken place according to the custom which has been approved by chiefs of their religion. The occurrence of the noble verse 'Today there is made lawful for you the good things, and the food of those who have been given the Book is lawful for you,' etc. [sura 5:5], after the verse declaring unlawful that which has died of itself and that which has been devoted to other gods than Allah, is in the nature of a refutation of any wrong opinions that might be held in the way of declaring the food of the People of the Book to be unlawful because they believe in the deity of `Isa [Jesus]. For they all were in that state [of belief] in the time of the Prophet, except those of them who turned Muslims. Moreover, the expression 'the People of the Book' is unlimited, and it is not proper to interpret it as applying only to this small, individual group [i.e. the Muslims in the time of Muhammad]. Consequently, this verse is like an explicit verse in declaring their food lawful, so long as they, in their religion, hold it to be lawful, in order to prevent embarrassment in intercourse with them and dealings with them.

In regard to the prayer of the Shafi`ite behind the Hanafite, there is no doubt in my mind concerning its correctness, so long as the prayer of the Hanafite is correct according to his own rite; for the religion of Islam is one. It is the duty of the Shafi`ite to know that his Imam is a Muslim, correct in the performance of the prayers, without showing intolerance in his regard for his Imam. Whosoever seeks for anything else than this, regards Islam as a number of religions not one religion. And it is not permissible for an intelligent person to entertain such an idea among Muslims, few in number, in a land all the inhabitants of which are non-Muslims, except those unfortunate few.

Commenting on the fatwa, there are three issues that concern Muslims regarding the verse "the food of those who have been given the Book is lawful for you" when applied to Christians:

1. The meats they eat.
2. The method (or mechanics) of slaughter,
3. *Tasmiyah*, that is the mentioning of Allah's name on the animal. A variation of this concern is that because Christians believe in the divinity of Jesus and ascribe partnership to Allah in a trinitarian concept, their invoking Jesus or a trinitarian notion of God may be equivalent to naming a false god. This raises a final question,
4. If the mechanics of slaughter and the tasmiyah is mentioned according to the Islamic procedure, does it matter if the slaughterer is a Muslim or not?

The second and third items above concern Muslims generally regarding the animals they slaughter themselves. However, we shall discuss each issue separately in order to explain more fully both what makes meat halal or haram.

### 1. Meats consumed by Christians

A number of Qur'ânic and Hadith passages have a bearing upon this topic; and since Shaikh `Abduh builds part of his argument upon them, we shall quote them

The Qur'ân reads:

> *He has only forbidden for you what is dead, and blood, and flesh of swine, and whatsoever has been consecrated to other than Allah. 2:173.*

This verse absolutely forbids the meat of the pig and liquid blood (even from a permitted animal). Pork in any form, such as ham, bacon, or a pork chop is forbidden. So are Irish blood pies, or Italian blood sausages, even if made from the blood of beef, and even if the Christians, including their clergy, consume these items.

The Hadith additionally prohibits eating the meat of domestic donkeys[151] and animals with fangs[152]. From this comes the general idea that carnivorous animals are prohibited. The rest of the categories are not prohibited meats as much as they are "prohibited methods of slaughtering."

## 2. The Mechanics of Slaughter

> *Forbidden to you is that which dies of itself [al-maytah], and blood, and the flesh of swine, and that on which other than the name of Allah has been invoked, and the strangled [al-munkhaniqah] and the beaten to death [al-mawqūdhah], and that killed by a fall [al-mutarāddiyah] and the gored [an-naṭiḥah], and what wild beasts have eaten—except what you slaughter in time [mā dhakkaytum] —and what is sacrificed to idols, and dividing carcasses by arrows. 5:3*

The term for slaughtering properly is called in Islamic law *tadhkiyah.* Many Muslims believe that for meat to be halal, it has to be exclusively "*dhabīḥa.*" This is not precisely so, for *dhabīḥa* is a technical term indicating a particular technique of slaughtering, as we shall define below. What is more generally true is that the animal has to be "*dhakka-ed.*"[153]

---

[151] Bukhari, Book 67, Chapter 14.

[152] Ibid, Book 67, Chapters 28 and 29.

[153] The above conditions only apply to land and air animals, not to sea food. All sea food is permitted per verse 5:96 which reads: "Lawful to you is the game of the sea and its food,..." All aqauatic life is lawful regardless of its method of death. The Prophet said "Two *maytahs* are lawful for us, fish and locust; and two bloods, the liver and the spleen [Qurtubi, II, p. 217]. If the seafood dies naturally out of the water, like fish or prawns, that is permitted. If it remains alive out of the water, like crabs, then any humane manner of killing is acceptable, unless it is a larger animal like a turtle on which dhabh or nahr may be performed.

*Tadhkiyah* is the noun form of the word; *dhakkā* is the verbal form, the root is *dhkw*. All this term means is "slaughtered in accordance with the law." Any of the following are forms of *tadhkiyah*:

1. *Dhabḥ* (this is the noun form, *dhabaha* is the verbal form). The meaning is slaughtering by completely severing the gullet and the jugular vein with a sharp instrument, cutting from the front of the neck without lifting the instrument until the act is completed. This is done usually for smaller animals like poultry, lambs and goats, and up to the size of a cow.
2. *Naḥr*. This is another method of slaughtering, usually performed on larger animals like camels or cows. This is done by stabbing the animal in the throat, severing the windpipe.

The requirements for *tadhkiyah* are:

1. That the intention in slaughtering the animal be for eating.
2. That Allah's name be mentioned,
3. That the animal's blood flows,
4. That you are responsible for terminating the life of the animal, provided that no nail or tooth is used. (These limitations are based on Hadith, for which see below.)

The following hadith demonstrates that, under certain circumstances, the animal does not necessarily have to be killed by dhabh or nahr. Ibn `Abbas is quoted to have said:

> *Wa fi ba`irin taradda fi bi'rin min ḥaythu qadarta fa'dhakkih;*
>
> ...And if a camel falls down a well, dhakkih it (i.e. slaughter it) at any place of its body that will be easy for you to reach. `Ali, Ibn `Umar and `A'isha thought similarly.[154]

---

[154] Ibid, chapter 23. Since this hadith is a statement by Ibn `Abbas, and not by the Prophet, it is a *ḥadīth ṣaḥīḥ mawqūf*.

From this use of the term *dhakkā* we learn that *dhakkā* does not only mean *dhabḥ* or *naḥr*, it means ending the life of the animal, even if the act of terminating the life of the animal occurs at another part of its anatomy.

Moreover, an undomesticated animal may be killed by hunting. If the animal is subdued while still alive and you slaughter it by dhabh or nahr, you have performed *tadhkiyah* on it. A hunted prey may be killed in either of two ways:

i) By an arrow (in modern times by a gun).

ii) By a trained hunting animal like a hound dog.

The above is explained by the following Qur'ânic verse:

*They will ask you what is lawful for them? Say, 'Lawful for you are the good things and what you have taught beasts of prey (to catch, training them to hunt) like dogs;—you teach them of what Allah has taught you—so eat of what they catch for you, and mention the name of Allah over it, and fear Allah.' (5:4)*

This verse is further explained by several ahadith, and here we shall quote from Bukhari, Book 67, The Book of Slaughtering and Hunting (*Kitāb adh-Dhabā 'iḥ wa 'ṣṣayḍ*):

> `Adi b. Hatim relates that he said: "O Messenger of Allah! We let our trained hound dogs on the game." He (the Prophet) said, "Eat what they catch for you." I said, "Even if they killed the game?" He replied, "Even if they killed the game." I said, "We also hit (game) with the *mi`rāḍ* (a kind of arrow without feathers or arrowhead)." He said, "Eat of the animal which the *mi`rāḍ* kills by piercing its body, but do not meat of the animal which is killed by the shaft of the *mi`rāḍ*."[155]

Two ahadith down in Bukhari is another in which the Prophet said:

> If you hunt an animal with your bow after mentioning Allah's name on it, eat of it, and if you hunt with your trained dog after mentioning Allah's name on it, eat of it, and if you hunt

155 Ibid, Chapter 2.

> something with your untrained dog and you catch its *dhakāh*, eat of it.

This means that if the prey was killed by your arrow or trained dog, you may eat of it. But if your untrained dog catches a prey and kills it, you may not eat of it unless it does not kill it, and you reach it before it has died, then you mention Allah's name on it and slaughter it; then it is *ḥalal*. This is because the arrow or the trained dog is your tool for slaughtering the animal, whereas an untrained dog may have killed the animal for its own eating. The core meaning of "catching the *dhakāh*" of the animal is that you were responsible for ending the life of the animal, and that you mentioned Allah's name on it, whether you accomplish this by *dhabḥ*, *naḥr*, or a weapon like an arrow or a hunting dog.

Going back to verse 5:3, the exception *mā dhakkaytim* [except what you slaughter in time] may apply to all the five classes mentioned, and the meaning is that if the animal partly eaten by wild beasts is found while yet alive, and is slaughtered in the proper manner, its flesh is permitted. Applying this exception to the previous four classes, if an animal strangled, beaten, fallen, or gored has not yet died, and you slaughter it properly in time, its flesh is allowed.[156]

The following hadith is instructive regarding the manner of slaughtering the animal:

> Narrated Rafi` bin Khadij: While we were with the Prophet on a journey, one of the camels ran away. A man shot it with an arrow and stopped it. The Prophet said, "Of these camels some are as wild as wild beasts, so if one of them runs away and you cannot catch it, then do like this (meaning shoot it with an arrow)." I said, "O Allah's Apostle! Sometimes when we are in battles or on a journey we want to slaughter (*fa nurīdu an-nadhbaḥa*) but we have no knives." He (the

156 According to Ibn `Abbas "*al-munkhaniqah* is the animal killed by choking; *al-mawqūdhah* is the one killed by a piece of wood [or by some kind of impact, like a deer killed by a car for example]; *al-mutaraddiyah* is the one that dies by falling down a mountain; *an-naṭīḥah* is an animal killed by being gored; but if you find an animal still moving its tail or eyes, slaughter it and eat it (*fa'dhbaḥ wa kul*)." Ibid, Chapter 1.

Prophet) said, "Listen! That which causes the blood to flow and if Allah's name is mentioned, eat of it (*mā anhara `ddama wa dhukira'smu 'llahi fa-kul*) provided that it is not a tooth or a nail…"[157]

In this hadith of a camel considered wild and felled by an arrow, the Prophet did not use a term like *dhabḥ* or *naḥr*, but says *mā anhara `ddama wa dhukira'smu 'llahi fa-kul*, meaning "eat of an animal killed by flow of its blood, the conditions being that Allah's name is mentioned on it and that it was killed neither by a tooth or nail," thus confirming expanded possibilities beyond dhabh and nahr. This hadith combined with the hadith quoted above of Ibn `Abbas of the camel fallen into a well being slaughtered at any part of its anatomy, shows that the circumstances of the situation allow for *tadhkiyah* to be more than just *dhabḥ* or *naḥr*.[158]

From the above we can conclude that the mechanics of slaughtering the animal in the Transvaal was within the embrace of the Islamic requirements of *tadhkiyah.*

## 3. The mentioning of God's name (tasmiyah)

The remaining question is:

If the slaughterer does not pronounce the *basmalah*, is the meat forbidden? And if an animal killed by a *hunting dog* is allowed, should not an animal slaughtered by a human being be allowed—even if the one performing the slaughter is not a Muslim?

---

[157] Ibid., Chapter 37.

[158] The following hadith expands the possibilities regarding the instrument with which the animal is slaughtered:

Ka`b narrated that a slave girl of theirs used to shepherd some sheep at Sal`. On seeing one of her sheep dying, she broke a stone and slaughtered it. Ka`b said to his family, "do not eat of it till I go to the Prophet and ask him, or, till I send someone to ask him." So he went to the Prophet or sent someone to him. The Prophet permitted it to be eaten.

The Muslim's concern with forgetting the basmalah is because of verses 6:119-122 of the Qur'ân which read:

> *Eat then, of that on which Allah's name has been mentioned, if you are believers in His signs. And why should you not eat of that on which Allah's name is mentioned, when He has already made plain to you what He has forbidden to you—excepting that which you are compelled to?...*
>
> *Eat not of that which Allah's name has not been mentioned on; and it is certainly sinfulness (*fisq*)...*

The pagan Quraysh during the Prophet's time used to sacrifice animals to their idols on altar stones set up around the Ka`bah. Not only sacrificial animals but also those intended for common consumption were often slaughtered on these altar stones for the sake of a supposed blessing. *The pagans believed in Allah, but their sinfulness was in ascribing partners to Allah.* A possible meaning of the above verse is that some Muslims may have been reticent to consume meat slaughtered by the pagan Quraysh in the name of Allah.[159] This verse distinguishes between an animal slaughtered by them in the name of Allah and one slaughtered in the name of another god; the first is permitted and even encouraged, while the second is forbidden. There is agreement among the jurists that fisq here refers not to the forgetfulness of mentioning Allah's name, but the mentioning the name of another (false) god, as defined in verse 146 of the same Qur'ânic chapter:

> *Say, I do not find in what is revealed to me forbidden for an eater to eat of, except that it be what dies of itself, or liquid blood, or flesh of swine—for that is certainly unclean—or a sinfulness (fisqan) on which other than Allah's name has been invoked. 6:146.*

In a hadith in Bukhari, Ibn `Abbas said: Whoever forgets to mention Allah's name while slaughtering, there is no harm in it.

---

[159] This suggests that the meat of an animal slaughtered by a non-Muslim who utters the Islamic tasmiyah is halal.

The hadith then quotes verse 6:121 and Ibn `Abbas adds: He who forgets Allah's name is not called sinful (*fasiqan*).[160]

In other words, *fisq* does not embrace the act of forgetfulness; it is not the *omission* of mentioning God's name but is limited to the deliberate *commission* of the sin of invoking another god's name. The following hadith narrated by the Prophet's wife shows that the lack of mentioning Allah's name on slaughtering an animal is not fisq:

Narrated Aisha: A group of people said to the Prophet, "Some people bring us meat and we do not know whether they have mentioned Allah's name or not on slaughtering the animal." He said, "Mention Allah's name on it and eat." Those people had embraced Islam recently.[161]

From this hadith we conclude that the animal on whose slaughtering no name was mentioned is allowed; we just mention Allah's name on it and eat.

Finally, Chapter 22 of Bukhari's Book 67 quotes the following hadith:

Az-Zuhri said: There is no harm in eating animals slaughtered by Arab Christians. If you hear the one who slaughters the animals mentioning other than Allah's name, don't eat of it, but if you do not hear that, then Allah has allowed the eating of animals slaughtered by them, though he knows their disbelief.

It is narrated that `Ali gave a similar verdict.

We now return and comment on Shaikh `Abduh's fatwa. He quotes the Qur'ânic verse:

> *This day good things are made lawful for you; and the food of those who have been given the Book is lawful for you and your food is lawful for them. 5:5*

Shaikh `Abduh gives this verse as the basis of a blanket permission to eat the food (including the meats) of the People of the

---

[160] Ibid, chapter 15.

[161] Ibid, chapter 21

Book (ahl al-Kitāb) with no conditions other than what the Qur'an explicitly prohibits. (Clearly ham or bacon is haram even when it is offered by a Jew or a Christian, or consumed by their clergy. This should cause the Muslim no doubt.) This verse comes after the verse prohibiting the eating of that which died of itself [*al-maytah* (5:3)], thereby showing that the Qur'ân has anticipated the possibility that difficulties might arise in the minds of some Muslims regarding such a permission. The difficulty is that the Christians believe in the deity of Jesus in a trinitarian concept; therefore it is part of the intent of this verse to "ward off" any suspicions regarding the lawfulness of eating Christian food, since it is essentially an explicit verse. Modern Christians are no less trinitarian or less believing in the divinity of Jesus than they were at the Prophet's time. Moreover, the absolute form of the statement in the verse does not allow limitation of the permission to the Christians existing in the time of the Prophet. The permission contemplates the food of Christians, understanding "Christians" in the widest and most general sense. One limitation `Abduh attaches to this permission, by referring to a fatwa on this subject delivered by one of the earliest Maliki Imams, Abu Bakr Ibn al-`Arabi. This interpretation stipulates that the animals intended for food should be considered lawful according to the requirements of the religion of the "People of the Book" and should be slain in the manner prescribed therein and that not only the laity but also the clergy should eat from the meat. There would thus be no doubt that the meat was lawful from their point of view and could be called without question "food of the People of the Book" and would thus be lawful for Muslims.

It will be noted that Shaikh `Abduh's fatwa does not discuss the technical details, although we have done so above for the reader's benefit. Two points regarding the Christian method of slaughtering in the Transvaal differed from the traditional Muslim manner and which may seem to make the food unlawful according to Islamic law:

1. The larger animals are first struck with an axe (*bulṭ*), presumably upon the head, although this is not stated. This manner of killing would seem to place them in the class called *al-mawqūdhah* ('knocked down'), the eating of which is forbidden. (See sura 5:3 above.) The animal is then slaughtered, that is, dhabh is then performed. As we have seen from the hadiths quoted above, and this is agreed upon by all the *madhāhib*, if dhabh occurs before the last spark of life has disappeared, then tadhkiyah has occurred, and the eating of the animal's flesh is lawful. If it is known for sure that the animal died as a result of the impact, thus died a *mawqudhah*, then its flesh is unlawful. However, if it is not known whether tadhkiyah took place in time or not, the presumption is that the animal was still alive when dhabh was performed, and thus, according to the general agreement of the *madhāhib*, the food of Christians is lawful. (In other words, unless something is known for sure that makes it unlawful, the presumption is that it is lawful.)
2. Christians do not repeat the name of God (*tasmiyah*) over the victim when they slaughter. This must accompany the act of slaughtering, and in hunting it must accompany the shooting of the arrow or the loosing of the hunting dogs upon the prey. It is considered essential to *tadhkiyah* by the majority of the madhhabs, but as we have seen above, its absence does not make the meat unlawful. The Shafi`is and the Hanbalis permit its omission either intentionally or through negligence, both by the Muslim or the *Kitābi* (a person of Ahli'l-Kitāb, the People of the Book); the Malikis do not make it a condition for the Kitābi, while the Hanafis make it a condition not to be omitted intentionally, but its omission through negligence or through ignorance of its being a condition is permitted. All these regulations, however, apply specifically to Muslims and it is generally agreed that Christians and Jews are not held responsible for the practice of them. Accordingly, the majority of the great jurists, both earlier and later, have held it lawful to eat animals slain by Christians and Jews, even though they did not repeat

the name of Allah over the animals, and even if they repeated the name of some other, as `Isa (Jesus) or `Uzair (Ezra). The agreement (*ijmā`*) which holds that the food of the Kitābis is lawful if the manner of tadhkiyah is unknown, covers not only the general situation in the Transvaal at the time of Shaikh `Abduh, but also in the other Christian and Jewish countries. The stipulation that `Abduh added, that the meat should be eaten by the clergy as well as the laity, is not one that is required by the majority of the jurists, although the apparent reason he did so was to place a limiting boundary on those who called themselves Christian.

# GLOSSARY

***āḥād*:** A ḥadīth given by only one chain of authority.

***'ālim*** (pl. *`ulama*): This means a scholar, a learned man, from the root `ilm. A *mujtahid* or a *faqih* would be considered a *'ālim.*

***aṣl*** (pl. *uṣūl*): Literally, "source, or root." Technically, the sources of law or the principles of jurisprudence.

***`azīz*:** This is a ḥadīth transmitted by at least two authorities and was not so generally disseminated as a *mutawātir* or *mashhūr ḥadīth.*

***ḍa'if*:** Weak. This is a ḥadīth against which serious doubts can be raised, either by reason of its contents or because one or more of its transmitters is considered unreliable.

***faqīh*:** A person who has studied *fiqh*, i.e. jurisprudence; a legal scholar.

***farḍ*:** A religious obligation. A *farḍ `ayn* is an obligation that falls upon everyone; for example, the five-time-daily-prayer is a *farḍ `ayn.* No one can pray this prayer on your behalf. A *farḍ kifāyah* is an obligation upon the whole community that can be fulfilled by one or a few individuals; for example, the funeral prayer upon a deceased Muslim is an obligation that the whole community is responsible for, but a few members of the community can do it on behalf of the whole community.

***fatwā*** (pl. *fatāwā*): a formal legal opinion by a jurist.

***fiqh*:** Literally, "understanding," jurisprudence.

***gharīb*:** A rare ḥadīth. When in reference to its contents rather than its *isnād*, *gharīb* refers also to a ḥadīth that contains foreign or rare expressions.

***ḥadīth*** (pl. *aḥādīth*): A report, a tradition, usually about the Prophet but also on some of his companions or some other early authority.

***ḥarām*:** Forbidden.

***ḥasan*:** Literally, "beautiful". This is a ḥadīth that is not absolutely faultless, either because its *isnād* is not quite complete, or because there is no perfect agreement regarding the reliability of its authorities.

***ḥila*** (pl. *ḥiyal*): A legal device or stratagem, therefore a legal fiction.

***ḥukm*:** A legal ruling, sometimes called a *ḥukm shar`i.*

***ijmā'*:** Consensus of opinion.

***ijtihād*:** The effort expended in inferring the rules of the *Sharī'ah* from the textual sources, or the implementation and applying of these rules towards the formulation of a legal opinion or judgment.

***`illah*:** In the science of *fiqh*, the effective cause. The ascertainment of the reason or *`illah* underlying a legal rule is an essential step in the process of reasoning by analogy (*qiyās*). A legal principle established by an original case is extended to cover new cases on the ground that they possess a common *`illah.* The word also means weakness, and is used in this sense in the science of Ḥadīth.

***isnād*** (or *sanad*): Literally, "support." The chain of authorities reporting a ḥadīth.

***istiḥsān*:** Juristic preference. Used in cases not regulated by any incontrovertible authority of the Qur'ān, Ḥadīth or ijmā', where equitable considerations may override the results of strict analogical reasoning.

***istiṣḥāb*:** Continuance, i.e. the presumption in the laws of evidence that a state of affairs known to exist in the past continues to exist until the contrary is proved.

***istiṣlāḥ*:** The principle of jurisprudence that "consideration of the public interest" is a criterion for the elaboration of legal rules.

***jihād*:** A holy struggle or war.

***khabar*:** news report, used as a synonym for ḥadīth.

***madhhab*** (pl. *madhāhib*): One of the schools of Islamic law. There were as many as thirteen sunni schools of law, but the sunni *madhāhib* boiled down to four, the Shāfi`i, the Ḥanafi, the Maliki and the Ḥanbali, with the Ja`fari being the predominant Shi`i madhhab.

***makrūh*:** An action deemed blameworthy.

***mandūb*:** A praiseworthy action.

***maqtū`*:** A ḥadīth in which the text deals with the doings of the first generation after the Prophet (*tābi'ūn*).

***marfū`*:** A ḥadīth in which the text relates a story about the Prophet.

***mashhūr*:** Literally, "well known." A ḥadīth that is reported by at least three different chains of authority.

***maşlaḥa*:** The public interest.

***matn*:** The text of a ḥadīth.

***matrūk*:** Abandoned, i.e. no longer considered or accepted. A ḥadīth transmitted by only one informant, whose authority is also considered weak.

***mawḍū`*:** A fabricated ḥadīth, and considered absolutely false.

***mawqūf*:** A ḥadīth whose text deals with the doings or sayings of the companions of the Prophet (*ṣaḥābī's*).

***mu'allal*:** A ḥadīth which may appear sound but has some not readily apparent weakness (*`illah*).

***mubāḥ*:** A permitted action.

***mubham*:** Literally, vague, doubtful. A ḥadīth in whose chain of authorities one of the transmitter's names is not mentioned.

***mudraj*:** A ḥadīth whose value is uncertain because some remarks by the transmitter have been interpolated among the words of the Prophet, it is impossible to accurately separate these two components of the text.

***mufti*:** A jurisconsult competent to deliver a *fatwā.*

***mujtahid*:** A person who exercises *ijtihād.*

***munqaṭi`* :** Literally, "cut off." A ḥadīth whose chain of authorities is not complete.

***muqallid*:** An imitator who follows a given school of law, a person who performs *taqlīd.*

***mursal* :** A ḥadīth in which the last authority in its isnād is a *tābi'ī*, in which the name of the companion who heard it from the Prophet is missing.

***musnad*:** Literally, "supported." A ḥadīth whose *isnād* is *muttaṣil* (complete and unbroken) and in which the last authority is a companion of the Prophet.

***mutawātir*:** A ḥadīth which is universally known, or that became frequently quoted and known from very early times, and to which objections have never been raised.

***muttaṣil*:** Literally, "connected." A ḥadīth whose isnād is complete and unbroken.

***nāfilah*:** (pl. *nawāfil*): A non-obligatory (supererogatory) action that is deemed good to do, and which will be rewarded.

***qāḍī*:** A judge.

***qiyās*:** Analogy used in juristic reasoning.

***ribā*:** Literally, "increase." Interest or usury. Any unequal transaction of a particular commodity.

***ṣaḥābī*:** A companion of the Prophet.

***saḥīḥ*:** Literally, "sound". This name is given to the utterly faultless ḥadīth in whose text and isnād there is no weakness (*`illah*).

***shādhdh* :** Literally, "anomalous, strange." A ḥadīth coming from a single transmitter and contradicting another ḥadīth.

***sharī'ah*:** Divine law. (*Shar`i* is the adjective or adverb of the word *Sharī'ah.*)

***sunnah***: Literally, "trodden path," precedent, local custom or traditional practice. It is usually used to apply to the normative practice of the Prophet. They have been categorized as follows:

1. *sunnah fi`liyyah*: the actions of the Prophet.
2. *sunnah qawliyyah*: the speech of the Prophet.
3. *sunnah taqrīriyyah*: the silence or tacit approval of the Prophet.

The *sunnah* of the Prophet has also been categorized by their normative value as:

1. *sunnah tashrī`iyyah*: that which has juridical or normative value,
2. *sunnah ghayr tashrī`iyyah*: that which has no normative value.

***tābi`ī*** (pl. *tābi'ūn*): the first generation after the Prophet.

***takhayyur***: The modern process of selecting a course of legal action from the various juristic opinions of the different *madhāhib*.

***talfīq***: The process of patching together or combining the views of different schools and jurists, or aspects therefrom, to form a single legal rule.

***taqlīd***: Imitation in matters of law; it is the opposite of *ijtihād*. It is the following of the opinions of others, sometimes with the connotation that one follows without understanding or scrutiny, or accepting the rulings of others when such rulings are not coupled with a conclusive argument. Although it has acquired a negative connotation, it should not be so, for there is nothing wrong or shameful in imitating others more knowledgeable than we are.

***tayammum***: ablution with clean sand, earth or a stone when no water is available. It consists of wiping the hands upon the sand, earth or stone, and with them wiping the hands, the face, and in some *madhāhib*, the arms up to the elbows.

***ummah*:** The body-politic, or nation, or sum total of Muslims. It is not defined by geography, but by the people

***`urf*:** Literally, "what is known about a thing." Pre- or post-Islamic custom or laws.

***uṣūl al-fiqh*:** The philosophy of Islamic jurisprudence.

***wājib*:** Obligatory, in most schools synonymous with *farḍ*.

***waqf*:** A charitable endowment of property under which ownership of the property is immobilized, and the use of the property, or its proceeds, is devoted to a charitable cause.

***wuḍū'*:** Ablution with ritually pure water.

## Imam Feisal Abdul Rauf

For the past sixteen years, Feisal Abdul Rauf has been the Imam of Al-Farah Mosque in New York City. He is the author of *Islam: A Search for Meaning*, in which he defines Islam as the universal religion that transcends the cultural settings of the Prophet Muhammad's seventh century Arabia.

He is President of ASMA (American Sufi Muslim Association), an association dedicated to developing individuals seeking to travel on the *spiritual path*. He is a member of the Board of Trustees of the Islamic Center of New York and of the Interfaith Center of New York, lecturing regularly at Mosques, Synagogues, Churches and at the New York Seminary, an institute dedicated to training interfaith ministers.

Imam Abdul-Rauf was educated in England, Egypt, Malaysia and the United States, and is a graduate of Columbia University in New York. He speaks Arabic, English and Malay/Indonesian.